Daughters of
DIVINITY

Daughters of DIVINITY

EVANGELICAL PROTESTANT CHRISTIANITY AND THE MAKING OF A NEW SOUTHERN WOMAN, 1830–1930

KATHERINE E. ROHRER

Louisiana State University Press

BATON ROUGE

Published by Louisiana State University Press
lsupress.org

Designer: Kaelin Chappell Broaddus
Typefaces: Bunyan Pro, text;
Annabelle, Engravers Roman BT, Espiritu Condensed, display

Cover image: Woman's Missionary Union Training School group photo, c. 1909.
Courtesy Archives, Special Collections, and Digital Initiatives,
Jack Tarver Library, Mercer University.

Library of Congress Cataloging-in-Publication Data

Names: Rohrer, Katherine E., author.
Title: Daughters of divinity : evangelical Protestant Christianity and the
    making of a new southern woman, 1830–1930 / Katherine E. Rohrer.
Description: Baton Rouge : Louisiana State University Press, [2025] |
    Includes bibliographical references and index.
Identifiers: LCCN 2025018335 (print) | LCCN 2025018336 (ebook) |
    ISBN 978-0-8071-8488-2 (cloth) | ISBN 978-0-8071-8526-1 (epub) |
    ISBN 978-0-8071-8527-8 (pdf)
Subjects: LCSH: Women, White—Southern States—History. | Women,
    White—Religious life—Southern States. | Women, White—Southern
    States—Social conditions. | Women, White—Education—Southern
    States—History. | Protestantism—Southern States—History. | Southern
    States—Religion.
Classification: LCC HQ1438.S63 R64 2025 (print) | LCC HQ1438.S63 (ebook)
    | DDC 305.40975—dc23/eng/20250513
LC record available at https://lccn.loc.gov/2025018335
LC ebook record available at https://lccn.loc.gov/20

FOR MY MOTHER,

Elizabeth Lytle Rohrer

CONTENTS

ACKNOWLEDGMENTS

Daughters of Divinity grew out of the work I completed at the University of Georgia. UGA and the history department in particular were crucial to my development into the person that I am today. Since the fall of 2001, when I began my relationship with this institution at age eighteen, I have grown as a reader, writer, thinker, researcher, critic, public speaker, teacher, and professional. I attribute my success and maturation to a number of scholars, educators, administrators, and colleagues. I particularly wish to recognize, with heartfelt thanks, my doctoral adviser, professional mentor, and friend John C. Inscoe. My relationship with him stretches back to the summer of 2003 when I had the very good fortune to be enrolled in his antebellum South class. I was immediately mesmerized by John's skill as a lecturer, his eclectic knowledge of, and insight into, southern history, and his demonstrated passion for his subject. Literally over the course of a few weeks, John altered my scholarly focus and, ultimately, my professional goals … and life. I jettisoned the idea of law school and decided that I would pursue a graduate degree in history.

I thank John for his guidance throughout graduate school, particularly his consistently sound conceptual advice and editorial assistance. I am likewise grateful to him for helping me navigate through many processes in the historical field, including those related to publishing, grant and fellowship applications, conferences, and the academic job market. No other scholar in UGA's history department offered the same multidimensional talents in scholarship, teaching, and professional service as did John Inscoe. It is my honor to be counted among those whom he has touched. Three other scholars in the history department at UGA shaped me in significant ways. They are Diane

Batts Morrow, Stephen Mihm, and Stephen Berry, each of whom contributed breadth and depth to my development as a historian.

Many individuals and organizations generously supported my research for this project. Beyond the assistance provided by the UGA history department in the form of travel awards and the Greg and Amanda Gregory research awards, I am indebted to the Willson Center for Humanities and Arts at the University of Georgia, which awarded me the Graduate Research Award; the Virginia Museum of History and Culture, which awarded me the Frances Lewis Fellowship in Gender and Women's Studies; and the North Caroliniana Society, which awarded me the Archie K. Davis Fellowship. Without their financial backing, this book would not be based upon the breadth and depth of sources to the extent that it is. I wish to acknowledge the innumerable staff who assisted me at the following libraries and research centers: the Virginia Museum of History and Culture, the Southern Historical Collection at the University of North Carolina, the South Caroliniana Library at the University of South Carolina, the Special Collections and Archives at Furman University, the Hargrett Rare Book and Manuscript Library at the University of Georgia, the Georgia Historical Society, and the Archives, Special Collection, & Digital Initiatives Department of the Mercer University Libraries.

I am very grateful that *Daughters of Divinity* found a home with LSU Press. I have long respected the scholarship that the Press has produced, and I am honored to be part of that tradition. My relationship with the Press has been smooth and without glitches, and I am sure that Rand Dotson has a lot to do with that. Thank you, Rand, for your early interest in my book manuscript. I likewise wish to acknowledge my two anonymous reviewers, who offered thorough, yet encouraging, constructive criticism. Their comments have only made my finished product clearer and more impactful. Finally, I wish to recognize my skillful copy editor, Jo Ann Kiser, as well as the entire production team at the Press.

I was fortunate to land a job in the History, Anthropology, and Philosophy Department at the University of North Georgia, where I have continued to develop, particularly as a teacher and mentor. I wish to give thanks to my colleagues at UNG who have offered me their friendship, advice, and support, particularly Ann Tucker, Deanna "Dee" Gillespie, John Paul Hill, and Michael Buseman. Michael, you deserve special recognition. One of the greatest highlights of this job has been my friendship with you over the past seven-plus years. Whether we're playing trivia, attending a concert, venting about life's vicissitudes, or just shooting the breeze about politics or sports or teaching, I always enjoy your company and appreciate your diehard loyalty. I also wish to recognize the generous support provided to me in the form of travel grants by two departmental chairs, Jeffrey Pardue and Tamara Spike. Budgets at UNG have been very tight over the last several years, yet Jeff and Tam have worked hard to lighten my financial burden. Thanks to their support, I have presented portions of this research at various conferences across the United States.

I completed an early version of this manuscript while reclining in an old red beanbag chair that I was given during my sophomore year at UGA. That well-worn beanbag kept (and continues to keep) me in close physical proximity to my dear canine children. Redford (2006–2017), my handsome labradoodle, remained by my side for nearly every hour while I worked, providing support and (at times) a welcome diversion. Rutherford, my much smaller and spunkier aussiedoodle, can never replace Redford but offers his unique gifts. A highly affectionate "snuggler," Rutherford has remained on my lap (in the beanbag chair) for much of the book revision process. Together, Redford and Rutherford have kept me sane, even relaxed, during some stressful times.

In May 2020, during the early months of the COVID-19 pandemic, I met my now husband, Matthew J. Smith. Since that time, we've been virtually inseparable. I cannot imagine meeting another man with as many exceptional attributes as you. Your kindness, emotional support, patience, magnanimity, playful spirit, and love have made my life better in so many ways, both tangible and intangible. You are the consummate life partner, and I look forward to our many adventures ahead. When I married Matt, I gained not only a husband but a large family, and they immediately welcomed me into their "tribe." Special thanks go to my parents-in-law, J. LaMont and Caroline Smith, for their support, warm hospitality, generosity, and love.

Lastly, I want to acknowledge my parents, Frederick J. Rohrer III and Elizabeth Lytle Rohrer, and the preeminent place they assume in my heart. I never had the opportunity to share the vast majority of my University of Georgia experience with my father, who passed away at the end of my freshman year. Ironically, he envisioned me becoming an historian when, as a teenager, I viewed such a career path as borderline asinine and impractical. I wish he could reappear for a day so that I could inform him that I had earned a PhD and become a history professor after all. But most of all, I wish to thank my mother, who has been with me every step of my life. She has provided me with all the support, attention, guidance, assistance, humor, and love that I could ever imagine humanly possible. She not only encouraged my early interest in southern and nineteenth-century history, taking me to countless historical sites in Virginia and introducing me to genealogical research (through which I could "meet" and begin to historically contextualize all of those many family members I never met), but also shaped my curiosity, analytical mind, and work ethic. More than anyone else, my mother has molded me into the person that I am. This book reflects all that she is and all that she has given me.

Daughters of
DIVINITY

INTRODUCTION

In 1860, young Sallie Didd Beck was a student enrolled at Griffin Synodical Female College (also known as Griffin Collegiate Seminary) in Griffin, Georgia, an up-and-coming commercial and cotton-market town located between Atlanta and Macon. Founded by the Flint River Presbytery in 1852, Griffin Synodical Female College coexisted with dozens of other female colleges, seminaries, and academies that had been established by evangelical Protestant churches across the antebellum South.[1] Such institutions offered young women the earliest opportunities for a new kind of education, one that fused a (more) rigorous academic curriculum with evangelical Christianity.

Attendance at such schools civilized and uplifted young women intellectually and spiritually as well as reinforced their status as members of the elite or emerging elite of the region. These institutions did not intend that their students would seek admission at a degree-granting college, nor did they prepare students for any career or profession. However, these religiously founded institutions functioned as crucial stepping stones for intellectual and professional advancement among the next several generations of white southern women. Such schools sowed seeds that would ignite southern women's passion for domestic and foreign mission work, work that would eventually catapult many such women from the private to public sphere and would redefine ideals of white southern womanhood.

Griffin Synodical Female College operated on an aesthetically pleasing four-acre campus. The main academic building was brick, two stories in height, and boasted an impressive castellated square belltower on its roof. Annual enrollment likely did not exceed a couple of dozen students. Sallie took coursework in literature, music, French, German, drawing, printing, and religion from both male and female instructors. As a religiously affiliated school, Griffin Synodical Female College held its female students to a high moral standard. Students attended church and Sabbath School every Sunday. Students were not permitted to "correspond with, receive calls from, or be gallanted by a gentleman, unless a blood relation" nor could they attend a party, fair, or show without permission from the college president. And, students were held to a strict dress code, one that included provisions regarding wardrobe material, color, and length.[2]

This austere code of conduct, however, did not deter students from forging strong bonds with classmates. Sallie Didd Beck, known affectionately as "Didd" by her classmates, kept a commonplace book during her years at Griffin Synodical College. The pages brim with creative poems and sentimental letters written to her by fellow students. Anna, one such student, penned the following poem:

> To Didd,
>
> Oh would that what I'd wish might unto thee be given,
> Maiden! I'd wish for thee the kindly care of heaven,
> that every earthly joy might cluster round thy head,
> And every heavenly blessing be on thy pathway shed.
>
> I would not wish for the long, life nor constant health,
> Nor pleasure, unalloyed nor joy, nor boundless wealth
> Nor bright far famed beauty for that will soon decay
> And pleasure, joy and wealth, they soon will pass away.
>
> But I would wish for thee the gift of love divine,
> Sweeter by far than pleasure, richer than golden mind,
> Whose ever brightening light will never pass away
> Leading thee safely through the straight and narrow ways
>
> When affliction o'er thee costs a dark and fearful cloud
> And sorrow's tempest round thee gather and thunder loud

This heaven light will guide thee o'er life's tempestuous sea
And moor thy bask in safety in a blest Eternity.

Your classmate,
Anna[3]

Anna's last name may be lost to history, but her sage and inspirational words live on. They reinforce the profound impact that evangelical Protestant Christianity had on her life. Her faith shaped her worldview, her priorities, and her relationships with others. Likely only fourteen or fifteen years of age, Anna had already internalized that her earthly life paled in comparison to the eternal one waiting for her in heaven. In Anna's eyes, one should not dwell on frivolous matters. One's appearance, health, wealth, and fun times were ephemeral. Rather, Anna stood firm in her belief that the greatest gift bestowed upon her was God's never-ending love. She wished for those close to her—Sallie Didd Beck included—to share those same feelings for and from God. Quite simply, Anna was an evangelizer. She was spreading the Gospel of Jesus Christ, if only to her classmates and perhaps to members of her household.

Unfortunately, Griffin Synodical Female College's existence was even more fleeting than the earthly life referred to by Anna. The Presbyterian college closed just twelve years after it opened. In wake of the Battle of Atlanta during the late summer of 1864, the Confederate government transformed the school into a hospital. Then, the devastating economic conditions in the Civil War's aftermath made a revival of the school unfeasible. However, the evangelical zeal ignited among young women at Griffin Synodical Female College and institutions like it only grew stronger and more demonstrable in the postbellum era and beyond. Fortunately, Griffin Synodical Female College's fate was not felt at all of the other female colleges, seminaries, and academies across the South. Indeed, those institutions that remained open faced monumental financial challenges during Reconstruction, but, in time, they rebounded and expanded, educating new generations of southern females who shared their evangelical fervor beyond the private or domestic sphere. By the later nineteenth century, such women spread their Christian values and worldview to more public arenas across the South and around the world. In so doing, they embraced more autonomy, exercised more authority, and wielded more agency. This book traces the transformative religious, intellectual, and professional journey experienced by a subset of white southern women who were profoundly molded by evangelical Christianity.

✝

Evangelical Protestant Christianity shaped the development of the post–American Revolution South in innumerable and far-reaching ways. In this faith-based society, Protestant clerics operated as the region's intelligentsia. According to historian Timothy L. Wesley, preachers "were influential because they were the acknowledged point men of organized religion, and in both the North and the South by 1860 religious sensibilities and beliefs exerted a greater influence on American public and political life" than at any other point in its history.[4] This view is shared by other scholars of religion in the South, including Mark A. Noll, John B. Boles, Luke E. Harlow, and Charity R. Carney.[5] Such high-profile men were not simply religious figures but were the region's scholars, educators, indoctrinators, and, in many cases, politicians.

This raises the question as to precisely what complementary religious roles their white female counterparts embraced during the nineteenth and early twentieth centuries. In what ways did such interaction with religion afford such women a degree of independence, agency, and fulfillment? How did their roles change over time as their region underwent tremendous political, social, and economic transformation? And how did such women's interface with religion in both private and public settings shape—and perhaps even change—notions of gender within the South? *Daughters of Divinity* offers answers to these three broad questions. It analyzes white women's religious expressions and actions in a South forever changed by the democratizing influences of the Second Great Awakening yet perpetually confined by deep-seated beliefs in racial and sexual subordination.

A nationwide religious revival movement during the first half of the nineteenth century, the Second Great Awakening emphasized emotional expression and democracy as well as salvation and a sense of mission. New Protestant denominations emerged, while older ones reconceptualized themselves in ways that reflected these new egalitarian values. Evangelical churches mirrored those same democratic values that structured American civil government during the early republic era and beyond. They expanded opportunities in church leadership, though women did not immediately benefit from this. They emphasized man's (and even woman's) equality before God, a so-called spiritual equality. They believed that salvation is a free gift offered by God, with the only condition for eternal life being faith. They rejected some of the rituals of a more traditional or staid Christianity in favor of less-structured services. And, they encouraged parishioners to forge direct, personal relationships with Christ. In this religious environment, ministers assumed a warm and familial role, not an emotionally distant and authoritarian one.

The egalitarian rhetoric and practices of the thriving evangelical Protestant denominations—Baptists, Methodists, Presbyterians, but even Episcopalians— spurred many women to think more seriously about their relationships with this new form of Christian fellowship and their place in southern society. Yet at the same time, strict gender and racial hierarchies limited southern women's progression and acceptance within religious and professional circles. Nonetheless, evangelical Protestantism presented an outlet through which many white southern women redefined themselves and southern womanhood.

Similarly, evangelical Protestantism offered Black women in the South ample opportunities through which they helped (re)define racial and gender norms, often very publicly. For example, in 1900, Black Baptist women established the Woman's Convention, an auxiliary to the National Baptist Convention, through which they demanded civil rights and educational opportunities as well as protested against lynching, segregation, and discrimination. The Woman's Convention organized after nearly thirty years of religious work by Black women's organizations at the local and state levels.[6] Black Protestant women also served as missionaries in Africa where they sought to shape Black identity around the globe. This study does not address the religious identities and experiences of Black women, although they are inextricably tied to those of white southern women between 1830 and 1930.[7]

✝

Scholarship on the religious expression of educated white southern women during the nineteenth and early twentieth centuries remains in its earliest stages. In spite of this, a vast literature on such women exists that collectively considers their roles as daughters, wives, mothers, caretakers, students, teachers, managers of the enslaved, consumers, correspondents, intellectuals, writers and journalists, members of and leaders in organizations, suffragists, and even preservers of their southern culture. This book offers a narrative that engages in a nuanced dialogue with a number of scholars, while offering an alternate lens of analysis and discussion of new topics and individuals.

Looking through a predominantly gendered lens, *Daughters of Divinity* studies the ways some well-educated white women of the South used evangelical Protestant Christianity as an instrument to expand their intellectual and professional capacities as well as their agency and influence at home and throughout the world. In telling this story, I have tried to balance the use of official denominational accounts, records, and publications with personal sources—for example, diaries, journals, and correspondence. Employing the same chronological span as did pioneering women's historian Anne Firor Scott in *The Southern Lady,* I trace both change and continuity in women's religious identities and experiences from the antebellum period through the 1920s.[8] Alternately, I use female mission work as a looking glass into religious and cultural values of the American South. I examine southern women's motivations, experiences, and the impact of their missions on both themselves and the communities they served.[9] Between 1830 and 1930, southern women assumed faith-based roles that increasingly fell in the public sphere and they occupied positions in religious work in which they exercised more authority. The employment of such a vast chronological span is necessary to fully appreciate this subtle, yet revolutionary, transformation that such white southern women underwent.

Over this century, such women slowly but steadily increased their influence and responsibilities within the public sphere, while often maintaining and even promoting their adherence to strict racial and gender hierarchies. On other occasions, however, some women did express themselves and behave in ways that exposed a more moderate, even progressive, southerner. Such women were often in the minority. Indeed, southern female missionaries were contradictory figures, modern and progressive in some regards while staunchly conservative, even reactionary, in others. *Daughters of Divinity* argues that this tension experienced by such women echoed similar anxiety experienced not only by and within religious denominations but by the South as a whole. This study underscores the duality of insularity and retrenchment versus growth and cosmopolitanism.

In spite of this ever-present tension, such white southern women who pursued roles ensconced in the religious sphere shared many similarities. These included their solid education, middle-class and elite status, conservative politics, and membership in elitist social and "heritage" organizations. Female mission workers also tended to be ambitious, committed, and self-righteous. A disproportionate number of such women, especially those engaged in long-term, faith-based careers, were single. This book thus contributes to our burgeoning understanding of the unique experiences and worldviews of single southern women. It complements recent scholarship by Angela Esco Elder, Allison Fredette, Marie S. Molloy, and Kirsten E. Wood. These scholars have explored female singleness with regards to nonmarriage, widowhood, separation, and divorce in the nineteenth-century South.[10] A large percentage of women in this study either chose not to marry or engaged in faith-based pursuits as widows. While this book sheds light on the lives of those southern women who never married, it also explores southern women who balanced marriage with a public life in Christian work.

This study centers, though not exclusively, upon those white women who lived, worshipped, and worked in what famed landscape architect and social critic Frederick Law Olmsted labeled the "seaboard slave states," namely Virginia, North Carolina, South Carolina, and Georgia.[11] All among the original thirteen colonies, these four states were more established politically, socially, economically, and particularly religiously in 1830 than were the southern states west of the Appalachians. These four states offered greater religious and educational opportunities which undoubtedly fueled southern women's faith-based interests and professions. In particular, a greater number of Protestant churches and denominationally founded women's academies and colleges existed in Virginia, North Carolina, South Carolina, and Georgia than in other parts of the South.[12]

✝

Before the Civil War, southern women engaged in a number of religious activities, the majority ensconced in the private sphere. While many of their activities during the antebellum years operated in the private sphere, southern women began to acknowledge themselves as spiritual equals to men. Concurrently, they explored the boundaries of their religious authority through their legalistic interpretations of scripture. Chapter 1, "The Formative Years," explores a panoply of topics related to the early religious expressions of southern women, precursors for the more public-minded female religious figure. These include women who sustained their role as spiritual mentor to their children through composition of religious advice, guidance, essays, and poetry; women who entered in the study of religion at the burgeoning denominationally backed female academies and colleges in the South like that of Griffin Synodical Female College; and a few women who organized and assumed positions within mite societies, the forerunners to denomination-wide missionary societies that flourished after the Civil War. While it is this latter group that makes up a focus of this study, this chapter addresses more private activities that transpired within the homes and educational institutions of southern women between the early nineteenth century and the end of the Civil War.

Chapter 2, "Evangelizing the Enslaved," remains in the private sphere, looking at slaveholding women who shared their religious knowledge and mentorship with the enslaved. In so doing, these women often saw the religious education of enslaved people as an exploitative means to reinforce racial and gender hierarchies through their promotion of paternalist values. While such women felt obligated to live up to the model of idealized antebellum womanhood of service and submission as represented by those like playwright Louisa S. McCord, they encountered many obstacles which limited their control and cultural influence over the enslaved.

Chapter 3, "Foreign Mission Work in Liberia," offers a case study of Martha Jane Williford, an Episcopal missionary from Georgia, and her twenty-year career in Liberia. Williford distinguished herself as she was one of the first southern women to enter the mission field as a single woman. Although influenced by, and even limited by, the racist and sexist southern environment of which she was a product, Williford's capacious correspondence offers insights into the educated or intellectual southern woman's views, opinions, and aspirations during the middle of the nineteenth century. This missionary's letters do not focus on the quotidian realities of mission life in West Africa nor do they even dwell on her Episcopal faith. Rather, and more significantly, her epistles shed light on women's roles in southern, American, and African society; race relations; cultural and physical differences between Black Americans and Africans; and church ideology and politics. While hardly a feminist, Williford's words showcase ways in which southern women could and did apply regionally permissible gender roles to a greater good within a religious public sphere. Williford married fellow Episcopal missionary Bishop John Payne in 1858 and continued to labor for the church in Liberia until her husband's retirement in 1869.

✝

The Civil War brought significant change to southern women, yet the conflict did not dismantle the southern culture to which they had bonded. Responding to the harsh realities of military conflict and social upheaval during the war years, many southern women had no choice but to adopt roles that assigned them more agency and responsibility while exposing them to the workings of a more masculine culture. According to Drew Gilpin Faust, some accepted positions in the War Department, Post Office, the Quartermaster Department, the Office of the Commissary General, and the Treasury Department. Women also assumed greater authority in domestic matters, including the management of enslaved people, and took on work in the fields of education and nursing. Despite an exposure to new roles and lines of work, Faust concludes, women who had long been accustomed to living a privileged life neither welcomed nor accepted these changes.[13] Gender lay at the heart of such discomfort. Women were reticent to embrace an identity that questioned their femininity and their place in southern society. Corroborating Faust is LeeAnn Whites, who interpreted the Civil War as a crisis in gender. For Whites, the war not only challenged gender roles but altered and confused them in a South defined by privileged white males.[14] Southern men and women did not wish to bury them in the past.

Daughters of Divinity does not entirely reject Faust's and Whites's interpretations of southern womanhood. Instead, it complicates and expands our collective understanding of concepts of gender and ideas about women's public and/or professional lives. It reveals that many elite, well-educated southern women embraced growing opportunities in faith-based work beginning with the Civil War and continuing well into the twentieth century. In this regard, this study belongs in an historiographical discussion with such scholars of postbellum southern women as Sarah E. Gardner, Caroline E. Janney, and

Karen L. Cox. Gardner identifies what she labeled "pen and ink warriors"—elite, middle-class women who participated in the production of a narrative of the antebellum South and Civil War that reflected the conservative values of their region, race, and class.[15] Janney examines white women across the South who organized Ladies' Memorial Associations (MLAs), through which such women assisted the indigent and injured, memorialized the Confederate dead, and arranged for bodies of dead Confederate soldiers to be brought home for a proper burial. More broadly, Janney challenges the notion that white southern women were peripheral to the Lost Cause movement until the 1890s, revealing instead that such women played a crucial role beginning in 1865. According to Janney, these women were among the earliest creators and purveyors of a Confederate tradition.[16] Similarly, Cox underscores the ways in which the United Daughters of the Confederacy (UDC) perpetuated the values of the Old South by tangible activities such as caring for needy Confederate men and women as well as by monument building. Corroborating Janney, Cox maintains that postbellum southern women sought to ensure that future generations of white southerners would imbibe traditional Confederate values. Cox assigns such postbellum women a large degree of agency as conservatives, concluding that the UDC's perpetuation of Confederate political and social values played a vital role in delaying sectional reconciliation.[17] Female mission workers, in word and in action, echoed the politics and worldviews of those women whom Gardner, Janney, and Cox have closely examined.

During the war years, such women assumed greater roles at their denomination's quarterly meetings and revivals; they organized drives at their local churches, collecting Bibles for distribution to Confederate soldiers; and they provided religious guidance and general assistance to recent new widows. Women engaged in these religious pursuits were not simply "mothers of invention," who, out of necessity, took jobs and positions to aid the Confederate war effort. Rather, they sought to expand their feminine influence across the South and the world through faith-based activities and careers. Yet during these years, Protestant denominations in the South failed to develop, let alone expand upon, their wartime mission projects. This reality limited women's opportunities in faith-based work or, in some cases, left projects to individual churches. Consequently, this study does not center upon women's missionary efforts during the Civil War, although it discusses them as background to the women's postbellum pursuits.

Women faced meager years after the war ended. The years between 1865 and the end of Reconstruction were lean ones for most southerners, including the once-flourishing churches. During this time of economic uncertainty, including a devastating depression in the early 1870s, denominations faced nearly empty coffers. They struggled to financially support their home and foreign mission efforts as well as their academic institutions and presses. The generation of southern women who reached young adulthood during the 1860s and 1870s faced a dearth of opportunities in many lines of faith-based work. However, by the early 1880s, Protestant women of the South achieved new professional breakthroughs on a level never seen before. Most significantly, these years witnessed the establishment of women's home and foreign missionary societies. In the last two decades of the nineteenth and first three decades of the twentieth century, southern women assumed, through their churches, a number of roles. These included everything from volunteer work with their neighborhood churches to long-term careers in education, accounting, administration, publishing, nursing, and social work that their respective denominations assigned them.

Chapters 4, 5, 6, and 7 tell the postbellum story. Chapter 4, "Interregnum and Transition," serves two purposes. First, it expounds on those reasons why white southern women faced limited opportunities in religious work during the financially and emotionally challenging years of Reconstruction. Second, it traces the emergence of a New South and specifically white southern women's new religious roles in it.

Chapter 4 unearths such women's growing interest in, and action within, their churches, religious organizations, and faith-based professional pursuits in the latter nineteenth and early twentieth centuries. During the 1880s, Protestant denominations organized hundreds of mission societies (at least when one considers local chapters or associations of larger organizations) through which southern women established schools, hospitals, Mothers' Clubs, recreational facilities, and other elements of the Social Gospel—the religious arm of the progressive movement whose aim was to combat poverty and injustice—both in the South and abroad. Under examination here are women who participated in home mission societies, particularly in administrative positions. Underscored is southern women's enthusiasm for activities that placed them in more public settings where they wielded some authority and agency.

In 1941, journalist W. J. Cash published *The Mind of the South,* an influential study of southern identity. Cash characterized the South as a relatively static region that intertwined honor, self-defense, and hostility toward centralized control along with an extreme racial hierarchy and a resistance toward societal progress. What Cash provided was a blueprint for better comprehending the collective mind of the South.[18] In decades since, historians have imagined not just one mind, but many southern minds. Using finer strokes than did Cash, they have carefully studied the minds of southerners of all races, classes, and genders. Chapter 5, "Home Mission Work Meets Conservative Progressivism," provides insight into the minds of postbellum white southern women who engaged in religious work. It emphasizes such women's embrace and fierce defense of a conservative worldview, both socially and politically, as well as the agency they exercised to reinforce such a worldview.

By the late nineteenth century, mission work had emerged as a respectable, fulfilling, and even powerful outlet for southern white women. Chapter 6, "Recruitment," examines the crucial roles southern women played in the recruitment of additional workers and expansion of home and foreign mission programs. To successfully interest other women, such women exercised three broad methods: 1) organizing and administering mission training colleges, 2) speeches delivered to churches or regional and statewide denominational meetings about opportunities in home and foreign missions, and 3) published and unpublished writings, some of which found their place in religious magazines and newspapers with large circulations. Finally, chapter 7, "Foreign Mission Work at Home and in the Field," introduces readers to four southern female foreign missionary workers after the Civil War: Laura Haygood, a Methodist missionary serving in China; Lula Whilden, a Baptist missionary also serving in China; Margaret Douglas, a Presbyterian missionary serving in Brazil; and Frances Worth, a Presbyterian missionary serving in the Belgian Congo. The first three women serve as paragons of southern womanhood of this era. Through their faith-based careers, women like Haygood, Whilden, and Douglas embodied female traits idealized in southern society. They were maternal, feminine, and devout but also ambitious, hardworking, patient, and savvy. (In contrast, Worth exhibited traits that fell far short of this feminine ideal, and she thus serves as a counterpoint to Haygood, Whilden, and Douglas.) Long-term vocations in foreign mission work offered to such women fulfilling, challenging careers that did not question gender roles but rather identified appropriate outlets for female professional contributions.

I close the Introduction with a note on region and gender. Regardless of their individual focus, scholars of southern history often consider in what ways and for what reasons the South differed from the North. Relative to female missionaries in the South, the answer is equivocal and not an appreciable concern of this study. While missionary women—from the South, the North, and beyond—have found personal liberation and spiritual inspiration from sharing the gospel across cultures, they have all struggled against gender limitations, imposed by the mission societies that sent them, the churches they served, and the families that shaped them. In Dana L. Robert's words, such women also found "themselves caught between secular scholarship that characterizes mission work as unwarranted proselytism and cultural imperialism, and doctrinal conservatives who condemn aspects of their work as illegitimate simply because it is being done by women."[19] Northern and southern missionaries shared similarities relative to their responsibilities, service, obstacles, politics, and reception. However, the focus on southern missionaries is significant because by virtue of their education, heritage, initiative, ambition, and employment they were more exceptional among white southern women at large than were their counterparts in the North. Yet they duly resembled their elite southern sisters outside of faith-based activities in their quest to uphold the Old South while exercising a degree of control and influence over poor whites, enslaved people, free Blacks, and foreigners both within and outside of their communities.

One

THE FORMATIVE YEARS

Between the very late eighteenth century and 1830, an unprecedented number of men and women, representing all social classes and races, embraced evangelical Protestant Christianity. According to historian Christine Leigh Heyrman's "most generous" estimate, "fewer than one-fifth of southern whites over the age of sixteen had formally joined Baptist, Methodist, or Presbyterian churches by the 1810s." However, just two decades later, the percentage of white southerners who belonged to a church among these three evangelical denominations exceeded 50 percent. By 1835, nearly 66 percent of white southerners "had regular contact with evangelical preaching." Among those exposed to "regular" evangelical preaching, 60 to 65 percent were women. The Second Great Awakening was a tremendous Protestant revival movement that transpired over the first four decades of the nineteenth century. It had a democratizing effect—religiously, politically, and socially—on southern culture and religious practices. Fundamentally, those who accepted evangelism rejected the tenets of Calvinism, believing instead that individuals could choose to be saved. Religious practices, displayed most conspicuously at large revivals, exuded democracy. In theory, in God's eyes, all were worthy of salvation. As a result of this equalizing trend, southerners across the racial, class, and gender spectrum thought about and responded to evangelical Christianity in myriad ways.[1]

White southern women reacted to and participated in this evolving evangelical society. The democratic nature of thriving evangelical Protestant denominations spurred these women to think more seriously about their own relationships with this new form of Christian fellowship and their place in southern society. Despite this trend toward democracy within the religious sphere and beyond, white southern women with solid educations and from landed or elite families were far more likely to engage in evangelical religion in ways that permitted them greater intellectual opportunities and at times greater public—or nondomestic—involvement than their less well educated and less socially elite counterparts.

These more educated and/or elite white southern women interacted with evangelical Protestantism in a variety of ways that were direct products of the Second Great Awakening. Some sustained their role as spiritual mentor to their (often many) children through composition of religious advice, guidance, essays, and poetry. Some studied religion at the burgeoning denominationally backed female academies and colleges in the South or with tutors. Some instigated meaningful, even intellectual, relationships with local ministers. Some attended religious lectures given by clerics who represented different denominations, regions of the nation, and political views. Some, including those who inhabited the more remote parts of the South and faced limited access to "live" religious events, read religious lectures and sermons reprinted in their local newspapers. And finally, a few southern women stepped into a more public, nondomestic, environment by organizing and assuming positions in mite societies, forerunners to denomination-wide missionary societies that flourished after the Civil War. While this latter group makes up the focus of this study, this chapter centers on more private activities that transpired within the homes and educational institutions between the early nineteenth century and the end of the Civil War.

These new, more cerebral, and more public religious expressions exhibited by southern women fell within the realm of acceptable southern femininity. Such expressions did not challenge gender roles or the gender hierarchy of the antebellum and Civil War South. Heyrman asserts that, over the course of the first four decades of the nineteenth century, southern evangelical churches increasingly "tailored their teachings to uphold, ever more equivocally, the authority of male heads of household, particularly over godly women."[2] Throughout the nineteenth century, southern women inhabited a society whose very existence depended upon strict racial and gender hierarchies.

What Heyrman neglects to fully recognize, however, is the increasing influence, if not power, of southern women within the religious sphere. Such women typically held moderate to conservative views on religion, race, and class, which were commensurate with the views of antebellum white southern society at large. This reality did not inhibit women from actively engaging in religious circles, readings, debates, and organizations. Rather, antebellum-era southern women emerged with the skills, confidence, and experience to assume more demanding and more public roles within the religious sphere throughout the remainder of the nineteenth century and beyond.

Southern women held no official capacities or positions within any Protestant church. However, clerics, including the influential Methodist bishop Francis Asbury, recognized women's crucial contributions to the livelihood of these nascent evangelical churches. Some clerics celebrated pious southern women as "heroines of Christ." Although southern women could not participate in any official capacity within their churches, some experienced their first taste of equality and public oratory at camp meetings, popular beginning around 1800. The positive and energizing nature of camp meetings, coupled with an emphasis on the equality of each person's soul before God, afforded such women unprecedented freedom. At such events, many southern women felt comfortable expressing themselves publicly, sometimes about very private matters. Similarly, while females held no official role at camp or quarterly meetings, they might exhort or present a prayer following a minister's sermon. Referring to a quarterly meeting during his travels through Virginia, Asbury stated, "We had a gracious time at quarterly meeting, especially at the sacrament. The words of our excellent Sister Jones, both in speaking and in prayer were sweetly and powerfully felt."[3]

Religion likewise afforded antebellum southern women opportunities to exert some influence, even control, over domestic matters. Historian Scott Stephan finds that domestic religious rituals—for example, consecrating new-borns to God's care, spiritually guiding dying kin through life's final stages, or crafting deathbed narratives—offered such women other forms of agency. Clergymen across the antebellum South upheld the contributions of these pious women.[4] For clerics, devout southern women served as key instruments in expanding evangelical Protestant Christianity throughout the first several decades of the nineteenth century. Because of this new-found domestic authority, especially with regard to moral matters, evangelical women did not entirely assume subordinate positions within southern households. Such women may have been members of a highly patriarchal slave society, but this did not entirely preclude them from exercising religious and/or moral influence on their families and, indirectly, their communities.

WOMEN'S RELIGIOUS AND DOMESTIC ADVICE

Between 1822 and 1862, Episcopalian Elizabeth Willis Gloster Anderson of Warrenton, North Carolina, and La Grange, Tennessee, spiritually guided her nine children through a series of religious-themed "letters" or memoranda she wrote. Among the letters were scraps of religious advice, excerpts from sermons, hymns, and analysis of biblical scripture, especially the parables of Jesus, discussions of camp meetings, and her interpretations of current events through a religious lens. Anderson, a frail woman, commenced writing down religious advice, ideas, and prayers because she feared she would not live long enough to spiritually guide her children into adulthood. In the first letter to her young children, then numbering three, Elizabeth Anderson wrote in 1822:

> Thus, with ardour and anxiety of mind, I pen these admonitions for the purpose of striving to lead you to consider serious things so that, though it may please God in his wisdom to deny me the gratification of witnessing your growth in piety and personally endeavoring from my experience to instruct you, I may yet leave some little memorial of my love by which you may know what were my wishes for you and what my sentiments [were] on the most serious of all subjects.[5]

Fortunately, Anderson lived a full life, dying at the age of seventy-seven when her youngest son was nearing the age of forty. She felt a passion to instill evangelical values, discipline, guidance, and love in her many children from birth through adulthood.[6] Although she truly held her children's best interests at heart and exhibited a genuine emotional attachment toward them, Mrs. Anderson's assertive rhetoric confirms a level of authority within her household. In fact, her demonstrative rhetoric suggests that the Anderson children looked up to their mother as an important—even commanding—spiritual guide or, at times, as an instiller of fear and admonition. Some of the recurring themes in Elizabeth Anderson's religious letters were the fulfillment gained from choosing God as a guiding light; self-restraint and the practice of moderation (to avoid "worldly pleasures which [her children] esteem[ed] innocent"); obedience to God, parents, husbands, wives, and ministers; the omnipresence of pain and suffering ("Afflictions are no mark of God's displeasure. Jesus loved Mary and Lazarus, yet they were both afflicted." Inspired by John 11); the importance of proselytizing, mission work, and sharing God's Word; the absence of privacy or independence that one should expect as a child of God ("let nothing be done without th[e] sentence and appropriation of ... the Bishop, Presbyters, Deacons and to God Himself"); the actions or circumstances that would lead one to Hell; the gravity of meditation and reflective reading of scripture; and even matters concerning daily happiness, like surrounding oneself with good company, steering clear of procrastination, and maintaining marital fidelity. In each letter, Anderson grounded in scripture her advice and guidance on such seemingly mundane and nonreligious matters as friendship.

The Anderson children were born between 1815 and 1835, and, as such there was overlap and repetition in Elizabeth's letters. Tellingly, Anderson made little to no direct differentiation between her male and female children, nor did she address any letter to a specific child. Perhaps in this southern mother's eyes, her entire household's devotion to God—and the promise of immortal souls as reward for such devotion—trumped the adherence to a strict temporal sexual hierarchy found in the Old South that consistently placed women in subordinate positions. Finally, Elizabeth Anderson's compendium of religious letters showcases this southern woman's mental acuity and ability to weave scripture, religious themes, and excerpts from sermons with church and domestic politics as well as literature. Thus, for the Anderson children, their mother's demonstrated intelligence may have reinforced her power and respect within the domestic sphere.

Elizabeth Willis Gloster Anderson was not an anomaly. While extant religious collections like Anderson's are rare, innumerable white southern women frequently corresponded with their children as a means to impart religious values and advice. However, many southern women of her era embraced the intellectual outlets that religious study afforded them. Intellectual opportunities for privileged white girls and young women abounded throughout the nineteenth century, especially within the walls of the emerging private female academies and colleges in the antebellum South.

A "HIGHER" EDUCATION

In fact, aside from attending church, Sunday School, and revivals, young white southern females' initial academic exposure to religion likely transpired at female academies and colleges that catered to the region's well-to-do.[7] Higher education was an option only for those girls and young women whose families believed in female access to higher learning and whose families could afford to send, what likely was to be, several male children to private schools before addressing the private educational needs of female children. By 1800, educators had founded female academies in only the more established sections of the South but most notably in Maryland, Virginia, and South Carolina.[8] Annie Belle Northen—an alumna of Mt. Zion Academy in LaGrange, Georgia, who composed a history of her alma mater—stressed the paucity of women's schools in areas of the South designated as "upcountry" during the 1800s and 1810s. She wrote: "In 1812 when the Mt. Zion Academy was founded there was no other classical school in all the Up Country, the College itself at Athens being in a state of collapse that lasted for years."[9]

Despite obstacles in establishing female academies and colleges during the first two decades of the nineteenth century, by the 1840s many such schools had opened across much of the South. By this time, most southerners embraced the notion of female intellectual equality. Many, however, did not go as far as accepting female educational equality.[10] Although expansion of female higher education during the antebellum era remained controversial in some circles, the South far outdistanced the North and Midwest relative to the establishment of female colleges in the 1840s and 1850s. Between 1850 and 1859 thirty-two of the thirty-nine American chartered female colleges were located in the South. Most of these schools held ties to a specific religious denomination.[11] Even those institutions not officially tied to a denomination, such as the well-known South Carolina Female Collegiate Institute, typically installed a Protestant minister as its president and thus nurtured an evangelical environment.

A discussion of female higher learning contributes to a broader discussion on women's literacy in the antebellum South. In contrast to the derisive stereotypes regarding southern illiteracy that were perpetuated by northerners, historians, particularly Beth Barton Schweiger and Jonathan Daniel Wells, have concluded that southern women were, in fact, avid readers who read the same authors and works as did their northern counterparts. In 1850, it is estimated that approximately four out of five free people living in slave states were literate. Before their admittance to female academies and colleges, young southern girls acquired basic education through such pedagogical texts as spellers, grammars, and rhetorics. The skills gained through these texts allowed them to enjoy more popular texts, such as songs, stories, hymnbooks and songbooks, biographies, and fiction as well as religious tracts and pamphlets. Even in the rural South, the printed word was ubiquitous. Increased access to print was made possible thanks to advances in production and circulation but also to the ministers of all denominations who worked to disseminate printed materials across the South.[12]

North Carolinian Frances Moore Webb Bumpass offers an exceptional example of a woman who not only embraced the power of literacy but employed it to stake her intellectual and moral authority. Her husband, Sidney D. Bumpass, a Methodist minister, died in 1851 when Frances was only thirty-two years old. At that time, she boldly assumed editorship of her late husband's religious paper, the *Weekly Message*. Crossing gender boundaries, Bumpass was the only southern woman to edit a publication with a doctrinal agenda before the Civil War. To appease those who were uncomfortable with a female editor, she acquiesced to a man serving as the paper's managing editor. Bumpass used the *Weekly Message* to promote women's religious agency. In particular, she advanced a version of holiness doctrine, a theological perspective that emphasizes personal holiness and the quest of a sanctified life, that impelled morally and spiritually pure women to speak and to assume roles as activist Christians. While not a recipient of an academy or college education, she clearly valued education. She taught school in Granville County, North Carolina, and enthusiastically supported Greensboro Female College, a Methodist institution, at which Sidney Bumpass had served as a trustee.[13] Southern female journalists like Bumpass used their intellect and rhetorical might to advocate for more varied roles for women in addition to critiquing slavery, lamenting over the region's intellectual and economic backwardness, or promoting expanded educational opportunities. The proliferation of female-authored publications, including those of a religious nature, in the antebellum era slowly eroded gendered private/public sphere divisions that had confined women to domestic spaces.[14]

Annual student enrollment at female academies and colleges hovered anywhere from a couple dozen to in excess of one hundred pupils. The larger academies and colleges offered a curriculum that included composition, logic, rhetoric, botany, natural philosophy, astronomy, chemistry, algebra, geometry, history, geography, moral philosophy, and world religions.[15] The curricula at such institutions did not include Greek or Latin, subjects emphasized at male colleges in the antebellum South, but rather offered what has become to be known as a liberal arts education. Such southern girls' academies and women's colleges instituted more rigorous curricula than they had during the eighteenth century under the French school model, under the premise that there existed an equality of intellect between the sexes. In spite of these more democratic views regarding women's education, wealthy southerners were ultimately looking to send their daughters to educational environments in which, though they would develop into more pious, benevolent, artistic, intelligent, and capable persons, they would not become assertive members of society. Such an image did not dismantle the status quo, neither slavery nor patriarchy.[16]

Furman Theological Institution graduate J. Edwin Spears, who delivered a speech at the 1859 public examination of the Baptist female college at Bennettsville, South Carolina, asserted that God "endowed [women] with capacities equal with man."[17] Clerics across the antebellum South echoed these sentiments regarding female intellect, although they did not promote equal opportunities nor advocated identical religious expressions between the sexes. Regardless, it was these elite and/or educated, as opposed to the illiterate or the functionally literate, southern women who led adult lives in which they actively engaged religion as something more than a purely emotional or spiritual outlet.

Martha Elizabeth Coons, a student at the Richmond Female Institute in Richmond, Virginia, in the late 1850s, illustrates the deep thinking that individuals like J. Edwin Spears promoted for pupils at female academies and colleges. According to copious notes in one academic notebook kept by Miss Coons in 1859, she and her peers spent much time studying religious archaeology and ancient history in conjunction with their studies in Christianity and world religions. The curriculum required students to consider the views and religious culture of non-Christians, to consider the definition and purpose of religion as an abstract, and to interpret and apply the Bible based upon tenets of logic.[18]

Among the questions Coons pondered and attempted to answer were: "What does Christianity represent to other religions?"; "What must a system of religion have in order to influence men?"; "What does modern discovery show [in relation to archaeological findings in Assyria and Biblical history]?"; and "What are the proofs of the genuineness of the miracles of the Bible?"[19]

Also included in Martha Coons's book were notes she had taken at the many religious lectures she had attended. Coons recorded her thoughts about several religious lectures, including one given by a famed Baptist minister, the Reverend J. Lansing Burrows, best known for the stirring sermon he later delivered at the Battle of Shiloh in April 1862.

Educational opportunities for young women temporarily dried up during and after the Civil War. During Reconstruction, fewer southern families could afford to send their daughters to academies and colleges. Those young women who were fortunate enough to receive an advanced education continued to seriously ponder higher-level religious, ethical, and philosophical concepts, issues, and dilemmas. The antebellum model that benefited young women like Martha Elizabeth Coons was not deemed irrelevant or outmoded after the war. For example, Ellen McAlpin, a Savannah native, attended the exclusive Madame Le Fevre's School in Baltimore during the early 1870s, where she excelled in religious studies. In addition to the myriad recorded Bible lessons, inspirational Bible passages, hymns and sermon analyses, her notebook includes several of her essays such as "The Master's Questions," "The Burial of Moses" and "Healing by Faith."[20]

Addressing many of the same broad religious questions that Martha Coons did, McAlpin exhibited an impressive, analytical appreciation for scripture and ancient history. Her essay "Healing by Faith" showcased her sharp prose, her air-tight arguments reminiscent of those of skilled attorneys, and her deep knowledge of the Old and New Testaments. In this one essay, Coons examined such questions as these: Was it within our rights as children of God to seek bodily healing from Him? Was such healing sought in the early Church? Was such healing a part of Christ's mission according to prophecy? How did the Apostles teach the concept of bodily healing from God? Was the sickness of believers connected with sin? How are we to regard death? Such essays and religious materials as recorded by Ellen McAlpin, Martha Coons, and others during their later adolescence challenge those who have equated evangelical Protestantism, especially as exhibited by women, with anti-intellectualism and excessive emotionalism.[21]

In the eighteenth and early nineteenth centuries, Deists, Unitarians, and other arch-rationalists often associated evangelical religiosity with emotion rather than intellect, viewing biblical revelation as a greater truth than reason and logic. In the later nineteenth century and beyond, evangelical Christians received criticism for their emotions-based religious practices from diverse individuals, including atheists, Jews, Catholics, Quakers, Congregationalists, Lutherans, and other nonfundamentalists. McAlpin and Coons, two evangelical Protestants, suggest that scholars and laypeople have exaggerated the extent to which these assumptions about evangelical emotions-based religious practices are valid. In particular, these two women substantiate that they ascended mere emotions in their interpretation of the Bible and religion more generally. This is significant in that these two women, and their counterparts across the South, directly influenced the religious ideology and practice of their families and indirectly influenced the religious ideology and practice of their communities. Southern women shaped the ways their families and community members interpreted and practiced their faiths. That said, poor and yeoman women of the South were not recipients of any higher education and, as a result, did not teach or express these more logical and intellectual renditions of evangelical Christianity associated with McAlpin and Coons.

RELIGIOUS EXPRESSIONS IN
DIARIES AND JOURNALS

While many southern females demonstrated a high level of thinking on religion within the setting of private academies and colleges, likely many more recorded their deeper religious insights and questions in their journals and diaries.[22] This is not to suggest that some white southern women were not simultaneously exhibiting their intellectual prowess in their academic work. However, and especially for adult women whose formal instruction was behind them, journals or diaries provided a private space in which to ruminate over their deepest thoughts. Journal writing often occurred on Sunday afternoons after church services when religious ideas were stirring within the minds of white southern women.[23] For such women, religion was not simply interchangeable with church services. Rather, diaries offered space to critique sermons, assess their applicability to current events, hone their writers' skills in argument, as well as consider issues that transcended the quotidian. They were safe spaces to ponder sermons, especially those that touched upon such omnipresent political issues as slavery and states' rights. Finally, they unveil southern women's conceptions of gender and femininity in a religious context.

Women's journals and other private writings further reveal that many kept a reasonably open mind about sermons and religious lectures, even those that were given (or written) by clerics whose politics, region, or denomination differed from theirs.[24] Among educated and elite white southern women, ecumenicalism—the principle that Christians who belong to different Christian denominations should collaborate to engender closer relationships among their churches and aspire to Christian unity—played a palpable role. For example, women like Ann Elizabeth Nowlan MacDonnell of Savannah, Georgia, the wife of a Methodist minister, discussed her frequent attendance at religious events hosted by at least four different denominations, including the Presbyterian, Lutheran, Episcopal, and Baptist. It is likely that this ecumenical culture, combined with their increasing access to formal education, encouraged such women to keep their insularity and (some of) their prejudices in check. That said, although these white southern women deserve a degree of praise for their open-mindedness on some issues, more often than not, they exhibited highly racist beliefs that harmonized with those articulated by men.

Sarah Lois Wadley, the adolescent daughter of the Central Railroad (Georgia) superintendent William Morrill Wadley, offers evidence relative to the religious topics educated and/or elite women of the era addressed in such private realms as dairies and journals. Sarah's three volumes of journals, spanning the years 1859 to 1865 and written from several different places in the South, reflect her interpretations of, thoughts about, and questions regarding the Civil War through a religious lens. Mr. Wadley's job with the railroad often uprooted the family, and, as a result, Sarah lived in several communities in Georgia and Louisiana during the war.[25] Despite these challenges, Sarah Wadley, a devout Methodist and later an Episcopalian, demonstrated intellectual prowess from a young age. Aiding her intellectual development during adolescence were the series of hired private tutors and family's fine library to which she had access on the eve of the Civil War and during the conflict.[26]

Wadley filled a few hundred pages of her journals analyzing a variety of religious themes and topics. Religion grounded all her observations and descriptions of social, cultural, political, economic, military, and educational phenomena. As Wadley wrote, "whenever I for a moment lose sight of the bible and of religion, my mind becomes involved in mazy labyrinths of doubt 'till I almost question the fact of my existence and wonder if I was not one of the fabled creations of ancient days ..."[27] A discussion of her collection of religious pamphlets by proslavery southern ministers and her subsequent critique of their logic, "Christian reasoning," structure, and rhetoric received particular attention in her journal. Wadley's many pamphlets included reprinted sermons by ministers from several different Protestant denominations.

While Sarah typically praised proslavery southern ministers, the young intellect worked to find logical fallacies—or flaws within scriptural inter-pretation—in the sermons of abolitionist or pro-Union northern ministers. Nonetheless, Sarah did not let her decidedly pro-Confederate politics entirely color her religious views and critiques of those who opposed hers. In Janu-ary 1861, Sarah wrote in her journal that she had "read ... a very interesting sermon delivered by the Rev. Mr. Vandyke in the first Presbyterian Church, Brooklyn, New York, upon the subject of slavery," concluding, "it was a very able discourse treating abolitionism on scriptural ground and only touching lightly upon Political subjects."[28]

More than a year later, when Sarah faced limited access to religious pam-phlets and newspapers as a result of the war's growing intensity, she turned to analyzing the religious undertones of varied works of literature, philosophy, and science. Presumably, these were volumes in the family library or those belonging to her tutors. Such works ranged from Alexander von Humboldt's *Cosmos* to the more melodramatic *Les Misérables, by Victor Hugo.* Apart from these secular works, Wadley found solace and mental stimulation in several works of religious poetry and philosophy. One was John Milton's *Paradise Lost,* the epic poem concerning the biblical story of the temptation of Adam and Eve by Satan and their expulsion from the Garden of Eden. Referring to it, Sarah noted in November 1862: "What a sublime work *Paradise Lost* is, and there are touches of exquisite beauty as well as grandeur. I closed the book with a clearer conception of the divine scheme of redemption, and a deeper love of Christ in my heart."[29] Other analyzed works of religious poetry and philosophy she discussed included Alphonse de Lamartine's poetry on the Holy Land and Thomas à Kempis's *Following of Christ,* a treatise imbued in the rhetoric of the Devotio Moderna (Modern Devotion) movement, which stressed apostolic renewal through rediscovery of such pious practices as humility and simplicity of life.[30]

The analysis and insight in the academy notebooks of Martha Elizabeth Coons and Ellen McAlpin and in the diaries of Sarah Wadley reveal highly intellectual young women which while no means typical were not exceptional either. While southern society readily accepted women's embrace of religion, especially relative to Christian service, it was reticent to encourage these same women onto an excessively intellectual or authoritarian path. It was one thing to encourage women to bring Christian instruction into the lives of their enslaved people, to deliver sermons, and teach Sunday School to their communities in the absence of clerics, or to volunteer for one of the many denominational aid societies during the Civil War, some of which will be explored in subsequent chapters. However, it was quite another to spur such women to read and respond to the Bible in nonconformist ways that were more reminiscent of rebellious, independent, or unorthodox forms of worship. In fact, Sarah Wadley's father recognized the potential dangers of a woman's mental acuity and excessive religious interest. Referring to a conversation between her mother and father, Sarah Wadley wrote in her diary in January 1861:

> In one of her letters Mother jestingly asked Father how he would like a minister for a soninlaw, he answered her remark in earnest, he said, "Whenever Sarah marries, which I hope may not be before she is twenty years old, I should prefer that her husband be engaged in some active out of doors business, not that I object particularly to a parson, except that I suppose she will take an interest in her husband's profession and I think it best that her mind should be turned from metaphysics to which I think she is rather too much inclined."[31]

On several occasions, Sarah Wadley berated herself for exhibiting religious behaviors and practices that challenged conventional gender expectations. For example, Sarah realized that it was not appropriate for the "fairer sex" to pray that death befall enemy Yankee soldiers. Nor did Wadley believe it appropriate for women to adopt excessively authoritarian, masculine tones with those whom they religiously instructed, particularly young boys.[32] Wadley's latter comment regarding women's assertive tone with disciples contradicts the content and affect of Elizabeth Willis Gloster Anderson's authoritative religious advice that she compiled for her family members. The disconnect between Anderson and Wadley suggests that evangelical Protestantism over time backed away from tenets of equality that in theory offered women more agency. Wadley's reservations suggest that southern women contemplated

26

their femininity and sought to religiously express themselves in ways that upheld the elite South's expectations of womanhood.

Southern society did not deem most religious expressions among women as inappropriate. Very likely, cautious southern white males acknowledged, perhaps feared, their daughters and wives combining intellect, logic, and religion. While such southern men were probably not comparing their female relatives to iconoclasts of the Middle Ages or intellects during the Protestant Reformation, they may have observed evidence of religious opposition, at least by their own definition, on their own plantations. In particular, they recognized that the African American 'brand' of Christianity—a highly syncretic religion that combined elements of Christianity, African religions, and Islam with aspects of their African American culture—could lead to insubordination, rebellion, and even flight among their enslaved.

Reinforcing acceptable gendered expressions of religion were religious addresses, or "discourses," that southern clerics delivered to female audiences. Reverend Thomas Verner Moore's February 1852 address, "Adaptation of Religion to Female Character: A Discourse to Young Ladies," offers one such example. Delivering his address to "young ladies" at his home church, the First Presbyterian Church in Richmond, Virginia, Moore presented young women with insight into their distinct roles as female religious beings. Although Moore consistently praised women, particularly their contributions to society and their deep influence on their families, he discouraged them from pursuing religious paths that might be construed as masculine. A masculine religious path, to Moore, would be an intellectual one, one that relied too much upon logic. This, however, did not signify women as inferior, incapable, or ineffectual. Rather, according to Moore, while men possessed a more "noble mind," women claimed a more "noble heart." The cleric asserted that society at large "esteem[ed] a noble heart to rank above a noble mind."[33]

Following this train of thought, man, with his pioneering spirit, was intended to "subdue the earth" as well as "conquer nature in those rude and intractable forms" in which mankind found "it congealed and petrified by the curse [of Eve.]" God intended that man would assume positions of authority and power on earth. Moore maintained that woman, in contrast, possessed "the intuitional powers of the mind, and the higher attributes of the heart" that "did not qualify her to bear the rule in the circumstances in which the human race [was] placed."[34] These gendered differences, in Moore's interpretation of scripture, dictated disparate civil and religious roles for the sexes.[35]

Sarah Wadley's quandary over gender coupled with the content of such an address to young women by Reverend Moore suggest that southern women, despite their demonstrated embrace of religion as an intellectual and both private and public outlet, still felt the need to act in ways that supported society's expectations of them. Generally, such women accepted this with few complaints, although someone like Wadley bristled at the thought that their opinions, including those on religious matters, held less weight than those of men. However, other evangelical southern women, especially those who readily acknowledged the brevity of life on Earth, probably relished religious roles that afforded them such influence on the eternal existences of their family members' souls.[36] Frances Todd Johnson of Orange County, Virginia, conveyed such views regarding gendered expressions of evangelical Protestantism through some of her religious poetry. At age seventeen, Johnson penned in 1851:

> I have not wealth, or power, or skill,
> To broadcast all around;
> The world's wide field I may not till,
> Nor sow its fallow ground;
> But little spots are here and there,
> Which I may weed of grief and care.[37]

Johnson appears to accept that while she, as a female, will not wield religious power or influence, as would a cleric whose writings could sway an entire Protestant denomination, she will serve society in another, important godly way by "weed[ing it] of grief" and exerting her soft, feminine, caring touch.

Complementing Johnson's poetry are poems received by Sallie "Didd" Beck in 1860, while she was a student at Synodical Female College in Griffin, Georgia. Composed by a few of her friends at the College, these religiously themed poems—although not part of the formal curriculum—stressed the feminine influence that the fairer sex exhibited. Significantly, these young women in such unpublished works emphasized the fleeting nature of life on earth in contrast to the everlasting life that was yet to come. Through these poems, which they wrote and exchanged with one another during times of leisure, young pupils bestowed "the gift of love divine" that was "sweeter by far than pleasure, richer than golden mind." While the former was made possible by acceptance of Jesus Christ and feminine piety and religious expression, the latter was a product of more masculine and hedonistic behaviors.[38]

RELIGIOUS MENTORSHIP WITH CLERICS

Although diaries and journals were an important outlet for adolescent and adult southern women, some of these women also encouraged intimate conversations with their ministers on religious and even controversial or sensitive political matters. Interestingly, southern women, other than those who were married to preachers, rarely referred to a discussion of religious matters with their husbands. Instead, such women typically shared personal religious thoughts, opinions, questions, and struggles with female friends, female family members, as well as with their male and female children. Some, however, transcended such unofficial "sexual boundaries" through deep dialogue with male ministers. Not surprisingly, this practice was especially common during the Civil War when such adolescent and adult women, whose fathers, brothers, and sons were out on the battlefront, sought spiritual comfort and a sympathetic ear from an inspiring minister.

Plantation mistress Mary Mildred Jeffreys Bethell of Rockingham County, North Carolina, a devout Methodist and alumna of Salem Academy—a well-known and respected Moravian-founded school in Winston-Salem—recorded in her diary a number of "crucial" conversations she shared with a few local pastors throughout the Civil War years, a period that brought her and her community much pain.[39] Bethell's husband and two sons served in the Confederate Army, one of whom was captured by the Union Army and imprisoned at Johnson's Island in Ohio. She agonized over her responsibilities as a Christian to local Blacks, both as enslaved people and then as freedpeople. She obsessed over God's solemn message, including His destruction on the battlefield. Bethell's diary revealed a sensitive woman who lived in a constant state of anxiety. In spite of endless emotional turmoil and her severe hearing impairment, Bethell's journal highlighted her active participation in church and community activities. These included her participation at Methodist quarterly meetings and revivals, collecting Bibles to distribute to Confederate soldiers, and assistance and religious guidance to new widows. Additionally, she nursed the sick and disabled, cared for new orphans, and fed passing Confederate troops at her home. These traumatic and fulfilling war experiences were mitigated by the candid discussions Bethell had with church members, including three clerics.

Bethell's diary revealed a particular fondness for the intimate conversations and religious soul-searching she shared with Brothers Bruton, Pepper, and Reid. Discussion of her religious soul-searching occupied much space in her journal. For example, in the summer of 1861, when her two sons had recently joined the Confederacy, Bethell sought religious advice from her mentors Brothers Bruton and Reid. At Bruton's home, Bethell benefited not only from Brother Reid's war news but from the context he provided her in understanding her sacrifice. Ministers like Reverend Reid served as nearly perfect conduits between God and Bethell by conveying God's messages. Bethell wrote in July 1861:

> I returned home yesterday from the Parsonage at Wentworth, I spent a day and two nights with Sister and Brother Bruton, our minister. Our time passed off pleasantly. Brother Fletcher Reid came to see us while there, he is one of my favorites. I felt it to be a privilege and an honor to be with God's ministers, and hear them talk. Bro. Reid spoke fluently about the war, he comforted me by his conversation. Brother Reid sympathized with me in giving up my dear boys to go to the army, he encouraged me to trust in God, and commit them to God. I was greatly comforted by his conversation, my soul thrilled with tender emotions of love and joy. I thank God for comforting me through dear Brother Reid.[40]

Bethell referred to another "profitable and pleasant conversation on the subject of religion" she sustained with Reverend Pepper in February 1863.[41] At this time, Bethell, who viewed herself as an evangelizer whose mission was to "advance [H]is kingdom here on earth," felt inadequate. Stressed over the religious welfare of others within her community and her extended family, she worried that her sincere efforts at evangelizing were not enough in the eyes of her Savior.[42] Her February 1863 exchange with Pepper, in which the two addressed her struggles with self-doubt and "melancholy" through a focus on "the 4th Chap Hebrews, 16 verse," served as a welcoming and stimulating salve for Bethell's weakened soul.[43] Bethell and a number of circuit-riding Methodist preachers during and after the war considered many topics. They assessed the war in biblical terms, believing that "perhaps the Lord [was] chastising his church." They likewise discussed Bethell's Christian works and private religious study, and they extrapolated on particular sermons.[44]

Almost all of the activities described within this chapter have related to white southern women's private religious activities. Such pursuits have included their religious instruction and guidance to family members; private study at religious academies; their recording of religious insights within their diaries and journals; their maintenance of correspondence, significant portions of which covered such topics as events at church, new clergymen, and reprinted sermons and lectures with families and friends; and their scripturally based conversations with clerics. Through such means, these white southern women, most of whom, as we have seen, were highly educated and grew up in middle-class and elite homes, readily demonstrated their penchants for religious thought and action. Some even displayed marked domestic authority over household religious matters.

MITE SOCIETIES

White southern women's experiences, however, were not entirely confined to the domestic sphere. In those several decades before the Civil War, white southern women, representing various Protestant denominations, involved themselves in such religious organizations as female mite societies, whose purpose was in "raising money for home and foreign missions and local benevolence."[45] Such organizations acquired the name "mite society" after the story of the widow's mite in Mark 12:41–44. A mite, or lepton, was a common coin exchanged in Jesus's Palestine. Appropriately, female members in mite societies paid weekly dues, usually a few cents, and engaged in fundraising campaigns for worthy projects. Female mite societies existed outside the South, but they enjoyed much success south of the Mason-Dixon Line during the antebellum years.[46] Similar organizations, not all of which used the "mite society" label, existed in other southern locations. For example, beginning in the early 1830s, the Female Education Society of the First Baptist Church of Richmond, Virginia, raised money for scholarship funds for the benefit of struggling ministerial students at the Virginia Baptist Seminary, later Richmond College (and ultimately the University of Richmond).

Baptist mite societies appeared as early as the 1810s in such South Carolina locales as Beaufort, Charleston, Greenville, and Lawtonville (present-day Estill) and operated independently of one another.[47] Members of mite societies engaged in fundraising, such as raising money for scholarships for male students at Furman Academy or Furman Theological Seminary, for church construction and repair, for expansion of the Baptist Tract Society (the main publishing arm of the Baptist denomination), for aid to impoverished divinity students, and suffering members within the community, especially widows and orphaned children, and for educating women in such foreign locations as Burma.[48]

According to the partial minute book of the Greenwood, South Carolina, mite society, the Mount Moriah Female Missionary and Benevolent Society, the organization wrote and adopted a constitution and elected a "directress," a "secretary," and a "treasurer." At its inception in 1833, the Mount Moriah society boasted fifty-five members, all of whom were required to attend any meeting organized by the directress and participate in fundraising efforts throughout the community.[49] At these semi-regular meetings, mite society members might hear a sermon delivered by a minister, re-read or tweak their constitution, invite and welcome new members, give reports regarding their progress and goals, and engage in religious study. Some mite societies pushed for representation at their respective state denominational annual or quarterly meetings. In such instances, members nominated and then voted on a favorable male church member to present any updates or ask any questions. Although mite societies experienced their peak in membership and influence in the years immediately before the Civil War, many lasted through the Civil War and beyond or morphed into other aid and benevolence societies.

South Carolina appeared to be an epicenter of mite society activity. While extant mite society records are spotty, the societies operated across the "seaboard slave states" in such locales as Augusta, Columbus, Milledgeville, and Savannah, Georgia; Fayetteville, Raleigh, and Wilmington, North Carolina; and Alexandria, Petersburg, Richmond, and Winchester, Virginia.[50] These female-led societies attest to a focus on community that the Second Great Awakening emphasized. Evangelical Christianity, while directed toward the individual, exerted a strong communal dimension. Conversion beckoned the believer out from the world, but evangelicalism "did not leave him alone, nor did it celebrate his isolation. It brought him immediately into a community established on rules and regulations."[51] Ironically, sectional schism of Methodist and Baptist churches during the 1840s impelled ministers to foster this emphasis on community to an even greater degree than they had before. It was at this time that Baptist and Methodist leaders promoted expansion of missionary enterprises, Sunday schools, and education as a means to recast perceptions regarding the southern social and religious order. Southern ministers "endorsed not a 'pro-slavery' Christianity but a Christian slavery."[52] Female mite and benevolence societies are part of this broader movement of institutional building that took place among southern evangelicals before the Civil War.[53]

Although mite societies had only a limited effect on the southern religious landscape, they were significant stepping stones along the long trajectory—one that reached back to the turn of the nineteenth century and stretched into the twentieth century—of evolving intellectual and public spiritual opportunities for generations of white Protestant southern women. Holding official positions within mite societies, coupled with their experiences as religious students, mentors, educators, and conversationalists, prepared such white southern women for a diverse array of religious roles.

Significantly, many roles afforded these white southern women more authority, independence, and access to decision making, skills all ensconced within the public, nondomestic sphere. Organized benevolence societies brought white southern women several benefits.[54] They provided women with a magnified sense of their personal value, a deeper appreciation for the contributions and thoughts of other women, an opportunity to develop leadership and administrative skills, and a place in which to participate in democratic decision making.[55] However, such change occurred slowly and southern women faced a number of gendered obstacles along the way. Nonetheless, in the decades following the Civil War, these white southern women engaged in new spiritual activities and adopted new religious roles, for example, as home and foreign missionaries or evangelical Christian crusaders in the later Progressive movement.

Before turning toward these more public expressions of religiosity among elite and educated white southern women of the Protestant South during the postbellum years, it is necessary to more closely examine how such women continued to wield religious authority within the domestic sphere. The religious instruction of enslaved people by slaveholding women thus offers a revealing case study through which the latter's (not always noble) mission, motives, and methods can be determined and assessed alongside realities of the antebellum South, a society dependent on racial and sexual subordination.

Two

EVANGELIZING THE ENSLAVED

Educated, elite women in the antebellum South found that their evangelical Protestant faith brought them intellectual and emotional fulfillment. Some gained a degree of authority within their households and in their communities. Among those, some served as religious guides to family members, while others administered mite societies. An additional, largely unexplored, instance in which slaveholding women exercised religious dominion was through Christian instruction of their enslaved people.[1] In this role, they not only honed their skills as educators but furthered their own study of religion and promoted morals and religion—albeit on their own terms—on their properties and in their greater communities. Simultaneously, slaveholding women, both religiously and intellectually, found themselves directly confronting the dilemma of slaveholding.

The egalitarian rhetoric of the early years of the Second Great Awakening had been largely discarded by 1830. Historians, particularly Donald Mathews, have thoroughly documented white southern evangelicals' shift from egalitarianism and democracy to authoritarianism and materialism.[2] With this transformation, the South ascribed to a more rigidly hierarchical society. Particular to elite and educated white southern women, sexist values permitted them few public roles, few authoritarian positions beyond the day-to-day management of the enslaved, and few intellectual pursuits beyond the religious instruction of enslaved people. Perhaps the latter was, at first glance, a welcome outlet. Nonetheless, regardless of whether slaveholding women embraced their role as religious instructor, tried to avoid it, or fell some place in between, they had to grapple with ideas, responsibilities, and realities beyond the confines of their homes, plantations, or farms. Exploring this specific role of some slaveholding women fosters a more nuanced and complete understanding of them as religious and even intellectual beings, albeit ones who were typically ideologically and socially conservative.

✝

As late as 1800, most enslaved people in the United States had not been converted to Christianity.[3] Before that time, southern evangelical preachers had opposed slavery but quickly reversed their view as slavery grew more entrenched in the region. And, by 1830, Protestant clergymen in the South were fiercely defending the institution. This coincided with the emergence of the abolitionist movement in the North. Leaders of the abolitionist movement argued that slavery was a national sin, and that it was the moral obligation of Americans to eradicate the institution. In an attempt to counter northern accusations regarding the inhumanity of slavery, southern clerics promoted proselytization of the enslaved as part of a greater civilizing mission. Innumerable Christians were needed to make conversion of the enslaved masses a reality. Southern slaveholding women were among those who responded to their ministers' plea. By the 1830s, these women were ever more committed to evangelizing their enslaved people.[4]

The emerging abolitionist movement was not the only impetus for the religious instruction of the enslaved after 1830. Paternalism was just as much at play. Widely accepted in the antebellum South, paternalism dictated that the enslaved were dependents who needed protection and guidance, in the same manner as biological children. Slaveholding men and women were thus materially, morally, and spiritually responsible for the welfare of their enslaved. Paternalism was not a reflection of genuine kindness or compassion on the part of slaveholders. Rather, it was a means to reinforce discipline as well as to morally justify slavery.

Drawing upon European socialist scholarship, slaveholding whites in the American South concluded that all laborers, whether white or Black, were victims of de facto slavery. The South, however, boasted a "Christian slavery" that was comparatively more humane.[5] In practical terms, most male slaveholders were seldom willing or able to attend personally to the material care and religious guidance expected by their paternalistic social order. Instead,

36

they typically assigned those duties to a female family member who regularly took charge of the material, moral, and spiritual needs of her enslaved people. Some historians, including Anne Firor Scott and Marli Weiner, have concluded that an expanded definition of feminine "benevolence" evolved from this ideology of paternalism.[6] Ironically, by converting to evangelical Christianity and perhaps even partaking in religious services with whites, enslaved people strengthened a paternalistic justification for slavery. This justification, whereby slavery came to be viewed as a prerequisite for Black conversion, was part of a larger mission by white evangelicals to reconcile the democratic ideology of the Revolution with the reality of slavery.[7]

Not all slaveholding women, however, embraced the role of evangelizer to the enslaved. Many felt serious frustration and encountered obstacles in their efforts to fully live up to this idealized model of antebellum womanhood and to evangelize their enslaved people. As their diaries divulged, many such women felt inadequate and lost in their role as religious educator. In contrast, others recorded significant frustrations not from feelings of personal inadequacy but from their serious discontent with the politics of slavery.

Before one can fully appreciate slaveholding women's dissatisfaction as evangelizers to their enslaved people, one must consider the medium through which women directly confronted their responsibilities and frustration, namely their diaries and journals. Particularly worth stressing is the reality that slaveholding women's diaries and journals are more likely to expose the actuality of southern women's religious ideas and expression than do other types of sources, particularly the antebellum narratives of the enslaved and postbellum mistress memoirs, whose agenda-driven authors wrote them for an outside audience. Rather, slaveholding women typically kept diaries for themselves or for their children. In the privacy of their diaries and journals, slaveholding women highlight their successes, but they also regularly express a spectrum of negative feelings, ones ranging from guilt to exasperation to resentment. In contrast, mistress memoirs published during the Lost Cause movement of the late nineteenth and early twentieth centuries routinely idealize the religious instruction they had provided decades before, and they almost universally characterize mistress-enslaved relationships in a positive, warm, and even nostalgic manner.[8] Meanwhile, pre–Civil War enslaved narratives typically projected an abolitionist agenda and sought to discredit mistress-directed religious education.

While there were some topics about which women were relatively silent or discussed only obliquely, they were candid about the trials they experienced in their roles as wives, mothers, and mistresses. Repeatedly, the opening passage in antebellum diary after antebellum diary attested to its author's commitment to honesty and candor. New Year's Day, in particular, was a predictable and popular time for a mistress to reaffirm written veracity and commitment to serving God by bringing perceived sinners to Him. For example, Lucilla Agnes Gamble McCorkle of Talladega, Alabama, wrote in 1858: "May this old account book witness my honesty and sincerity in this transaction and may it ever remind me of the Great Day of Accounts—where the Judge of Quick and Dead will sit upon the great white Heaven and open the Lord's Book of Life!"[9] Similar sentiments appeared throughout antebellum mistress diaries.[10]

One must also gain an appreciation for some of those individuals, influences, and institutions that reinforced or promoted paternalistic values, more generally, and women's role as religious figures, more specifically. Many individuals encouraged slaveholding women to express female benevolence by embracing their essential role as religious instructors and mentors to their enslaved. These included southern religious leaders, male and female slaveholders from across the South, and even northern visitors to the South.

Among these, leaders within churches were the most outwardly supportive of slaveholding mistresses' efforts to bring God to their enslaved people. Through their paternalistic language and exclusively male authorship, such figures, in speech and in publication, challenged elite southern women to take on an evangelizing role and to establish Sunday school activities into which they would bring their enslaved people. The Reverend Francis Hanson, rector of St. Andrew's and St. Michael's Episcopal Churches near Demopolis, Alabama, for example, praised several plantation mistresses of his acquaintance who "devoted much time and care to the religious instruction of [their] servants."[11]

In 1849, the Baptist State Convention of Alabama offered a premium of $200 for the best essay on the duties of Christian masters to their servants. Methodist minister Reverend Holland Nimmons McTyeire won the contest with his *Duties of Christian Masters to their Servants*, a treatise which outlined the basic human, social, and religious needs of the enslaved. The son of slaveholders who knew the institution firsthand, Rev. McTyeire acknowledged that it was not always feasible for slaveholders to engage an ordained minister to lead religious services for their enslaved people. In his eyes, individual slave-holders assumed the greatest responsibility of all for the spiritual welfare of their enslaved people: "Remember that you have a charge of the souls in your family, and are as a priest and teacher in your house, and therefore see that you keep them to the constant worshipping of God, especially on the Lord's Day in public and private, and that you teach them the things that concern their salvation."[12] Books and pamphlets like *Duties of Christian Masters to their Servants* were widely distributed across the region, and slaveholding women took suggestions and inspiration from their contents.

Beyond religious figures, fellow female southerners were vocal in their support of fellow plantation mistresses who adhered to the model of female benevolence and who assumed roles as Christian educators. In so doing, such women were able to enter a more public and/or intellectual sphere than was customary. One notable woman was South Carolinian Louisa S. McCord. McCord was an accomplished playwright and poet who associated with the male faculty at South Carolina College (now the University of South Carolina), married at the advanced age of thirty, and even held property in her name after her marriage. Yet, despite such unorthodoxy, she passionately supported conventional ideas about the submission of women, marriage and mother-hood, paternalism, and slaveholding women's roles as "parent" and "teacher" of their enslaved people. McCord conveyed her conviction that the role of plantation mistress and the role of caretaker went hand-in-hand. This is seen in her 1853 poem "Woman's Progress," which was published in the *Southern Literary Magazine* in November 1853 and reached a large readership among elite southern women:

> Sweet sister! Stoop not thou to be a man!
> Man has his place as woman hers; and she,
> As made to comfort, minister, and help,
> Moulded for gentler duties, ill fulfils
> His jarring destinies. Her mission is
> To labour and to pray; to help, to heal,
> To soothe, to bear; patient, with smiles, to suffer;

Further into the poem, McCord continued:

She is a living sermon of that truth,
Which ever through her gentle actions speaks,
That life is given to labour and to love.
Through this rough world her angel ministry to all,
Like sweetest water bubbling through the sands
Of arid desert, cheers the weary heart,
And leads the restless soul which cursed its fate
To pause, to think, and learn to love that God
Who, midst the parching waste of suffering,
Has dropped this comfort like a boon from Heaven
To bid him drink and live.[13]

Whether McCord included the enslaved in her vision of a woman's informal Christian ministry is unclear. However, it is significant that McCord emphasized women's role as religious educators, "through this rough world her angel ministry to all," and did not specifically exclude enslaved people from her model for elite white women as evangelizers.

Although relatively few women spoke publicly about evangelization of enslaved people, many slaveholding women did address the topic in other venues. Pupils at elite finishing schools in such places as Baltimore, Charleston, Nashville, and New Orleans, and later at southern female colleges like Wesleyan Female College in Macon, Georgia, wrote essays that discussed their future obligations as wives in a privileged class. In them, they identified those duties expected of them: obedience to God and to men, industry, cheerfulness, and serving as moral examples for their families and their enslaved communities. Ella Noland MacKenzie's essay "On Obedience" illustrates the sentiments these young women expressed. In 1849, from a Baltimore female academy, MacKenzie, of Leesburg, Virginia, wrote that as an adult she would "embrace with constant devotion her duties as a virtuous Christian woman, always mindful of her duties to her family and servants and that she pitied the woman who did not obey God or men."[14] Had MacKenzie read McCord, she would have felt reassured by McCord's philosophies, as would many other slaveholding women. Detractors of antebellum southern elitism, however, are quick to identify these ideologies as mechanisms that controlled both the Black race and the female gender.[15]

Some slaveholding women exhibited their devotion to a higher calling by collecting clippings from various publications and affixing them to their diaries. These clippings outlined the requirements of propriety, particularly religious propriety. For example, between 1846 and 1858 Lucilla McCorkle, the wife of a Presbyterian minister who founded a religious-affiliated college for women in Talladega, Alabama, filled one journal with material which she both quoted and clipped from newspapers and periodicals. They defined those virtues to which proper women should aspire. McCorkle's material also included citations from northerner Catherine Maria Sedgwick as well as other champions of the ideology of domesticity. Various southern periodicals frequently reprinted such pieces. Those works emphasized patience, tenderness, firmness, and devotion to Christ, offering tangible directives which female religious educators could incorporate into their efforts. One such piece McCorkle saved contained the following instruction: "Perhaps one of the most indispensable and endearing qualifications of the feminine character is an amiable temper with servants."[16] Plantation women like McCorkle could assess their own successes and failures in living up to those ideals presented to them by such publications. Although slaveholding women often worried about falling short of their goals, they also described their efforts to improve themselves, especially in the role of dutiful Christian and religious educator.

Similarly, elite white southern women had ready access to northern-authored "advice books" written specifically for bourgeois young women. Such volumes typically emphasized the "Cult of True Womanhood" and its corollary, the doctrine of separate spheres. The "Cult of True Womanhood," also known as the "Culture of Domesticity," refers to an idealized set of standards imposed on middle- and upper-class American women during the nineteenth century. Such expectations included female domesticity, purity, piety, submissiveness, and acceptance of masculine shortcomings. A "true woman's" supposed physical frailty belied her moral strength. Some of these "advice books" also stressed the importance of "godly" servants and a lady's role in converting her servants to Christ.[17] One publication, *Bridal Greetings: A Marriage Gift, in Which the Marital Duties of the Husband and Wife are Familiarly Illustrated and Enforced*, warned elite women of the dangers of "heathenish" servants who would instill an "unhappy moral element in the family:" "The influence of a wicked domestic is still more potent in that family which has children among its members.

41

The fact is unquestionable, that a servant's influence has ruined many a child. Ghost stories, licentious anecdotes, and even unchaste habits, have been taught by such servants to the unwary children, until they have fallen victims to superstitious fears or destructive vices."[18] Of course, as a northern publication, the word "servant" did not refer to an enslaved person. However, southern women surely internalized the potential dangers posed by their enslaved people, particularly domestic ones, who had not been proselytized.

Antebellum society urged women to embrace the Cult of True Womanhood and to lead godly, moralistic lives, devoted to others. Innumerable slaveholding women accepted this. Southern women's diaries reveal that many felt obligated to provide religious instruction to their enslaved and were committed to doing so. Some devout mistresses held daily morning prayer services for their enslaved before breakfast and observed Sunday as a strictly religious occasion, a day of rest that prohibited performing most physical tasks.[19] In 1863, Kentuckian Maria Southgate Hawes wrote during a visit to Shreveport, Louisiana: "The young ladies taught some of the brighter ones among the house servants to read from the Bible; every morning several little colored children would gather for their lessons."[20] Predictably, the more devout the mistress, the more committed she was to structure a religious framework consciously and conscientiously to benefit her enslaved people. Faith played a central role in the daily lives of many mistresses. They had attended denominational academies, and those experiences gave them the knowledge, intellectual interest, and confidence to proceed in that undertaking. For countless slaveholding women, religion represented one of the few—albeit limited—intellectual outlets encouraged for them to pursue.

Although slaveholding women attested to the frequency of their religious instruction, they were far less thorough in their discussion of the actual content and form of their religious teachings. Some slaveholding women set up Sunday schools on their plantations and met with a few dozen at once, while others preferred intimate one-on-one or small group instruction. While form of religious instruction varied widely, one constant was a deep reluctance among women to teach their enslaved to read. Slaveholders feared that literacy would empower their enslaved people to recognize the dehumanization and manipulation to which they were being subjected. On a practical level, between 1740 and 1834, all southern states had enacted antiliteracy laws, prohibiting anyone from teaching enslaved people to read or write.[21]

Regarding content, mistresses acknowledged that they introduced their enslaved to the Ten Commandments, the Apostles' Creed, the Lord's Prayer, various catechisms, and the concepts of heaven, hell, and salvation. That said, they rarely acknowledged discussion of specific biblical figures, other than Abraham, Isaac, Jacob, and those patriarchs' servants. As a result of this void, scholars may only make educated guesses relative to slaveholding women's instruction and are forced to consult other primary sources for additional insight. One such example is nineteenth-century slave narratives. In these sources, (former) enslaved people complained that those white preachers and mistresses with whom they had contact were typically selective in their biblical teachings and maintained that such figures usually emphasized teachings that reinforced enslaved subservience.

Some mistresses internalized the ideals of benevolent womanhood to the extent that they sincerely worried about the spiritual welfare of their enslaved people. A few, expressing an evangelical zeal to bring as many as possible to God, conveyed a desire that they would be with their enslaved in the world to come. As an aside, such slaveholding women did not specify whether their heaven would be a democratic one or not, in which all were equals. Nonetheless, some slaveholding women recorded genuine joy, reporting that their enslaved students were making good progress on their journey as Christians. Such advances were especially meaningful for mistresses who perceived themselves as instruments in civilizing and uplifting those whom they classified as pagans. Caroline Elizabeth Burgwin Clitherall, a schoolteacher and later plantation mistress, who, with her husband, owned enslaved people in both Carolinas and Alabama, described the spiritual journey of one young enslaved adolescent. Clitherall wrote with considerable pride: "My little servant is, I think, striving to be a *Christian*."[22]

In a similar vein, other slaveholding women reasoned that finding the road to salvation was as much the right of a Black person as of a white person. Maria Baker Taylor of Beaufort, South Carolina, and Osceola, Florida, affirmed that the Holy Scriptures clearly established the right of men to own enslaved people. She also believed that religious education of enslaved people was an obligatory duty of slaveholding women. In substantiating this, Taylor cited Colossians 4:1: "Masters, give unto your servants that which is just and equal, knowing that ye also have a Master in heaven." She reasoned, as did other mistresses, that although enslaved people were property, they were also human beings, guilty of sin but worthy of deliverance. They possessed immortal souls and were thus capable of obtaining their reward for eternity. Taylor was an impassioned Baptist, a wife, mother, and plantation mistress, who served for many years as the secretary of the Female Missionary Society in Lawtonville, South Carolina. She made repeated reference to her grandfather Richard Furman, founder of several southern colleges, president of the South Carolina Baptist State Convention, and creator of plantation "preaching stations" for his enslaved people. Taylor borrowed heavily from her grandfather's ideas, particularly (what was then considered) his more enlightened philosophy regarding slavery, when conceptualizing her own religious program.[23] That included frequent, even daily, religious meetings, open to all, in which she incorporated some of her grandfather's beliefs, some of her own, and those of two enslaved preachers.[24]

Also concerned with the religious salvation of enslaved people were Laura Alexander Baker and her husband, Everard Green Baker, of Jefferson County, Mississippi. A slaveholding couple, the Bakers frequently debated religion, especially weekly sermons, and they passionately supported the religious instruction of their enslaved. Adhering to an almost humanist philosophy, the couple reasoned that the enslaved person "who had never read or heard of God, & all his works as revealed to us in the Bible,—would nevertheless, if he conformed to the moral laws which every nation has in kind, for the promotion of good & repression of evil,—go to that Heaven which the Saints & good people in Civilized countries,—find their abode."[25] Instead of drilling their subservient subjects with very literal biblical messages, Laura Baker attempted to enlighten her enslaved spiritually with a more ethically based religious approach. Although antebellum diaries reveal that religious instruction of the enslaved was a priority, few mistresses would have concurred with Everard and Laura Baker concerning their possible path to salvation.

North Carolinian Mary Jeffreys Bethell was yet another mistress noteworthy for her degree of religiosity and dedication to enslaved religious education. Bethell established a strong relationship with God while a pupil at Salem Academy, a Moravian institution in Salem, North Carolina. A frequent attendee at evangelical camp meetings as a teenager and adult, Bethell often wrote in her diary about her efforts to maintain her covenant with her Lord. Like Caroline Clitherall, Bethell reflected upon, with genuine gratitude, the spiritual advancement of her enslaved people. In November 1856, she wrote:

44

> All at once Betty, the nurse (13 years old), broke out to saying Oh! Miss
> Mary I Believe God will have mercy on me. I was astonished I told her
> yes that God would bless her if she would believe after she got home,
> she professed religion. I felt very thankful, I hope God will convert all of
> my Negroes. I am praying for it. I read the bible to them Sunday nights
> and instruct them, and sing and pray with them, some of them listen
> attentively but all my labor will be in vain without the help of God.
> Abi has professed religion. Little Tommy Torian professed religion last
> winter 1856 thanks to God.[26]

On at least some level, Bethell believed all of her enslaved people could achieve salvation, especially young ones like Betty, the nurse, and "little" Tommy Torian who "professed" interest in religion.[27] Likely, Betty and Tommy Torian were favorites of Bethell. Furthermore, it is tenable Bethell considered that these children, by virtue of their age, were more receptive to her brand of religion.

It is difficult to determine whether, or to what degree, enslaved people agreed with their mistresses' assessments of their own purity of motive in their attempts at religious education or in their mistresses' effectiveness in bringing them to God. In the case of Mary Bethell, some of her former enslaved people attested to her uplifting influence in their lives. Ex-enslaved person William Bethell, a Works Progress Administration interviewee, reminisced that he "was quite a pet of the mistress, and [that] every morning and night my mistress would put her hand on my head and pray."[28]

Many evangelical slaveholding women embraced their missionary roles and executed them with conviction. As Mary Bethell penned in 1857, "I feel a determination to love and serve God as long as I live, I want to be instrumental in bringing many sinners to Christ. I want to do everything with an eye single to the glory of God. I want to be heavenly minded, and have the spirit of Christ, and grow in grace and in the knowledge of my Lord and Savior Jesus Christ."[29] Another plantation mistress disclosed to a northern governess visiting her plantation that she felt greater responsibility for elevating her enslaved people than she did for elevating her own biological children. "I tremble," the travel journal reported, "at the reflection that God will ask their souls' lives at my hands!"[30] Corroborating these sentiments, Caroline Clitherall remarked on her relationship with a young house servant: "What a responsibility upon me— who am her only friend and the only one she has to lead her and instruct her in the right way of her duty. Lord keep and teach me that I may teach her."[31] Many slaveholding women expressed similar feelings of accountability for the souls of their enslaved.

✝

Religion and religious mentorship brought emotional and intellectual benefits to a number of slaveholding women. However, and perhaps just as often, such women's forays into religion and religious mentorship exposed them to a darker, contentious, and/or superficial world, one which made them think about their race, class, gender, and philosophical and religious beliefs in new, often painful, ways. In a society that expected elite white women to be levelheaded, calm, abounding in patience, and serving as role models for others, they often expressed negative feelings or frustration with husbands, family members, the enslaved, and their lives in general. Slaveholding women found it impossible to live up to this idealized model all their adult lives.

Some plantation mistresses either made no reference whatsoever to their efforts to Christianize their enslaved people or plainly indicated no interest in doing so.[32] Many of those women who chose not to do so were candid in revealing their reasons. First, though fewer in number after 1830, some slaveholding women professed little interest in religion in their own lives and had little or no interest in it in the lives of others. Others feared for their own physical safety when alone with a group of Black men. Still for others, the choice to withdraw from the role of religious educator created feelings of guilt and doubt as women fought a moral battle within themselves. Keziah Goodwyn Hopkins Brevard of Columbia, South Carolina, described conflicted feelings toward her enslaved people and their access to religion on the eve of the Civil War: "Oh I wish I had been born in a Christian land & never seen or known of slaves of any colour. A degraded population is a curse to a country. Negroes are as deceitful & lying as any people can well be—Lord give me better feelings towards them. (Forgive me Lord, for unkind thoughts & have mercy on me!)." She later recorded:

> Oh My God help thy dear children from these low grounds—Oh help, help!! Help us up—help us up—the deception of my servants disheartens me—Oh it almost makes me hate them when I find out their feelings

46

for me—with all I have done for them—they seem at times to hate me as though I had satan's principles in me—all I can plead is Lord forgive me & Oh take me from this world to a better—it has been my constant desire to make my negroes Christians—& I am every now & then awakened to the fact that they hate me.[33]

In addition, a few women toyed with the idea that deliverance of enslaved persons to God might be antithetical to the keeping of those same persons in bondage or that slavery might have a demoralizing influence on themselves.[34] For example, Ella Gertrude Clanton Thomas confessed: "I have sometimes doubted on the subject of slavery. I have seen so many of its evils among which is the terribly demoralizing influence upon our [enslaved people] but of late I have become convinced the Negro *as a race* is better off with us as he has been than if he were free."[35] Keziah Brevard concurred. On the eve of the Civil War, she wrote: "Lord help me to holy feelings—make me love these more & more for Oh I mourn this difference—would I not be better in heart if I had no slaves? This is hard to answer—God has given them to us—Now Lord, help us do right with them."[36]

Evangelical slaveholding mistresses worked to transcend these negative feelings and trying dilemmas because of the importance that they placed upon bearing witness of Jesus Christ (John 15:26–27) as well as upon living up to the idealized model of antebellum womanhood. For those committed to proselytizing their enslaved people, many dealt with a number of thorny realities. Some lamented that their enslaved rejected their brand of faith or were too uncivilized to fully benefit from mistress religious instruction. Slaveholding women were unable or refused to accept that their enslaved did not wish to imbibe their religious advice and teachings. Second, many privately voiced anger toward male family members, emanating from female placement into the role of religious mentor which allowed them little or no decision-making power. Regardless of the specified complaint or obstacle, slaveholding women's private writings reveal that they vacillated among a panoply of complicated feelings, ranging from hatred for their enslaved or hatred for the institution of slavery to feelings of the superiority of their race, civilization, and religious culture.

Perhaps most disappointing to slaveholding women was the number of enslaved people who rejected their faith. The reasons why their enslaved openly chose to dismiss their mistresses' religious instruction are varied. Sometimes the enslaved formulated a syncretic version of Christianity more to their own liking and style. Others believed that religious instruction from their mistresses simply reinforced racial hierarchies and upheld enslaved subservience.[37] Former enslaved Reverend William H. Robinson, for example, mocked one of his mistress's sermons in which she uttered the line "God's wisdom is displayed in the system of slavery."[38] Other enslaved people denied Christianity entirely.[39]

While plantation mistresses rarely openly admitted that their enslaved people intentionally spurned their religious mentorship, their diaries are replete with comments on the inferior nature of enslaved religious practices. In reaction to these rejections, mistresses condemned the basic, even immoral nature of African American religious beliefs, customs, and behavior. Some women could not fathom why their supposedly genuine attempts at moral uplift were not appreciated by their enslaved people. Others felt that their enslaved people were of an inferior race and thus incapable of functioning as good, practicing Christians.

Susan Cornwall of Burke County, Georgia, offers lengthy insight into these realities. Using her diary as an intellectual outlet to explore religion, slavery, and politics, Cornwall repeatedly cited the uncivilized nature of the religious practices, beliefs, and behavior of her enslaved people as well as her continual frustration in their religious mentoring. In one entry from 1857, Cornwall recorded: "Their very religion seems to consist of feelings or impulses, more than principles. They have no law for the governance of their passions higher than the dread of punishment for an offense, or glimpses of a tangible reward for a correct course of conduct." Later, she added: "Their examples of chastity are the exception not the rule. They see this themselves, know that it is wrong, but at the same time yield to their temptations and laugh at their disgrace."[40] Some historians, notably Elizabeth Fox-Genovese, have faulted slaveholding women for their inability or unwillingness to consider the reasons for enslaved behavior, especially the dynamics which resulted in miscegenation. She argued that behaviors that mistresses often deemed unacceptable or sinful, namely sexual relations with the husband of the mistress, were not within the control of the enslaved.[41] Mistresses like Cornwall nonetheless found it difficult not to view such behaviors through the lens of their own religion and morality.

Still within the same entry, Cornwall compared the religious history of

Jews with that of the African race. Cornwall characterized Jews as a "nation of people" who had "been more oppressed in modern times" than virtually any other population. Though she conceded that Jews were "not slaves," they had "occupied through successive ages in most European countries [in] an inferior position." Citing specific instances in which Jews had "labored under peculiar disadvantages in a political as well as religious sense," Cornwall concluded that Jews had distinguished themselves and that they would "eventually fulfill their destiny in God's revealed way."[42]

In contrast, Cornwall doubted that those of African descent would follow the same progression as had Jews. In her words, "no encouragement can be found in the past or present of the African races for the hopes of those who pretend to look forward to a career of glory or even usefulness for them in a state of liberty." She argued that Africans had failed to distinguish themselves in poetry, "the art by which untutored minds first frame their budding germs of thought." Cornwall admitted that her enslaved people lacked any formal education but that they demonstrated little intellectual or moral potential. Cornwall further lamented that American enslaved people—hers included— were scarcely more morally elevated in the late 1850s than their ancestors had been when they first arrived on the American continent. She stated: "And if this is the condition of the Negro after so long a residence among a cultivated people enjoying, as most of them do, opportunities of learning what is right, what prospect is there of improvement if left to themselves?" Although Cornwall was obviously frustrated by the lack of progress of her enslaved people as religious and intellectual beings, her words also suggest that she believed African Americans were incapable of taking care of themselves and that emancipation would only hinder their advancement. Yet she exhibited evidence of inner turmoil as well as a trace of compassion for her enslaved people with respect to their religious experience: "I lift my voice and cry 'Teach me to be useful O Lord' for I am an unprofitable servant."[43] Cornwall thus valued the welfare of the enslaved and committed herself to making her teaching methodology more effective in spite of her inner emotional and intellectual conflicts.

Ann R. Page of Frederick County, Virginia, religious almost to the point of obsession, committed to her diary thoughts not dissimilar to Cornwall's:

> Ah! Thou hast seen that I should have gone to work in my own strength, and long ere this have given over through faintness and the discourage-

ments which arise from the perverseness and ungrateful behavior of those whom I desired to serve. Look upon those of my fellow-creatures in servitude in my family, who this day has given way to the temptation of their situation in murmuring and rebellious language toward me. Thou canst enlighten them and show them the error of their way. Thou canst convince them of sin, and subdue their spirits to bear with patience the trial of being under the guidance of one, who only from necessity, as they well know, is enduring, and that for their sakes, the task of urging them to such duties, as will lead to their temporal and eternal freedom.[44]

While both Cornwall and Page feel rejected, dejected, and frustrated, Page also conveys desperation and may believe that religious instruction for the enslaved is a lost cause. Likewise, Mary Carmichael of Augusta, Georgia, projected both scorn for aspects of her enslaved people's behaviors and anxiety about their needs for and rights to religious education, all within a single journal entry. Writing in March 1842, she described being deeply moved by an "excellent sermon about charity," expressing her desire to incorporate her minister's sentiments into those sermons that she delivered to her enslaved people, while at the same time, discussing the distress she felt when she chastised one of the house servants who had recently burned the new imported oriental carpet.[45]

Corroborating Cornwall and Page were those slaveholding women who believed that their enslaved possessed incorrect knowledge—or flawed ideas—about Christianity and were further incorrect in their practices of it. These phenomena vexed many mistresses and made them defensive about their efforts as Christian teachers. Reflecting the internalized superiority of their religious culture, these elite white women believed that their enslaved people were too superstitious and emotional, or that they retained elements of their animistic African religions and Islam in their religious rituals.[46] Although antebellum slaveholding women disapproved of and ridiculed some enslaved religious practices, some fought to overcome cultural differences. Northern-born Emily Wharton Sinkler, mistress on a large cotton plantation in South Carolina, sought to achieve religious salvation of her enslaved regardless of their beliefs, behaviors, or (lack of) knowledge. Rather, she viewed it as a primary mission in her earthly life to correct the religious beliefs of her enslaved people. Sinkler, referring to her religious efforts with her son's newly purchased maid, wrote: "I taught her a prayer which I made her say every night and gave her some general ideas. I found she had some previous ideas on the subject but as you can imagine it was a hard thing for me to preserve suitable gravity when listening to her answers."[47] Others, including Mary Boykin Chesnut, possessed wider worldviews and expressed interest in, and even admiration for, their enslaved people's faith. Chesnut recorded:

> Jim Nelson, the driver... was asked to lead in prayer. He became wildly excited, on his knees, facing us with his eyes shut. He clapped his hands at the end of every sentence, and his voice rose to the pitch of a shrill shriek, yet was strangely clear and musical, occasionally in a plaintive minor key that went to your heart. Sometimes it rang out like a trumpet. I wept bitterly.... The Negroes sobbed and shouted and swayed backward and forward, some with aprons to their eyes, most of them clapping their hands and responding in shrill tones: 'Yes God!' 'Jesus!' 'Bless de Lord, amen,' etc. It was a little too exciting for me. I would very much have liked to shout, too. Jim Nelson when he rose from his knees trembled and shook as one in a palsy, and from his eyes you could see the ecstasy had not left him yet. He could not stand at all, and sank back on his bench.[48]

Enslaved preachers constituted a crucial component of enslaved Christianity throughout the antebellum South. Plantation mistresses were well aware of them, some having personal interaction with them or witnessing their religious services. Likely, enslaved preachers had minimal impact on white women.[49] Some women did report in their diaries that Black preachers were intensely emotional in delivering uplifting sermons. Those who were particularly devout and comfortable with passionate physical and rhetorical expression were probably those who most appreciated the typical African American sermon and the entire service. Consequently, the intense crying, the shouting, and the physicality associated with the enslaved religious meeting would have seemed less extraordinary and would have been less uncomfortable for them to witness than those expressions would have been for a less impassioned woman.[50]

Conversely, for mistresses who resided in the Chesapeake region and Upper

South, who tended to be Episcopalian, Presbyterian, or even Roman Catholic, the structure and the content of the enslaved religious service probably would have seemed alien to the more formal, more predictable, and more ritualistic worship to which many of them were accustomed. Most slaveholding women cleaved to the superiority of their own religious traditions, believing it their duty to bring their brand of Christianity to their inferiors.

✝

A second theme directly tied to mistresses' frustration in their role as religious educator related to the (perceived) role of elite white men. Elite women resented the ways that white men, particularly their husbands, sought to control their responsibilities as religious instructors to the enslaved. Slaveholding women with northern or foreign roots were more likely to voice frustration and discontent regarding the limitations placed on them as religious educators. Philadelphia native Emily Wharton Sinkler stated that her husband exerted his strict control over the content of her teachings to their enslaved people on their South Carolina plantation. Genuinely interested in religion and in African American culture, she believed that Black children deserved both religious and basic academic instruction, though the latter was against the law. Her husband, Charles Sinkler, a vestryman for their Episcopal church, discouraged his wife from establishing a school on her plantation which would address both needs. A disappointed Emily Sinkler wrote in December 1842, "I only wish *I* could teach the little blackeys the ways of our Savior. I wish I could do what Frank [Wharton, her brother, in Philadelphia] says with regard to the black children or frogs as he calls them but it is impossible. It is entirely forbidden by the laws of South Carolina and it would be very wrong for me to attempt to instruct them especially as Mr. Sinkler entirely disapproves of it."[51]

Although constrained by her husband, the local clergy, as well as state law, Emily Sinkler tried to transcend such restrictions. In her private writings, she confided how she helped establish a church on the Sinklers' two plantations where their enslaved people could receive religious instruction. However, she possessed little to no control over the teachings, schedule, or management of the churches. Her husband insisted that only he and their minister, Reverend Dehon, were permitted to lead any Sunday religious activities for their enslaved. Emily Sinkler reluctantly accepted this reality and yet still praised a

Sunday service led by Reverend Dehon. Referring to one Sunday in December 1844, Emily Sinkler recorded, "After Church last Sunday Mr. Dehon came home with us to stay until the next day so as to have church for the servants in the afternoon. They behaved remarkably well, the women sitting on one side and the men on the other. There is something very wild in their tunes. It always makes me melancholy but they persist in curtseying after every thing."[52]

Like most men, Mr. Sinkler insisted on masculine jurisdiction over the religious instruction of enslaved people. That said, it is unlikely that Mr. Sinkler—especially if he were being reasonable—held his wife's intellect in low estimation. Emily Sinkler's voluminous correspondence with family members in Philadelphia reveals her to have been a voracious reader who frequently lamented the scarcity of books, newspapers, and magazines in the rural South. Rather, it is more likely that Mr. Sinkler sought authority over his wife's teachings because he felt that he—or his way of life—might be threatened by Emily Sinkler's strong opinions shaped by the sociopolitical culture of the North. Whether Emily Sinkler came to terms with the reality of male sovereignty remains unknown. She continued to commit herself to her enslaved people, especially domestic ones, and took an interest in their religious progress, albeit on an informal basis.

Pierce Butler—a Philadelphian who had inherited multiple cotton, rice, and tobacco plantations on St. Simon's Island, Georgia, and who married Frances "Fanny" Anne Kemble, a British-born actress—also reined in his wife in her efforts in Christian education. Like Sinkler, Kemble complained that her husband derailed her attempts to educate the enslaved. Both women expressed frustration with their husbands' controlling roles. Kemble pointedly criticized elite white southern men for their self-serving, paternalistic agendas. The elite, white male establishment within the antebellum South produced pamphlets largely intended for plantation masters' and mistresses' use as Christian educators. Those documents presented enslaved people in need of Christian "enlightenment" and presented white plantation women as elite white men's instruments to accomplish it.[53] Kemble, who viewed the enslaved more humanely than just as mere inferiors who were candidates for elevation, caustically mocked the elite white male paternalistic view in her diary:

> "Christian enlightenment," say they; and where shall they begin? "Whatsoever ye would that men should do unto you, do ye also unto them"?

No; but "Servants, obey you masters"; and there, I think, they naturally come to a full stop.... If these heaven-blinded Negro enlighteners persist in their pernicious plan of making Christians their cattle, something of the sort must be done, or they will infallibly cut their own throats with this two-edged sword of truth, to which they could in no wise have laid their hand, and would not, doubtless, but that it is now thrust at them so threateningly that they have no choice. Again and again, how much I do pity them!

Kemble attacked the recommendation that slaveholding females use a separate catechism and an enslaved version of the Bible in their teachings.[54] Kemble strongly implied that suggestions put forth by these pamphlets both assumed and perpetuated the phenomenon of subservience, subservience both of the wife/white female family member and all of the enslaved.

Emily Wharton Sinkler and Fanny Kemble were both outsiders, but southern society expected them to conform to its dictates. Both of these newcomers voiced hostility toward male family members and toward pamphlets which imposed a framework for conducting Sunday Schools to the enslaved. Perhaps this was not surprising since Sinkler and Kemble grew up in environments alien to the American South. Unlike their southern sisters, many of whom accepted the structure of southern society, those two women and other transplants like them felt constrained by southern elite society's expectations. As outsiders, some felt greater isolation on the plantation than perhaps did their native counterparts. Kemble left bustling London for life on a remote, sparsely populated Georgia Sea Island. Sinkler departed Philadelphia for a plantation in South Carolina. Both women, accustomed to social lives in thriving metropolises, experienced profound feelings of isolation, geographically and psychologically, in their new settings. Cut off much of the time from peer conversation and accustomed to urban activity and easy exchange of ideas, these two women found the role of mistress and all it entailed suffocating and unappreciated. In part as a reaction to their situation, Sinkler and Kemble and others, although not abolitionists, professed more enlightened views about a biracial society and its implications than many, but not all, southern mistresses. These views found their way into their attempts to provide religious instruction for their enslaved people and perhaps to stimulate their minds;

at the same time, they took a small stand against male society in order to promote the greater good.

✝

Mistresses' views of their enslaved ranged from godly to almost inhuman. In their eyes, enslaved people might be worthy of deliverance and possessing of souls or else be almost animal-like in their lack of humanity. More slaveholding women positioned enslaved people between these two extremes. While some slaveholding women viewed all enslaved people to be unworthy of, or unsuited for, religious instruction, a large number believed they could evangelize at least some of them. Religious education was widely perceived to be an important Christian and moral duty of slaveholding women. It offered thousands of women the opportunity to embrace their own intellectual and religious interests, even though such interests epitomized the values of a socially conservative South.

Similarly, it gave other disgruntled and frustrated women a brief moment to transcend their own stifling and subordinate position. Susan Dabney Smedes, the daughter of a Mississippi planter, observed that "the mistress of a plantation was the most complete slave on it."[55] Indeed serving as religious instructors to their enslaved people provided white women the chance to assume positions in which they could exercise some authority, garner some respect, and view themselves as something other than as the "slave of slaves."[56] Many slaveholding women who cared about the spiritual welfare of their enslaved took the responsibility seriously even as they anguished in the role and responded to their frustrations in a variety of ways.

Three

FOREIGN MISSION WORK IN LIBERIA

By 1850, American women, including southern women, had involved themselves in foreign missions for at least two generations. Such women accompanied their minister husbands to serve God in a myriad of locales, most prominently India, China, and the Middle East. While these women performed important duties as the wives of foreign mission workers, their wider contributions to the mission field and to those they served were often limited. In fact, for the first four decades of the nineteenth century, the overseas mission movement had been overshadowed by Protestant denominations' focus on domestic missions, specifically planting churches on the advancing frontier. This changed beginning in the mid-nineteenth century and would grow in the succeeding half century.

Georgian Martha Jane Williford was a pioneer in this emerging field of American foreign mission work. Not only did Williford leave lasting contributions to the community she served, but she was one of the first women—and definitely one of the first southern women—to enter the mission field as a single woman.[1] Between 1850 and 1870, Williford steadfastly served as an Episcopal missionary at Cavalla, Cape Palmas, in Liberia. Her passion for foreign mission work was tied to her perhaps naïve, yet intense, desire to "spread the ever lasting Gospel to those who are sitting in the 'darkness, and shadow of death.'"[2] This strain runs throughout many of the surviving letters Williford wrote while serving as a missionary. Even during those days, months, and even years of frustration, disappointment, and despair, she kept a determined, reasonably positive attitude.

Martha Jane Williford's letters reflect much more than one southern woman's commitment to serving God and those living in the perceived heart of darkness who she believed needed her spiritual and practical guidance. Rather, although influenced by, or even limited by, the racist and sexist southern environment of which she was a product, Williford's voluminous collection of letters offers insight into an educated or intellectual southern woman's views, opinions, and aspirations during the middle of the nineteenth century. Her writings diverge from the content of the diaries kept by many of her female contemporaries who presided over southern farms and plantations and who led insular, nonstimulatory lives. Williford, like so many of her evangelical "sisters" engaged in missionary work, redefined herself, and, in the process, expanded conceptions of southern womanhood.

Williford's letters do not focus on the quotidian realities of mission life in West Africa nor do they even dwell on her Episcopal faith. Rather, her epistles present one southern woman's thoughts on, and analysis of, such broader themes as women's roles in southern, American, and African society; race relations; cultural and physical differences between enslaved Americans and Africans; and church ideology and politics. In the process, Martha Williford pondered, reconsidered, and even (re)constructed her conceptions of race, gender, and southern identity, all during a twenty-year span when the American South experienced its own series of challenging transformations. These included the demise of slavery and antebellum culture, defeat in the Civil War, and deprivation and subordination during Reconstruction. While Williford's recorded thoughts divaricate from those of her southern female peers, Williford did not hold feminist ideals. Her missionary expressions did not appreciably fall outside the realm of acceptable southern femininity. However, they do showcase how southern women could and did apply regionally permissible gender roles to a greater good within the public sphere.

Ultimately, this chapter considers the ways by which Martha Williford's very identity as a white southern female was shaped, perhaps even altered, by her experiences in the mission field of Liberia between 1850 and 1870. Williford's contemplations, reconsiderations, and even reconstructions of race, gender, and regional identity stemmed from her racial and gendered status. Consequently, the focus of this chapter is not on the machinations of the Episcopal Church of the United States of America (ECUSA) in Liberia. However, the institution does serve as a crucial backdrop in Williford's transatlantic narrative.

One might consider an analysis of an *Episcopal* missionary out of place in a book focused on *evangelical* Protestant Christianity. However, the Episcopal Church of the nineteenth century exhibited many theological and cultural similarities with Methodists, Baptists, and Presbyterians. The Great Awakening of the mid-eighteenth century had sparked an evangelical movement within the Church (then known as the Anglican Church or the Church of England). In 1789, the Episcopal Church officially separated from the Church of England so that American clergy would no longer be obligated to recognize the supremacy of the British monarch. This break engendered a church that would evolve to emulate other evangelical Protestant denominations.

Nineteenth-century Episcopal evangelicals, also known as "low church" Episcopalians, reflected the broader tenets and practices of American evangelicalism in many ways. Most fundamentally, this included a staunch rejection of hierarchy. Likewise, the Episcopal Church encouraged emotional expression in services and personal conversion. It promoted the importance of justification by faith (the belief that faith alone makes a person righteous in the eyes of God), the preaching of the Word, and the study of the gospel. It stressed the authority of the Bible as shown in the revelation of God in Christ. It opposed ritual excess, which the denomination associated with the top-down Roman Catholic Church. Finally, Episcopal ministers took immense pride in assisting their parishioners forge direct, emotional relationships with God. Evangelical principles guided the establishment and growth of Virginia Theological Seminary in Alexandria, Virginia. This seminary educated a preponderance of the Episcopal preachers who ministered in the antebellum South, including Martha Williford's future husband, Reverend John W. Payne III.

✝

One of four children, Martha Jane Williford was born in 1817 in Chatham County, Georgia, to David and Martha Stackhouse Williford. Her father died sometime during her childhood, and her mother was remarried to J. H. J. Service, an English-born merchant and slaveholder in Richmond County, Georgia, by the late 1830s.[3] Little is known of Martha's childhood and early adulthood. She did spend several years during the 1840s employed as an instructor at the Montpelier Female Institute, a well-respected early women's academy and college established by the Episcopal Church, in Macon, Georgia.[4] No diary or trove of letters exists that reflect Williford's life as a teacher at Montpelier. Although little is known about Williford's tenure, including its precise length, at Montpelier Female Institute, one can surmise that this school offered a rigorous education. In fact, historian Christie Anne Farnham cites Jane Constance Miller, a student at Montpelier during the late 1840s, the approximate time at which Williford served as an instructor. Among the works Miller mastered were Shakespeare's *Henry VIII, Julius Caesar, Hamlet, Macbeth, Othello,* and the *Merchant of Venice,* as well as those of such authors as Longfellow and Homer.[5]

However, what one can surmise from Williford's life before her departure to Liberia comes from a letter to her mother dated August 4, 1849. In it, Martha revealed that she had long given thought to a career in foreign mission work. She endured significant resistance from her family, especially from her remarried mother. Her mother and stepfather worried about unreliable communication between two continents; the primitive nature of missions and mission facilities; the unhealthy climate of West Africa; and the lack of American (not to mention southern) mission workers in Liberia who could provide Williford with the comforts of her native soil.

What most troubled her family, aside from the possibility of never seeing their daughter or sister again, was Williford's status as a *single* woman serving a foreign mission. One striking feature of the American foreign missionary force in the nineteenth and on into the early twentieth century was that women comprised about 60 percent of it. However, the majority consisted of missionary wives. Far fewer single women served as foreign missionaries at the midpoint of the nineteenth century. Williford tried to convince her family that her unattached marital status was actually a positive attribute. In her eyes, single women could offer more direct contributions to mission work than could their married counterparts. In response to her mother's reservations, Williford wrote: "And you must not suppose, Dear Mother that as a single woman I would not be useful. In every mission, they single ladies for the most effective part of the body, so much so, that the Committee for Missions is calling loudly for them. Look at Miss Jones, who is in China, she is everything to that mission, and also Miss Milligan in Greece. Their influence is untold and can never be known, 'till at the Judgment seat of Christ."[6]

On the eve of her thirty-second birthday, Martha Jane Williford overcame her family's opposition. She departed the United States several months later, on December 17, 1849, to begin her nearly three-month journey from Savannah to West Africa. Two Episcopal clergymen, Reverend E. W. Hening and Reverend Elie W. Stokes, an African American, accompanied Williford.[7] All three were to serve in the Episcopal mission at Cape Palmas, Liberia. Their West Africa–bound vessel also included two Baptist clerics whose mission work would take them "into the interior of Africa ... at Bookoo."[8]

Numerous denominations, representing the United States as well as Great Britain, France, Germany, and the Netherlands, enthusiastically embraced foreign mission opportunities between 1820 and 1850. The so-called Scramble for Africa, when a handful of powerful and modern western European nations aggressively vied for territory, raw materials, markets, and influence on the African continent, occurred much later. It was a product of the imperialistic realities of the 1870s and 1880s. However, several decades before these same nations, as well as the United States, realized the full economic potential of Africa, the aforementioned denominations sought to establish a more informal influence on the continent through mission work. According to the 1850 edition of the *Missionary Register,* a journal published by the Church Missionary Society, in West Africa alone there existed a few hundred mission stations. Some African nations, including Sierra Leone, Gambia, and Gold Coast, boasted several dozen mission stations. American missions in West Africa included one Episcopal mission, sixteen Methodist missions, one Presbyterian mission, and several sponsored by the American Colonization Society (ACS).[9]

Of particular note to Martha Jane Williford's story is, of course, the Episcopal mission in Liberia. The Episcopal Church of the United States of America (ECUSA), under the leadership of Reverend John Payne, established its mission station at Cavalla, Cape Palmas, Liberia, in 1836. Cavalla included formerly enslaved African Americans and Greboes people, an ethnicity centered in southeastern Liberia and part of the larger Kru linguistic group. Geographically, Cape Palmas—a headland located on the far southeast end of the coast of Liberia—lies at the extreme southwest corner of the northern half of the African continent. Located near the equator, coastal Liberia falls within a tropical monsoon climate zone in which rainfall often exceeded two hundred inches annually.[10]

Reverend Payne played an important role in Williford's life and lengthy career in Liberia. Born in 1815 in Westmoreland County, Virginia, Payne graduated from the College of William and Mary in 1833 and Virginia Theological Seminary in 1836. Shortly after his ordination and upon his marriage to Anna Matilda Barroll in 1837, the Paynes left the United States for Liberia.

Between 1837 and 1841 or 1842, the Paynes exclusively served formerly enslaved African Americans. After its founding in 1817, ACS began sending volunteers there in the early 1820s.[11] During those first few years in Cape Palmas,
Payne mastered several local languages, and he started to minister to members
of several local tribes. By 1849, Reverend Payne's Liberian staff increased, and
notable progress occurred at the main stations—Mt. Vaughan, Cape Palmas,
and Half-Cavalla—while new ones were opened at Taboo, a town east of Cape
Palmas, and at Rockbookah, the capital of the Babo tribe.[12] In June 1851, Reverend Payne was consecrated the first bishop of Cape Palmas and parts adjacent in West Africa.[13] Throughout the 1850s and early 1860s, Payne published
several books on the Grebo people, including *History of the Greboes,* a text
that chronicled his personal experiences in Liberia and his interpretation of
Grebo history and culture.[14]

Reverend Payne was crucial to the successful establishment and growth
of the Mission at Cape Palmas.[15] During his tenure, the Episcopal Church
built five churches, two asylums, and one hospital, as well as ordained twenty
priests. Most significant was the Episcopal Church's ability to spread Christianity in West Africa. Payne translated most of the Bible into the Grebo language and played a vital role in the establishment of Liberia College, a theological school to train native West Africans for the clergy. Upon his return from
Africa in 1871, Payne initiated the first integrated school in Westmoreland
County, Virginia. This school taught Black and white children together during
the week and held church meetings on Sunday.[16]

Regardless of any role that Reverend and Mrs. Payne may have played in
missionaries' acclimation to life in West Africa, Martha Jane Williford tran-
sitioned smoothly into her new life as an Episcopal missionary in Liberia. In
the summer of 1850, Williford wrote to her mother that she "continue[d] to be
better and better pleased with [her] new home each day," adding that she inhabited "the pleasantest station belonging to [her] Mission." By this point, Williford
had been teaching for four months at a girls' boarding school, where she spent
"many happy hours in [her] little school room." Comparing her new teaching
experiences in Cavalla to her professional life back in Macon, Williford noted:
"I was happy at Montpelier [Institute], but not so happy as I am here."[17]

At the mission school, Williford taught and ministered to twenty-three
girls, "big and little," ranging from five to eighteen years in age.[18] These twenty-
three female students were all Greboes and not African Americans from the

States. Bible, grammar, geography, history, and arithmetic were the primary subjects taught at the mission school.[19] According to Anna M. Scott, a fellow missionary at Cape Palmas who wrote an account of the Cape Palmas Mission, Martha Williford's school was educating most of the native women of the Christian village at Cavalla, and "their children [by the late 1850s] were receiving in it the same advantages."[20] Unlike assimilationist boarding schools later established for Native American children, mission schools in Cape Palmas did not forcefully remove Grebo children from their homes. Pursuit of an education was entirely voluntary, and Grebo parents were enthusiastic supporters.[21]

In praise of Miss Williford's efforts, Bishop Payne, in an official Church report, wrote: "The department has been blessed, three quarters of the year, with a most devoted and efficient teacher in Miss M. J. Williford, who joined the mission in February [1850]. After five weeks, during which she had so little indisposition ... Miss W. took full charge of the school, and continued to discharge the duties connected with it." Bishop Payne viewed Williford as a paragon of teaching, concluding that "may the Lord of the harvest greatly multiply such sisters of charity for Heathen as well as Christian lands!"[22]

Williford's epistles highlight her re(constructions) of race. Her earliest letters to her family back in Georgia consistently praise her African pupils' advancement and Greboes' intellectual and cultural superiority in comparison to African Americans. Not present in Williford's letters are the omnipresent frustrations and criticisms found in the diaries of those southern slaveholding women who religiously instructed their enslaved. Such sentiments echo observations recorded by John Leighton Wilson and his wife, Jane Bayard Wilson, a missionary couple who served the American Board of Commissioners for Foreign Missions in West Africa during the 1830s and 1840s. The Wilsons worked with varied African peoples, including the Mandingo, the Fanti, and the Fang, but spent most of their time serving and living among the Greboes.[23]

In contrast to the commonly derogatory descriptions of enslaved people by plantation mistresses, Williford often described her girls as "very tractable" and indicated that they gave her "but little trouble." She repeatedly used the word "tractable" to characterize her students. Individuals of the twenty-first century typically associate "tractability" with such exploitative descriptors as docility, pliability, and complaisance. Instructors of the nineteenth century, somewhat in contrast, demanded obedience and submissiveness from their pupils. It is thus, unknown, whether Miss Williford characterized her Grebo students as "tractable" as a reflection of their (perceived) inferior race or status as students. What Williford constantly reinforced is her commitment to these children's welfare. Her frustrations were with limited resources—most significantly time and other teachers—rather than with boredom or dissatisfaction with her missionary career. Referring to a recent series of examinations at her school, Williford wrote her mother: "We have quarterly examinations. I had an examination of my girls … which was both satisfactory, and gratifying to me." Williford further recorded that she was "agreeably surprised by the capacity of this people," noting they were "far superior intellectually to the colored race at home."[24]

Further complementing Martha Williford's assessments of the Greboes' intellectual potential are descriptions that fellow missionary and southerner Anna M. Scott provided in *Day Dawns in Africa* (1858).[25] Scott stated that in the mission schools, Grebo children "learn[ed] rapidly," adding that she was especially "struck with the order, decorum, and mental acumen displayed."[26] While Williford notes the differences between Greboes and African Americans, Mrs. Scott compared the Greboes that the Cape Palmas mission served to various interior African tribes. In her words, the Grebo people "boast of being more active, wiser, and more civilized than their brethren of the interior, 'or the bush people,' as they somewhat contemptuously term them." Other labels Scott used to describe the Grebo, including Grebo women, include "orderly," "cleanly," "considerable energy of character," "graceful," "hospitable," and "affable."[27]

Why southern women like Martha Jane Williford, Anna Scott, and Jane Bayard Wilson shared such open and complimentary assessments of their pupils and Greboes at large deserves consideration. First, southern missionaries may have held lower expectations of West Africans they served than did those northern women who had little or no previous contact with African Americans. Such southern women were accustomed to a large percentage of enslaved people who were illiterate, who performed basic, highly regimented tasks, and who, at least in their eyes, led amoral lives. Southern missionaries like Martha Jane Williford thus used the enslaved as an instant population of comparison with sub-Saharan Africans. For such southern missionaries, the sub-Saharan Africans seemed more industrious, more promising, more attractive, and ultimately a less-degraded people.

The insightful Williford, however, acknowledged that the (perceived) superior status of the Greboes was attributable to several factors, the most obvious being that the Greboes had not been shipped to the New World in shackles. Williford accepted that, over the past several centuries, the institution of southern slavery had not only exploited millions of African Americans but that it had also stunted their growth, development, and potential for civilization. She did not entirely imbibe the southern message that slavery was an enlightening institution. Williford's understanding of African American culture appears to be limited. Although sympathetic to the plight of African Americans—both free and the enslaved—Williford was not familiar with, or chose not to comment upon, the rich enslaved cultures that did exist on hundreds of plantations across the antebellum South.[28] Referring to the superiority of the Grebo, when "compared to the colored race at home," Williford wrote: "You will hardly believe that I know, Dear Mother, but though the feathers are the same, the expression is very different. These are free men, and have always been so, and it does make a difference."[29]

Unfortunately, sources that could bring light to Williford's own racial politics do not exist. One does not know to what extent she believed in a racial hierarchy—ideas that scientists did not fully formulate until the latter decades of the nineteenth century. Nor are there extant sources that reveal much about the racial politics and/or records of ownership of enslaved people of her parents or siblings. Regardless of Williford's own personal experiences with slavery in Georgia, she had undoubtedly given the institution considerable thought. After all, her three previous homes, Macon, Augusta, and Savannah, were major political and economic centers of antebellum Georgian society. Likewise, Williford confronted slavery at the Montpelier Institute, a center of learning at which students were more likely than not to be children of slaveholders. What Williford's early letters do reveal is her relative openness and positive attitude toward "otherness," otherness whose descendants populated the southern fields and cabins of the enslaved.

A second, yet intertwined, reason to explain Martha Williford's consistently positive characterizations of native West Africans relates to the sexual dynamics present on antebellum southern plantations. Although Williford never married prior to her tenure in Liberia she likely knew—or knew of—women's husbands who had sustained sexual relationships with their enslaved women. Such infidelity fueled infamously tense relationships between slaveholding and enslaved women. Grebo women were not associated with such uncomfortable sexual dynamics and were thus not the source of any jealousy among southern female missionaries. For Williford, the young Grebo girls and women did not embody such negative traits as immorality, debauchery, and promiscuity, labels commonly placed on exploited enslaved women.

Rather, American missionary women like Williford, Scott, and Wilson exhibited a degree of sympathy toward Grebo women, all of whom lived in a polygamous society and were thus accustomed to being one of many women within the sexual lives of their husbands. Whereas southern white women often viewed female enslaved people as the sexual aggressors and their husbands as victims in biracial relationships on their plantations back home, white missionary women, in contrast, may have interpreted African women within polygamous relationships as exploited victims of forceful African men. Of course, such Caucasian women displayed no appreciation, let alone respect, for alternative social organizational systems like polygamy, but Williford, Scott, and Wilson were able to view females of color as something other than as sexually voracious objects. Anna Scott expressed her disappointment that one young Grebo girl would not attend Williford's boarding school because she had already "been bought from [her] parents . . . and carried home to be trained up in the house of [her] future husband." Scott wrote: "We remember on one occasion, being somewhat puzzled when we asked an interesting little heathen girl, not over six years old, if she would not like to come to our mission school, to hear her little companions cry out, pointing to her neck: 'She can't come; see, she has got a husband.'"[30]

A third reason why southern female missionaries may have characterized native West Africans in a positive light lies in their own teaching ability. Martha Williford may have internalized her students' progress as a direct reflection of her skill and patience as an instructor.[31] Quite simply, did the steady progress made by her pupils display Williford's own sense of superiority and importance? Exuding a degree of arrogance, Williford told her mother that while the "tractable" native girls and young women exhibited potential, both spiritually and intellectually, they required a "savior" like herself to bring them into a more enlightened environment: "Many are perishing for lack of knowledge, and few are here to supply their need. Dear Mother, every day convinces me that this is the work for which God has been preparing me. My position is one of great usefulness. I find my knowledge of various kinds of work invaluable to me as a missionary for all one's talents are in requisition here."[32] Regardless of why Martha Williford believed her mission school students, and the Greboes at large, to be a promising and accomplished people, she did not feel the anxiety, guilt, stress, and anger many slaveholding women confronted in their day-to-day interactions with their enslaved people.

Williford praised Christian efforts made by herself and her neighboring missionaries, especially by Reverend and Mrs. Payne. Adjectives and labels such as "indefatigable," "indispensable," and "helpmate" were among those descriptors Williford used in her correspondence back to Georgia. She acknowledged the key role Reverend Payne played in the Greboes' spiritual advancement. She stated that he preached, always in Grebo, to a Sabbath congregation of approximately two hundred. On weekdays, the minister traveled to twelve villages of ten miles within his circuit each fortnight. According to Williford, Payne's sermons sparked a change in the Greboes: "When Mr. Payne first came among them, they were like all heathen people, much addicted to thieving. But a great change has taken place, the Gospel has had its influence in making them more moral and politically a better people, for they are ashamed to do many things they once did, and there is more of justice among them."[33]

Martha Jane Williford's correspondence reveals that she was engaged in teaching, mentoring, and ministering mostly to Liberian natives and a few Liberian immigrants in her first several years of mission work. That work ceased when severe illness threatened her missionary career, even her life, four years into her tenure in Liberia. "A very severe attack of fever," followed by a "complication of diseases," all with inadequate medical care, forced Williford to resign as principal of the girls' school in Cavalla. Williford reluctantly concluded that her only hope for better health and her only hope that she might someday be of use to the Mission was to return home to Georgia. She did so in the summer of 1854.[34]

Fortunately, Martha Williford's health did improve enough that she could return to the Cape Palmas Mission. She left the United States from Norfolk, Virginia, in the late spring of 1855. While in that port city, she had helped supervise many dozen free African Americans, presumably very recently emancipated enslaved people, for emigration to Liberia. On the eight-week voyage from Norfolk to Cape Palmas, Williford further mentored these "more than 100 emigrants on board," most of whom were "just off plantations, and ha[d] heretofore received no instruction."[35] Among these many dozen former African American enslaved people, Williford and her fellow mission workers,

Reverend C. C. and Mrs. Hoffman, saw great potential and looked forward to the day when these people would become leaders in Liberian communities.

However, Williford also observed that former slave owners had severely neglected their enslaved people's basic needs, particularly their spiritual needs. She lamented that "their ignorance is indeed sad" and that she would "not like to stand in the place of their owners, who have so utterly neglected their religious instruction." Most concerning to Williford and the Hoffmans were those former enslaved who expressed deep reluctance to accept the missionaries' teachings of Christianity, teachings that their former masters and mistresses had supposedly strictly forbidden on their plantations. In response, the three missionaries commenced daily instruction of the Liberia-bound African Americans on the voyage.[36] Significantly, Williford's observations challenge the idealized portrayals of Black colonists in Liberia that many white political and religious leaders in the Upper South as well as such publications as the *African Repository and Colonial Journal,* an ACS paper, perpetuated. In the eyes of such people, those Blacks who did relocate to Liberia were paragons of the benevolent nature of American slavery. Whites celebrated both the successes of Black colonists as well as the successes of Liberia as a whole because they "confirmed a place in God's plan for whites' paternalist system of slavery."[37] Williford encountered some emigrants who did not display such evidence of white benevolence and chose to comment on it, and, perhaps in the process, champion herself and her efforts at Christian instruction.

Upon her arrival in West Africa in July 1855, Williford resumed charge of the native female boarding school at Cavalla. She found that her boarding school had been administered by several capable missionary women from the American South, some of whom had been assisted by educated native women. She was also pleased to find a vastly expanded and improved school premises: "A large and commodious building had taken the place of the low, damp, and dilapidated school-room, so long the refuge of lizards, spiders, and scorpions. Its walls [were] adorned with a set of fine maps, presented by a kind lady of Savannah; and it has recently been fitted up with suitable desks, globes, and other aids to study."[38]

Not only had the female boarding school at Cavalla flourished during Martha Williford's absence, but so had the Mission. In fact, the Cavalla Station experienced healthy growth during the mid-1850s. The Episcopal publication the *Spirit of Missions* provides insight into its growth. The number of "laborers" (the title given to more senior members of the mission) remained constant throughout the decade at three. These included the Bishop and Mrs. Payne and Martha Williford. However, the number of supporting teachers, clergy, and religious pupils expanded markedly. In 1856, the *Spirit of Missions* identified one native deacon, several American and native teaching assistants, 62 boarding scholars and village children, 200 Sunday-school children, and 43 newly baptized natives.[39]

Beginning in the spring of 1858, nearly eight years after Martha Jane Williford's original arrival in Liberia, Reverend Payne began to play a far more prominent role in Martha's life, as did she in his. Late that winter, Mrs. Anna Payne died, likely succumbing to a tropical illness. Reverend Payne had committed himself to a career in Liberia, and in order for him to remain there, he needed a helpmate with the utmost skill, patience, and foreign mission experience. Mrs. Payne's African diaries reveal a woman who made Reverend Payne's ministry such a success. Would there be a woman of equal skill, passion, dedication, and determination? Enter Martha Jane Williford, a woman who had embarked on the foreign mission field on her own, who held the same religious convictions as did Reverend Payne, who had spent much time in the minister's company, and who could boast nearly eight years' worth of practical experience on the African continent.

Reverend Payne and Martha Williford experienced a brief courtship before they married in the late spring of 1858. Writing to her half-sister, Emma Service, about their marriage, Williford, now nearly age forty-one, noted that she had never felt better in her life. She added: "I do feel that God has greatly blessed me in the husband he has given me. He is every thing I can desire. How truly and fully has the Blessed Savior fulfilled his promise, even for this life, to me."[40] The following year, in 1859, the Paynes returned to the United States for a visit to report to foreign missionary administrators in the Episcopal Church. He also attended regional conference meetings and delivered lectures to seminarians at Virginia Theological Seminary and to a large audience at the Church of the Incarnation, Madison Square, New York City, regarding the bountiful opportunities in foreign mission work. The couple most likely took a detour down to Georgia to visit with some of Martha's kinfolk, who now had a new son-in-law (or brother-in-law) to meet.[41]

Marriage to John Payne inevitably altered Martha's missionary experience, but correspondence to her mother, sisters, and friends confirms that Martha continued to keep a busy schedule. Referring to the first several weeks upon her return to West Africa in late 1860, the new Mrs. Payne wrote: "Such an amount of labor has devolved upon me. 'Tis wonderful how I have gotten through with it all, without a breakdown, but 'as my day, so has my strength been.'"[42] Administrative issues, catching up on several months' worth of correspondence, and providing physical and spiritual comfort to Miss Relph, a dying missionary, were among Martha's new pressing concerns.

Correspondence, especially related to mission fundraising, proved to be a constant duty for the bishop's wife. Writing to her sister in a rare moment of leisure, Martha indicated that she had "a large correspondence to keep up north, south, east and west, which must be kept up, if the interest in [their] work [was] to continue."[43] One of Martha's greatest challenges or noblest duties was her recruitment of men, and especially women, to the foreign mission field. She lamented that she faced generalized apathy toward and limited financial support for foreign mission work. These realities were likely outgrowths of the drama leading up to 1861. Writing on the eve of the Civil War, Martha complained that "few Christians to their shame be it spoken are interested in missions from principle," adding that their "overtaxed missionary must write and write to search the mere pittance which our self-styled *Apostolic Church* grudgingly doles out for the real work of the Church."[44]

Disappointingly, Martha Payne commented little on events transpiring in the many months leading up to the Civil War. Though Payne identified as a southerner, she was not a fire-eater and did not support southern secession. Referring to South Carolina's secession in December 1860, Payne grieved "for the reception of Carolina and wish[ed] that the other southern states would not be influenced by her to dissolve the Union." Further revealing her conciliatory nature, she added that she feared "that many hot-headed ones will find that it was a much easier matter to destroy than to remake."[45]

Inevitably, Martha Payne heard about the intensifying political, social, economic, and religious schisms in the United States from her family, her friends, her correspondents associated with the Episcopal Church, as well as from newspapers and church publications. Despite the dearth in existing commentary, she habitually hinted at the self-serving politics of the Episcopal Church with regard to the institution of slavery. Like their Baptist, Methodist, and Presbyterian counterparts, some Episcopal Church leaders proffered theological justifications for slavery, maintaining it was sanctioned by the Bible. Some Church leaders simply avoided taking a strong public stance against slavery in order to prevent offending parishioners, many of whom were slaveholders and who would financially support the Church. Finally, it was not unusual for Episcopal churches and dioceses in the South to own enslaved people or own property that employed enslaved labor. Although Martha Payne never formally condemned the institution of slavery, she did recognize the hypocrisy of her Church, specifically noting how the politics of the Civil War had too narrowly bound the interests of its members. Martha Payne feared that all of this had contributed to waning interest in the foreign mission field.

Martha Payne strongly believed that members of the Church should always focus upon and pursue the aims of the Church, transcending the temporally limited realities of life on Earth: "I often wonder how Christians can be content to live in a tiny enclosure, bounded by their own interests when such a vast world of thought and interest to stretch out before them. Immortal beings should seek to impress themselves on immorality to live for eternity." She insinuated that no church should let its livelihood be diminished by politics. For Martha Payne, "no church [would] prosper in itself, where there [was] no missionary interest" and where "no unchristened Christian [would] prosper spiritually, if his heart [did] not go out to the work of Christ over the whole earth."[46] Martha Payne's religious and political views about slavery—which undoubtedly had been colored by her southern heritage—did not appreciably affect her relationships with missionaries of northern origin and abolitionist leanings. Their shared commitment to the Mission transcended political and regional disagreements.[47]

Martha Williford Payne's comments prompt one to explore the Episcopal Church's relationship to slavery and the Civil War. In the twenty-five years leading up to the war, several of America's largest denominations faced internal struggles over slavery. Stretching back to the first two decades of the nineteenth century, the United States had developed a clear North/South divide over slavery, one that was based less on moral arguments than on economic realities. The cotton economy of the southern states depended largely on the low-cost labor provided by the enslaved. In the industrializing North, however, slavery had become only marginally economically viable. This divide was further reflected in the views of Christian denominations on abolition. The Episcopal Church complemented this trend. Nevertheless, the Church

never officially split—as did their Presbyterian, Baptist, and Methodist counterparts—over slavery. When the Civil War erupted in April 1861, Episcopalians
in the South formed their own Protestant Episcopal Church. In the North,
this separation was never officially recognized, and by May 1866, the southern
dioceses rejoined the national church.[48]

Many Christians in southern states, likely including Payne's southern kinfolk as well as those of her husband, viewed abolition as a massive attack on
their culture, economy, and religious views. Several Episcopal clerics debated
the issue. For example, in 1861, John Henry Hopkins, the eighth presiding
bishop of the Episcopal Church, authored a pamphlet, "A Scriptural, Ecclesiastical, and Historical View of Slavery," which justified slavery based on the New
Testament and gave a clear insight into the Episcopal Church's involvement in
slavery. However, two years later, G. W. Hyer, an influential Episcopal cleric,
countered Hopkins's pamphlet in his publication *Bishop Hopkins' Letter on
Slavery Ripped Up and His Misuse of the Sacred Scriptures Exposed.*[49]

Despite challenges related to limited funding and a ready supply of new
missionaries to West Africa, Martha Payne kept as busy a schedule during the
Civil War as she did in prior years. In fact, considering the administrative and
financial obstacles of the Episcopal Church and the deteriorating health of the
bishop, even more responsibility fell on Mrs. Payne. This meant that Martha
Payne was ever more involved in Mission duties, especially correspondence,
bookkeeping, organizing donated goods, and administering mission schools.
For example, in December 1861, a frustrated Martha wrote "that [she] need[ed]
all the help [she could] get in the way of boxes as [she] found the Mission
greatly involved. There had been such careless expenditure and very little
economy. But I am trying to get my department straight once more."[50] Debt,
in fact, appeared to be a constant obstacle that Mrs. Payne—as missionary
administrator—faced.

Above all of these administrative responsibilities, Martha Payne acknowledged that the Mission's goal of planting Christianity in West Africa was not
yet realized and that the trials exacerbated by the war were not an excuse
for any diminished expectations. While Martha expressed gratitude that "the
Gospel ha[d] been planted and had taken root" in Liberia, she also lamented
that, despite the missionaries' genuine fondness for many of those whom they
served, the Greboes had not yet entirely embraced their religious message.
Referring to the unrealized potential of "their people," she wrote: "Poor peo-

ple! They are I think really attached to us, but as yet they do not receive our message that is, as a people of God may have free course and be glorified."[51] For Martha Payne, the Mission's ultimate success was thus contingent upon recruitment of passionate and hard-working missionaries who would be more successful as proselytizers.

Discussion of their respective duties in mission work, especially the hardships and limitations, was a prevalent topic for Martha and her sister Emma, who resided in Augusta, Georgia, during the war years. One letter from December 1861 referred to Emma's work in an Episcopal "Society" in Augusta that prepared aid boxes for the Confederacy.[52] Emma may also have been involved in religious work at Saint Paul's, Augusta's largest and oldest Episcopal Church. Saint Paul operated an orphanage beginning in the 1850s, while the church building itself served as a Confederate hospital during the war years. Both ventures relied on female assistance.[53] Martha and Emma's mutual interest in, and respect for, missionary work likely served to solidify their relationship and further enhance their female consciousness. Martha reminded her sister of the sustaining importance of their collective efforts: "Let us seek first the kingdom of God and His righteousness and also seek to spend and be spent for the advancement of His cause on earth. Then will we rejoice when the blessed Savior comes to make up His jewels."[54]

Undoubtedly, the sisters' cultural ties lay in the American South, and thus to a rigidly race-based and patriarchal society. Nonetheless, their involvement in the public sphere during the Civil War, albeit in positions that reinforced acceptable southern gender roles, allowed ambitious and morally committed women like Martha and Emma to engage in more fulfilling lines of work. At the same time, such women who found themselves in the public sphere, in no way abandoned the dictates of patriarchy.[55]

The Civil War ended with no comment from Martha Payne; in fact, no letter written by Martha during the last two years of the war appears to exist. However, her postbellum correspondence confirms that she followed the developments of Reconstruction with strong feelings for what the South had experienced. Early letters showcase Martha's simultaneous feelings of despondency and anger. To her sister Margaret, Martha wrote in June 1866: "All seems so dark! I shrink kindly from the mental suffering I shall endure when I look upon the desolation of my Loved people and Land, for my heart beats warmly for every true southern heart and sings to every foot of southern soil!"[56] Martha ascribed blame to both sides and expressed disapproval for what the South had become—a greedy society with no heart—yet she remained intensely loyal to the region of her birthplace. In one 1868 epistle, Martha insisted "that punishment must come to that Yankee Nation," presumably for the ruination of her Southern nation, yet she also agreed that the South "needed chastening, and [that] God ha[d] seen fit to put them in a fiery furnace for their 'correction of profit.'"[57]

Mrs. Payne was a rabid opponent of Radical Reconstruction, reconstruction envisioned by Republicans in the United States Congress who pushed for both stricter punishment of ex-Confederates and Black civil rights. She did not believe that the federal government's intentions toward the newly freed Black people were genuine. In the same June 1866 letter to Margaret, Martha wrote: "Had the Yankees been consistent [toward their treatment of African Americans], I could respect them, but from Lincoln down, this quality is wanting in them and consequently I have but little patience ..." While Martha agreed that the South should have been punished for its excessively acquisitive nature and accepted blame on behalf of her region for perpetuating the institution of slavery, she also believed that God, not the federal government, should be the "institution" to determine the South's retribution: "I trust but the furnace may be broken to pieces when its work is done and such may be the case now. 'Tis safe to leave all in the hands of God: for cannot err but 'will make the wrath of man to praise Him' and 'the remainder of wrath He can and will restrain.'"[58]

The postwar years continued to present challenges to the Mission and obstacles and limitations for Martha Payne, in particular. In the fall of 1868, Payne informed her sister Emma: "Oh! I am so pressed. I never have a leisure moment."[59] She was habitually concerned about the diminishing strength of the Mission's personnel. Reverend Payne's health continued to decline, and, in 1868, the wife of a prominent cleric whom Martha labeled as "crucial to the realization of the Mission" died. Sickness and death were constants in the tropical climes of coastal West Africa. Mrs. Payne occasionally lost her patience when she realized that the number of "inefficient," healthy personnel always seemed to outnumber those with aptitude and "character, but [whose] health [wa]s miserable" and who "ha[d] not been able to do any thing."[60]

Martha further complained about the apathy and idleness exhibited by some of the newly recruited young female missionaries. In a 1868 letter, she wrote at length about one particularly lazy colleague: "[Miss Gregg] has never done anything of consequence. Has passed most of her time in idleness. I never have been so disappointed in any one as in Miss Gregg. Ignorant of all practical matters, yet thinking that she knows more than all other people put together." Martha Payne was anything but a weakling or a pushover and did not permit Miss Gregg to use her missionary duties as an extended adventure. Acknowledging that she did not possess the right authority to "berate her," Mrs. Payne used the power she had to remove the indolent missionary to a neighboring mission, Roiktown, where she would help establish some "vernacular schools." The pragmatic Martha Payne nevertheless recognized that Miss Gregg's new position would simply "prove [to be] the plaything of an hour."[61]

Adding to Martha Payne's stresses regarding diminishing missionary personnel strength were the increasing demands on the Mission associated with Black emigration. Her correspondence, in fact, cites the increasing numbers of Blacks from the American South that the Mission served in the first few years after the Civil War. Yet immigration to Liberia was modest. According to data supplied by the Episcopal Church, fewer than two thousand African Africans relocated to Liberia during the many years after the Civil War.[62] Nonetheless, Martha referred to an immigrant, Cornelia Boyer, as "a wise woman who came out from Macon about 18 months ago," likely in the fall of 1866, who happened to be an old acquaintance of her sister's. Speaking about Cornelia Boyer in more detail, Mrs. Payne wrote to Emma: "She lived in Mr. Rees' family and said she knew you. We have her little girl, 'Sarah Jane,' a nice child, but too small to be very useful. Cornelia lost her husband and two of her children in the acclimating fever and has married again, an old man 'Neyle' from Savannah. He is a fine man, but I suppose double her age."[63]

In addition to personnel problems within the Mission, the Episcopal Church, like its denominational counterparts, continued to suffer from empty coffers. William C. Burke, a former enslaved person on Arlington, the northern Virginia plantation with ties to the prominent Custis and Lee families, immigrated to the Liberian mission of Clay Ashland and wrote of such realities. In an 1867 letter, Burke, then a pastor at Clay Ashland, an Episcopal mission neighboring Cavalla, wrote to a friend in Virginia, "the southern Mission to which I belong has ceased to operate in Liberia from the Commencement of the war to the present time. Nor do I know that they will even be able to operate again. We have been left since 61, without any missionary aid."[64]

Perhaps funds that the Protestant churches could spare during these years went toward home mission efforts, including to newly freed African Americans in the South, Native Americans out on the Great Plains, Civil War widows, and the throngs of indigent immigrants who were swelling the urban Northeast. Martha Payne honed her fundraising skills, out of necessity if nothing else. If not directly begging the Episcopal Church for more funding, she spent countless hours preparing financial reports for the Church. Martha referred to being "kept intensely occupied," at past one o'clock in the morning, "copying the Bishop's Reports to the General Convention and Board of Missions."[65] In her reports, she bemoaned that the regular funding from the Episcopal Church could scarcely cover the food expenses for the Mission, let alone take care of any expenses incurred by the mission schools.

Showcasing Martha Payne's fundraising persistence is an excerpt of a letter to Emma in June 1868: "I wrote to a dear young friend of mine, and that letter made the good people of the Church approximately $100.00 towards a box which this friend Mrs. Clarkston is sending me by the same vessel which brings yours and two more are on board the same vessel and two or three more will soon be sent. We are very dependent upon these boxes now as it takes nearly all the appropriation to purchase food. Now, two or three prices compared with former times." The "box" to which Martha refers likely included Bibles, books and other instructional materials, basic medical supplies, and other essentials necessary for personal, but especially mission, use. In that same June 1868 epistle, she acknowledged having written "60 odd" letters to potential supporters over several weeks.[66] Financial issues continued to plague the Mission. One October 1868 letter revealed Martha's growing anxiety and stress as she confided to her sister that "the [missionary] committee [was] $11,000 in debt." Describing the Church's "coldness and darkness," Payne stated that she had "lost the confidence [in] the Church which is a very serious matter" but told Emma that she "of course must say nothing about this."[67] In spite of these perpetual obstacles, Martha Payne felt fulfilled in her efforts, if not a sense of self-importance.[68] As a result of some of these trying realities, Reverend Payne and the entire Mission came to increasingly rely upon Martha to sustain the Mission's aims.

In addition to personnel and funding issues, Martha Payne expressed discomfort with the structure of the governance of American missionary activity. Although the Episcopal Church was the religious-political body the Paynes and their Mission volunteers represented, oversight of American missionary activity was increasingly conducted by a nondenominational, northern-founded, voluntary organization, the American Board of Commissioners for Foreign Missions (ABCFM).[69] The ABCFM functioned independently, and not under any particular ecclesiastical body. To Martha, the ABCFM was excessively centralized, did not hold the support of the Episcopal Church, and exercised too much power. Martha's discontent with this centralized foreign missionary organization reached such a level that in June 1868 she implied that she and Reverend Payne had discussed the possibility of his leaving the Mission and returning to Virginia. Mrs. Payne blatantly discouraged Emma from seriously considering her own missionary experience in Liberia: "I cannot say a word to urge him to remain, and it is because there is such a Committee in charge of the Missionary work, that I do not wish you to come out here. I shall not be surprised if this *trying affair* causes a break up of this Committee. They have not the confidence of the Church and are not worthy of it."[70]

By the late 1860s, the Paynes were discussing the bishop's impending retirement and the couple's return to Virginia. Yet Martha felt reluctance to leave the Mission, especially in its then present underfunded and understaffed state. By this point, one might question her hesitation to return to the United States. She, after all, had spent a rather lengthy career in Liberia, especially by the standards of female missionaries, in which she had served in numerous roles, including educator, administrator, fundraiser, correspondent, and nurse/caretaker. In other words, she had lived through all sorts of experiences both within the boundaries of typical female missionary life and perhaps had even crossed such (unofficial) gendered boundaries. Was there anything new for Mrs. Payne to experience?

A second reason why a permanent return home may have been more attractive to the Paynes relates to the changes in the postbellum South. Quite simply, by the later 1860s, southern missionaries, like the Paynes, may have felt more inclined to return to a South that was not plagued by direct attack or the threat of attack. While the region faced significant political, economic, and social turmoil in 1868, the Civil War and the single decade's worth of political turmoil leading up to it, while still very fresh wounds, were now events of the past. A third reason that may explain the appeal of a southern homecoming ties to the availability of jobs and volunteer positions in southern home missions. During these years, the American South was at the cusp of what would be a long period of physical, political, and economic reconstruction and modernization. And in this region of limited state-funded organizations and programs, religious denominations could and did play a palpable role in the South's future, not simply with regard to its rebuilding but to issues of race, class, gender, and education. Surely, Reverend and Mrs. Payne could identify appropriate home missions—some of which served emancipated enslaved people—in which they could involve themselves and their interests. Finally, and taking into account practical issues, by the latter 1860s, the Paynes were no longer "young," and Reverend Payne, in particular, endured habitual poor health. The bishop's "precarious health," in fact, left Mrs. Payne "in a constant state of anxiety."[71] The Paynes were ready for a retirement, surrounded by family and friends they had left behind years before.

Despite the appeal of an American homecoming, Martha Payne continued to express her reservations about leaving West Africa and their Mission. In a spring 1869 epistle, in which Martha informed her sister of the bishop's departure plans, she wrote, "Tis a grievous trial to me—sometimes I feel tempted to let him go without me." Mrs. Payne pointed to more practical reasons why her continual direction of the Mission was so necessary. She was focused on female representation in and contribution to the Mission: "We leave the mission so weak, especially as regards female aspirants. Mrs. Ware does what she can but she is naturally inefficient except that she teaches well. Miss Scott does nothing of any consequence. Mrs. Auer is very industrious and efficient, but this is her first year, and I fear there will be other complications. Indeed that there are already such. Sometimes I fear this Mission will be broken up. Oh! That I could abide by it till death."[72]

Despite such feelings of commitment to the Mission, Martha Payne did not remain in West Africa. John Payne's weakness and deteriorating health proved to be too much for the fifty-three-year-old man. The Paynes left their West African mission in the late summer of 1869 to start a new life at John Payne's family home on the Northern Neck of Virginia. There is no doubt that Reverend Payne, with the help of Martha and his staff, had irrevocably altered the lives of West Africans whom his mission served. Reporting to the House of Bishops upon his departure for the United States, Reverend Payne remarked that, while at the Cavalla Mission, he had baptized 352 persons, confirmed 643 persons, and ordained fourteen Deacons and twenty-five ministers. With crucial assistance from Martha, the Mission had established nine churches, multiple common and Sunday schools, a high school for boys, a "training school" for young men, and an orphan asylum.[73]

✝

Martha Jane Williford Payne offers a paragon of white southern womanhood that would more fully emerge by the end of the nineteenth century. Payne was a transitory figure, living during turbulent decades when white southern women's accepted spheres of influence straddled the private and the public. While fully embracing antebellum conceptions of femininity, Payne took advantage of opportunities in which the world—in her case, the Cavalla Mission—and not simply her household was a space in which she exercised moral authority and professional agency. Significantly, Martha Payne actively chose such a life as a single woman, and, in so doing, set an example for future generations of southern women. It was thus ironic that, while she faced familial and, indirectly, societal and Church resistance toward her selection of a missionary career as a single woman, it was her status as a married woman that ultimately forced her to close the West African chapter of her life. Perhaps as a small consolation to this ambitious and devoted southern woman, the couple remained committed to issues of the Church, and particularly to issues of Black education and religion, in postbellum Virginia. Reverend Payne died in 1874 in Westmoreland County. Upon his death, Martha Payne returned to Augusta to be near family, dying in 1896 at the age of seventy-nine.

Four

INTERREGNUM AND TRANSITION

At the end of the Civil War, the South faced innumerable economic, political, and social challenges. It was coping with the psychologically painful impact of defeat. Its infrastructure was devastated. The economy was destroyed. Confederate currency was worthless, and southerners across class lines faced dire shortages and high inflation. Families were still recovering from displacement and loss. Slavery had been abolished, prompting shifts in labor practices. Newly emancipated Black people were carving out new lives, all the while facing serious discrimination and violence. Radical Republicans in Congress were relentless in their pursuit to punish the region and to strip it of political agency. And conceptions of gender were in flux. Men struggled with their masculinity, while women wondered whether they would reassume their antebellum identities or take on quite different roles. The fifteen years between 1865 and 1880 marked a time when the South was just beginning to reconceptualize itself. These years were the makings of the New South.

This chapter adopts the theme of reconceptualization, particularly as it relates to evolving conceptions of white southern womanhood as envisioned by postbellum women. Complementing previous and succeeding chapters, this one employs religious expression as the primary instrument through which to assess southern women's evolving identities. It explores the emergence of the first generation of white women who more fully engaged in mission work outside of the home in the postbellum South. However, before this new generation of female southern mission workers emerged, participation in mission work actually declined for a period. One might say there was an interregnum of such religious activity between the end of the Civil War and the end of

Reconstruction. Protestant churches, dependent on local donations, found their congregations struggling to operate at anything other than a most basic level. Continued economic instability across the region made it difficult for churches to plan for the future. Very little money existed for missionary pursuits, and opportunities in religious work for women failed to materialize. However, just as the South displayed its first signs of revitalization by 1880, so did the Protestant churches, in general, and mission activity, in particular. And it was at that time that a new generation of white southern women was primed to enter challenging, yet rewarding, careers in mission work.

LEAN YEARS IN MISSION WORK

Before focusing on women's significant advancements in both home and foreign mission work after Reconstruction, it is necessary to lay out the developments in, and realities related to, mission work in the South between the Civil War's outbreak and the mid-to-late 1870s. When southern Methodists, Baptists, and Presbyterians split from their northern peers in 1844, 1845, and 1861 respectively, they engaged in both home and foreign mission work. Until the beginning of the Civil War, they established foreign mission boards, the main administrative units overseeing such work, and collectively dispatched a few hundred missionaries across the globe.[1] Careers and outlets in foreign mission work, however, quickly dried up after the Confederate bombing of Fort Sumter in 1861.

That said, the Civil War did help to usher in a new era of southern women's participation in religious circles at home, both formally and informally. During the war years, evangelical Protestant denominations poured most of their efforts into proselytizing and nursing the physical and spiritual bodies of the hundreds of thousands of men serving in the Confederate armed forces. To avoid denominational friction, the Confederate government was initially reticent to appoint chaplains unless they were requested by a particular regiment. However, by 1863 southern denominations had grown more organized and had begun launching revivals for the troops and, to a lesser extent, civilians in different parts of the Confederacy, especially in northern Virginia and Tennessee.[2] Southern women, although not always properly acknowledged by the governing bodies of their respective denominations, played an important part in all of this. They assumed greater roles at their denomination's quarterly meetings and revivals; they organized drives at their local churches through which they collected Bibles for distribution to Confederate soldiers; and they provided religious guidance and general assistance to new widows. However, upon Robert E. Lee's surrender at Appomattox Court House in April 1865, most white southern women quickly retreated to the exclusively domestic roles they had held in the years prior to the war.[3]

A few white southern women, however, continued to engage in mission activities during those immediate months after the war, raising funds for seminary students and domestic missionaries, populations that had been and would continue to be poorly funded. In addition, some southern women toiled alongside their northern sisters, whose churches' coffers were much fuller, to establish Sunday Schools across the region. However, this interregional co-operation disintegrated by the early 1870s, at which time southerners voiced increasing resentment toward northern influences on their religious life.[4]

During Reconstruction, southern female religious workers understood that they faced uphill battles as home mission workers and that their efforts yielded very modest results. In the fall of 1865, Elizabeth Gilmer Grattan of Richmond, Virginia, corresponded with Virginia Campbell, a local Presbyterian preacher's wife, begging for financial and material contributions from members of her church. Such contributions would benefit seminary students, most likely those at Union Presbyterian Seminary. Grattan wrote: "The smallest donation will be very acceptable so that none need be deterred from taking part in the good work who can send a pound of meat, meal or dried fruit, a yard of cloth or a few cents." To allay any fears about improper use of donations, Grattan referred to a mutual friend who would oversee the contributions provided by the parishioners of Mrs. Campbell's church: "Mrs. Brown is really at the head of the Society so there is no doubt that the supplies sent here will be promptly and properly distributed."[5]

The struggles of Grattan's faith-based society in the months and years after the Civil War were not an anomaly. Mite societies continued to exist, at least on paper, after 1865. However, painfully little evidence survives attesting to specific actions committed by such mite societies in the ten years after the Confederacy's defeat. This lack of funding sources, not to mention the desperation conveyed in Mrs. Grattan's letter, could help explain the seeming lull or hiatus in home mission work performed by southern women during the second half of the 1860s and into the first half of the 1870s (and, in some cases, beyond). Concurrently, denominations ceased publication of many of their newspapers.[6]

As dire as the situation was for those involved in home mission work, the period also seriously disrupted expansion of foreign mission work for each of the Protestant denominations in the South. "Foreign missions languished as the tide of war rose," according to Fannie E. S. Heck, an early Baptist leader in mission work and a key proponent of women's role in it. Heck stated that contributions to Baptist foreign mission projects had exceeded $40,000 in 1860 but plummeted to $9,000 in 1863. The Baptists' financial situation remained discouraging for several years after the Civil War. In 1866, "a more hopeless year than all that had gone before, the lowest ebb was reached." It was in that year when the denomination received fewer than $7,000 in contributions for foreign missions.[7] The Baptists and their fellow Protestant denominations dispatched no or very few foreign missionaries between 1861 and the mid-1870s.[8]

Simultaneous with this financial shortfall among the denominations was a crisis of masculinity in the South, a reality that affected southern women's outlets in foreign religious work, in particular, and opportunities and acceptance within religious circles more generally. The Confederate defeat, including their lost mastery over the enslaved, seriously maimed white southern men's sense of self-worth and masculinity. White men now devised new notions of manhood that were in opposition to both northern ideals of masculinity and southern womanhood. This crisis in masculinity leached into southern churches and tangibly impacted women's participation within them.[9] By the early 1870s, southern men sought ways to limit women's roles in church organization and politics. Women's participation in religious groups, such as mite societies, might engender too much freedom and power for women. While such men probably gave little to no thought to women ever occupying the pulpit, many believed that churches needed to take a proactive role in the preservation and enforcement of strict gender norms that antebellum ministers had advocated.[10] For example, in 1871 South Carolinian James Petigru Boyce, a southern Baptist pastor, theologian, and professor at the Southern Baptist Theological Seminary in Greenville, vigorously advanced a motion that women no longer have any vote—and thus any appreciable voice—in Baptist churches. Fortunately for women, fellow Baptist minister Basil Manly Jr. opposed Boyce, and the motion lost.[11] Similarly, some scholars suggest, southern men feared that the organization of women's groups, including religious ones, would delegate too much economic control to the more delicate sex.[12]

PRECURSORS TO SUCCESS

Several factors beyond a stabilizing southern economy paved the way for female advancement in religious work after Reconstruction. These included growing opportunities in female higher education as well as evolving definitions of white southern womanhood and marriage, as conceptualized by women. The expansion of female higher education played a crucial role, catapulting some white southern women into more professional environments. As we have seen, Protestant denominations established several dozen academies and colleges across the South beginning in the 1830s. Most such schools remained open during the war and in the lean years thereafter. With an uncertain economic climate ahead, many southern women accepted that a college education might bring them a degree of financial security. Enrollments at such schools equaled or, more likely, exceeded what they had been before 1860. Educational priorities changed during these years, too. Before the Civil War, female higher education sought to provide an academic knowledge but, perhaps as importantly, the marks of a properly finished young lady. Women who strayed from this model were a threat to men and to themselves.[13] According to Baptist scholar A. J. Battle in 1857, "strong minded women unsex and degrade themselves, by their boisterous assumption of man's prerogatives and responsibilities."[14]

However, during and after the war, southern women remained in or returned to school in order to gain marketable skills, particularly ones to prepare them as teachers or secretaries. Religiously affiliated women's colleges across the New South raised rigor and expanded course offerings, yet sought to "create a Christian home-like atmosphere on campus" whereby faculty and staff assumed parental roles and emphasized communal, familial activities, including prayer, worship, religious lectures, and silent meditation.[15] By the time of the founding of women's denomination-wide foreign missionary organizations in the 1880s, female academies and colleges had graduated a couple of generations of educated southern women. Significantly, a disproportionate number of the early administrators in such societies had benefited from—and strongly promoted—college educations. Baptist Fannie E. S. Heck, who published a book in 1913 on the history and contributions of southern Baptist women in mission work, shared her views on the merits of female education: "Tennyson will voice the hope of many another woman when a little later he sings that woman should 'Learn and be All that not harms distinctive womanhood.'" According to Heck, educated women "should bless the wider world." However, while women engaged in mission work were on "equal footing" with men, they were not to jettison their femininity.[16]

Expansion in educational opportunities was not the only necessary precursor of southern women's advancement in religious work. More flexible conceptions of white southern womanhood, at least as conceived of by women, contributed to their interest in missionary endeavors. The Civil War had been the impetus for such change. It made white southern women both more visible and more independent. With fathers, brothers, and sons off at war, southern women could no longer expect protection, nor could they operate as though they were delicate pieces of fine china. Rather, if only initially out of necessity, these new "mothers of invention" fended for themselves but, in so doing, found inner sources of strength and resilience. In the postbellum years, white southern women displayed varying degrees of comfort with these changing conceptions of gender. For example, women who came of age prior to the war were not as welcome of change as those who came of age after 1861. Likewise, southern men, who were dealing with their own crisis of gender during these early postbellum years, were typically slow to accept such evolving conceptions of southern womanhood.

These broader observations concerning gender have been made by Anne Firor Scott and Jane Turner Censer.[17] Scott, in particular, found evidence of larger numbers of women who served as heads of household (which might even include management of vast plantations); as instructors at private institutions, public schools, and normal schools; as boardinghouse keepers; as journalists, including newspaper editors; as stenographers; and in other positions.[18] While some women "worked from necessity and would happily have returned to dependency," Scott concluded that many others embraced the chance for greater interface with the public world, where they would find "lasting satisfaction in independence."[19] Censer refined Scott's analysis by characterizing a polarized post-1865 South in which "white women from elite backgrounds experimented with different notions of women's proper role, notions that validated womanly independence and achievement." At the same time, "external forces and the contradictions within their position were making these notions untenable."[20] Censer, more often than Scott, recognized that white, elite southern women could and often did lead lives that were public and civic-minded while adhering to social and political values that did not contradict their antebellum pasts.

Alternately, elite white southern women still valued their role of "lady," even while they pushed to make the boundaries of womanhood more malleable. Anastatia Sims, in her study on North Carolina women engaged in voluntary associations at the turn of the twentieth century, maintained that southern women "cherished the southern lady as the most sacred ideal of woman-hood."[21] Small changes, however, hinted that modifying roles and expectations were in store for white southern women. For example, etiquette surrounding courtship loosened. No longer was it a requirement for young women to navigate the public world with a chaperone. Women enjoyed more flexibility surrounding their social lives. Newspapers reported on women's activities and contributions, and in the process, gave women more visibility.

Similarly, white southern women's relationship to marriage was in flux. Indeed, postwar demographics dictated that many tens of thousands of southern women would never marry. Over a quarter of a million Confederate men died in the Civil War, and, for many, spinsterhood was an assumed reality. However, for other women living in the postbellum South, marriage was deemed unnecessary, even unwise. Such women possessed no desire to be chained to an incompatible mate. Consciously rejecting marriage, they were content to remain with their families.[22] However, the decision to forgo marriage meant that women needed to identify paths that would lead to their financial independence. And, it was this reality that pushed such southern women into a limited number of professions, including that of religious work.

Sources of empowerment and inspiration, some women responded to their educations—including their exposure to new ideas, books, classmates, and instructors—as well as evolving thoughts surrounding womanhood articulated by their female friends and family members in meaningful ways. They began accepting their intellectual capacities; they thought about ways in which the world would benefit from their feminine contributions; and they looked for scriptural evidence to encourage them in religious and community uplift. In 1884, Methodist missionary Laura Askew Haygood delivered a speech to southern women that reflected such ideas of female self-realization. She declared: "I thank God that there is no longer a question as to woman's having a part in the world's work."[23] However, Haygood also acknowledged that society continued to question women's abilities and rights, many of which scripture supported: "We—the women, as well as our brothers—have been slow to understand that she, with all who should believe on Him through the ministry of the apostles and their successors, was included in the Savior's gracious words to the Father when He said: 'As thou hast sent me in the world, even so have I also sent them into the world.'" Specific to women's place in mission work, Haygood believed that God had instructed women as well as men "to teach and to testify to the risen Christ."[24] By 1880, southern women were more primed, more confident, and more committed to serve as leaders, administrators, teachers, nurses, and followers of Christ. A career in the home and foreign mission fields offered an appropriate place to combine their talents and passions with their strong views on the preservation of femininity.[25]

RELIGIOUS WORK AFTER 1880

Coming to terms with the physical, economic, social, emotional, and spiritual pain endured over the past generation, white southerners were ready to imagine a new religious landscape by the end of Reconstruction, one that would be defined by (the beginnings of) regional reconciliation and personal discipline, especially temperance, as well as a renewed commitment to benevolence.[26] While forward-looking in their attempts to accommodate encroaching modernity and industrialization, white religious leaders of the postbellum South embraced old values, too, particularly a rigid racial hierarchy.[27] In this new, yet evolving, religious environment, women gradually gained greater authority, greater independence, and ultimately greater public involvement.

Countless southern women engaged in home mission societies, particularly in administrative positions, between 1880 and the turn of the twentieth century. As has been shown, many faith-based religious organizations administered by southern women existed prior to 1880. However, in the years after 1880, women not only expanded upon these organizations, but organized countless others for the first time. An example of the former—a women's mission society that grew and furthered its objectives—was the Rappahannock

(VA) Baptist Association. According to a history of the association, presumably written by teacher-missionary Olive Elliott Bagby, the Rappahannock Baptist Association organized as early 1843 but witnessed continued, although uneven, progress. In Bagby's words, "It is possible to understand that the growth of work among women has been slow at times but never was the spark of interest extinguished."[28]

By 1880, some women publicly celebrated and supported their female colleagues who voiced their ideas on religion, community uplift, and politics. Some acknowledged the significant advancements made, and gender roles challenged by, southern women since the antebellum years. Essayist Mary Washington Cabell Early, of Lynchburg, Virginia, was one who articulated such views. Described as "a person of deep spiritual and intellectual gifts," Early enjoyed a lengthy tenure as a writer who expounded on an array of topics, particularly religion, southern artists and authors, race relations, women's issues, and politics. In one, undated newspaper article, she proclaimed: "Every one who lived in or visited the South before the war knows how tenderly the women of the better class were sheltered from contact with the outer world. Many women were left widows or fatherless by the casualties of the war and the men who survived have met with such serious changes in their fortunes that they are no longer able to shield the women of their household from care and poverty."[29] In Early's eyes, women had emerged as more independent and self-reliant, "often called on to think and decide and act for themselves," and carrying "on enterprises which were formerly considered to belong exclusively to the masculine sphere."[30]

This new generation of female workers for Christ belonged to well-established Protestant churches, most commonly Presbyterian, Methodist, and Baptist, but also others, for example, the Episcopal Church and the Evangelical Lutheran Church, lived comfortably within the middle or elite southern classes, and possessed academy or college educations. Specific to the latter, many believed strongly in the value of education. In correspondence with a close friend about a family member, a Virginia woman wrote: "*Educate,* no matter what the outlook. If Ada never marries, what you teach her will be, next to her faith in God, the solace of her life."[31] While both married and single women participated in religious pursuits, a disproportionate number of the most ambitious participants in mission work were single, some of whom never married and some of whom were widows.

A shared worldview and political agenda served as a glue for this community of southern female mission workers. While often more malleable on issues of gender, such women reflected conservatism in other regards. Most fundamentally, women sought to preserve racial and class hierarchies that had existed in the antebellum South. They participated in a more conservative Social Gospel than did their northern counterparts, but a less socially and theologically constricting one compared to their fundamentalist Christian sisters. Religious scholar Priscilla Pope-Levison maintains that divides grew wider between evangelical, mainline Protestants and fundamentalist Christians during the late nineteenth century. Evangelical Protestants followed a more pliable interpretation of the Bible and were more accepting of the coexistence of religion and modern science, while fundamentalists, who had been influenced by the Wesleyan-Holiness and Keswick movements, vehemently defended literalist interpretations of the Bible.[32] Southern women's religious work reflected these theological differences.

The number of southern women involved in home mission work increased markedly between the end of Reconstruction and the turn of the twentieth century. In the 1870s, only a handful of highly localized and informal mission societies (or mite societies) existed. However, by 1888 the Methodist Episcopal Church, South (MEC, South), for example, had organized 214 local home mission societies, with over 3,500 registered members.[33] Particular to the MEC, South, the number of southern women in home mission societies grew from a few thousand to approximately 60,000 just prior to the 1910 merger of home and foreign mission societies.[34] A majority of the members within these home and foreign mission societies were women, suggesting that mission work was a highly conspicuous and respectable place for ambitious and devout southern women.

Home mission activity was both diverse and inclusive during this era. It comprised faith-based work from rural Appalachia to bustling New South cities and catered to southerners of all ages and races. In Virginia, women in the MEC, South, participated in numerous projects through the Woman's Board of Home Missions between 1890 and World War I and beyond. Specifically under the administration of the MEC South's Woman's Missionary Council, women established settlement houses (often known as Wesley Houses) in fast-growing industrial areas. They provided religious and educational programs for working-class children whose parents labored in the textile mills in such locations as Danville, Portsmouth, and Richmond.[35] Under the direction of a deaconess, each typically offered a Mothers' Club, home economics and religious classes, kindergarten, recreational activities, and pageantry as means to uplift such disadvantaged community members. Other women of the MEC, South, served as teachers, mentors, and administrators in cooperative boarding homes, such as the Wilson Home, which catered to new female workers in Richmond's tobacco factories.

Other Methodist women served in various capacities in rural areas, including in the southern Blue Ridge Mountains, where communities often lacked any infrastructure, such as public schools. Institutions like the Ferrum Training School (later Ferrum College), a school founded by Methodists in 1913, provided primary, secondary, and eventually postsecondary education to underserved Appalachian southerners. It offered other professional, faith-based opportunities for ambitious white southern women. Most southern settlement houses, boarding homes, schools, and orphanages to which such women were connected opened their doors at the height of the Progressive era, between the late 1890s and 1910.[36]

Devout women throughout the South engaged in similar pursuits to those taken on by these enterprising Virginians. This included direct oversight of, and volunteer work with, orphanages, hospitals, schools, settlement houses, and women's boarding houses in mining and mill communities. In such environments, they worked as missionaries, home visitors, educators, office secretaries, and directors of social welfare.[37] Particularly determined women, like Kentuckian Lucinda Helm, founder of the Woman's Parsonage and Home Mission Society of the MEC, South, in 1886, took on positions through which they could expand their denomination's influence across the South through mission societies and home mission projects.[38] Some female-led religious organizations, such as the Woman's Missionary Union (WMU), founded by Southern Baptists in 1888, held annual drives through which they instituted weeks of self-denial as a time of praying for and financially contributing to home missions. One such drive was the Southern Baptists' Week of Prayer, also known as the Week of Prayer for Home Missions and the Annie Armstrong Offering. It was a triumph, and, in its first year raised in excess of $5,000, most of which went toward assisting colleagues in the debt-ridden Foreign Mission Board in addition to the continued exportation of their message about opportunities in home mission work.[39] The WMU also engaged in such activities and pursuits as raising

money for foreign missions, state missions, home missions, the WMU Train-
ing School (Louisville, Kentucky), the Sunday School Board, and the Connie
Maxwell Orphanage (Orangeburg, South Carolina). In addition, women in the
WMU delivered speeches to audiences of varying sizes to encourage women
to get involved in home and foreign missions; they participated in theological
debates about women's place in religious work; and they sent delegates to the
WMU Auxiliary of state conventions and the Southern Baptist Convention.
Male denominational leadership was reluctant to acknowledge the contributions of those women like Lucinda Helm who assumed more traditionally masculine, more administrative, and more authoritative roles than those women
who labored in more feminine, less "high stakes" religious activities. In fact,
their efforts were strikingly minimized or absent from many denominational
histories, including those specifically focused upon mission work, written in
the late nineteenth and early twentieth centuries.[40]

Female mission workers, however, received ample support and encouragement from their female colleagues. Abby Manly Gwathmey of Richmond,
Virginia, epitomized this spirit.[41] She hailed from a family committed to Christian service. Her father, Basil Manly, had been a prominent Baptist minister
and founding member of the Southern Baptist Convention, while her brothers
had served as college presidents. Her husband, William H. Gwathmey, filled
the position of (unpaid) recording secretary of the Foreign Mission Board, a
post he held for thirty-three years until his death in 1886. A resourceful widow,
she served as president of the Virginia subcommittee of the WMU during
the early 1890s and president of the WMU in 1894–95. Gwathmey addressed
her colleagues at the sixth annual Union convention in Washington, D.C., in
May 1895. With the following message of motivation, she pronounced: "Shall
we, for a moment, falter when such large opportunities confront us, inviting
to still greater zeal and activity? Nay, my sisters, let us rather go forward,
relying upon God encouraged . . . by the assurance that 'we can do all things
through Christ which strengthened us.'"[42] Further championing women's influence in the governance and expansion of mission work, Abby Gwathmey
spent the first decade of the twentieth century leading efforts to strengthen
the relationship of, and communication between, local WMU societies (also
called associations) and the statewide committee. As a result of her efforts,
the number of local WMU societies "multiplied" and fundraising reached an
all-time high.[43]

The WMU continued to experience healthy growth in the first decade of the twentieth century. According to a 1974 history of the WMU, between 1902 and 1907 there were 234 new Woman's Missionary Union societies and 165 new children's bands. The latter were sometimes referred to as Sunbeam bands. Established in Virginia in 1886, children's or Sunbeam bands were clubs in which children and teenagers "learned about the world from missionary articles," read "missionary stories and catechisms," recited "Bible verses and 'missionary pieces,'" and "helped to pack boxes for frontier missionaries." Women served as teachers and mentors to those in the Sunbeam bands, in the process reinforcing Baptist and southern values, while cultivating the next generation of Baptist leaders.[44]

Countless southern women also served their communities and Christ in less-involved, although vital, ways. In many instances, these women engaged in religious work through their local churches. They organized Black Sunday Schools. They assembled "bundles" of food and basic supplies for Blacks and poor whites, especially at Christmas time. They gathered and distributed Bibles and missionary literature. They created quilts for Native Americans in Indian Territory (Oklahoma). They collected money to build and repair parsonages. They held sales of children's second-hand clothing. They put together scrapbooks of old denominational newspapers and publications that were donated to orphans. They delivered lectures to groups about opportunities in home mission work. They corresponded with wealthy community members for donations to their home mission projects. And they worked as Bible readers (teachers) and religious mentors, consecrated women who ventured to rural localities where it was not possible to organize schools. Denominational societies, such as the Woman's Home and Foreign Missionary Society of the Evangelical Lutheran Synod, often adopted smaller projects with little or no oversight from men. In contrast, larger projects, ones tied to denomination-wide missions located in remote places, were more often dictated to such women.[45]

While most southern female mission workers who focused upon reform in the public sphere exerted their religious ideas and influence within their native region, a few did venture outside of the South. They served sparsely populated locales in the West or slums in northern cities. For example, Mississippian Susan Dabney Smedes (1840–1913) labored as a missionary and teacher in South Dakota and Montana during the late 1880s. Described as "gentle," "devout," and "ambitious," Dabney had expressed an early interest in missionary work. Her instructors at Mr. Ozanne's School in Jackson, Mississippi, and at Madame Desrayaux's School in New Orleans likely encouraged her religious and intellectual propensities while reinforcing conceptions of southern womanhood. In 1860, Dabney married North Carolinian Lyell Smedes, the son of an Episcopal minister. Unfortunately, the new Mrs. Smedes became a widow just eleven weeks after her wedding. The war years were erratic, and she lived in several locations across the South. In 1866, Smedes and her sisters helped establish an Episcopal church near Burleigh, Mississippi. She served as a fundraiser, even asking Episcopalians in the North for financial assistance. Their efforts to found a church were successful, and she oversaw its "church store for many years."[46]

Perhaps because of her single marital status and her father's death in 1885, Smedes seriously considered a career as a missionary. Indeed, her desire became a reality and at the age of forty-five she obtained a commission as "United States teacher in the Rosebud Agency, South Dakota Territory."[47] Smedes worked with the Sioux between the fall of 1886 and late 1887.[48] She not only taught the "3 R's" required by the federal government, but, more related to her personal interests, proselytized the local Native Americans with the use of a Bible translated into the Sioux language. However, the Dakota climate proved to be too severe for the Deep South native. Helena, Montana, offered a (somewhat) more moderate climate as well as plenty of opportunities to proselytize its Native American population. It was likewise home to her sister who was married to the United States Surveyor-General. Smedes moved there by the end of 1887 and secured a clerical position in the office of her brother-in-law as well as in that of his successor.

Excerpts from an extant diary kept between 1888 and 1889 allude to Smedes's work with Native Americans near Helena—most likely the Blackfoot or the Crow—but offers scant information about her missionary work there. In later life, Mrs. Smedes returned to the South, specifically to Sewanee, Tennessee, where she gave regular lectures to the University of the South community about her experiences as a western missionary. Smedes likewise led a Sunday School class of sixty or sixty-five mountain children at Otey, a village church, concurrent to serving as president of the Women's Auxiliary, the missionary society of the Episcopal Church.[49]

Other women, including Virginians Sara Agnes Rice Pryor (1830–1912) and her daughter, Marie Gordon "Gordy" Pryor Rice (1850–1928), took on professional, faith-based community activist and teaching roles in New York City. In 1867, Sara's husband, General Roger Atkinson Pryor, C.S.A., relocated to the North to start a fresh life, joining an established community of "Confederate carpetbaggers."[50] Living in an enclave of southerners in New York offered southern women like the Pryors social and professional opportunities that combined the comforts of their native southern culture with a northern, somewhat more progressive, outlook on women's potential. The Pryors identified as Presbyterians. Sara Rice Pryor displayed an exceptional penchant for religious study, at one point having read under the guidance of a Presbyterian clergyman attached to Union Presbyterian Seminary.[51]

Mrs. Sara Pryor was among the founders of, and primary teachers at, a home—opened at least as early as 1870—for women and children in Brooklyn.[52] While most of those whom the "home" served were northern-born, some destitute southerners also took advantage of its services.[53] According to her memoirs, published in 1909, "some women formerly of high position in the South found temporary refuge in this Home. The world would be surprised if I should give their names!"[54] Meanwhile, Roger Pryor established a successful law practice, and, as observed by historian Sven Beckert, in postbellum New York City, "no group of professionals became more important than lawyers."[55] Paid employment was not essential for Mrs. Pryor or her daughter; rather, both women desired to engage in voluntary work that kept them occupied spiritually and intellectually for many years.

Gordy Pryor's correspondence reveals that she worked at the school until late 1879 when she married Henry Crenshaw Rice and returned to Virginia. Sara Pryor's memoir confirms that she remained in Brooklyn and served women and children with the Home throughout the 1880s. Gordy Pryor wrote in 1878 to childhood friend Franklina "Lena" Bartlett, who was herself a missionary: "I have entered upon my busy 'half' at school. I have eighty three girls now, and have a constant succession of classes, with scarcely any intermission."[56] Ambitious and committed to materially and morally uplifting working-class New York youth and women, she nonetheless became discouraged by her lack of progress. Referring to a recent conversation with a friend, Gordy Pryor confided: "I was talking the other day, in a rather discouraged frame of mind about my Mission class. 'But you must not expect to metamorphose those girls,' she said, 'Their children will be, probably, brought up on a slightly higher plane, because of your teaching—and so the human race is raised by hair's breadths.' I confess I have neither largeness of heart nor faith enough, to find that result altogether satisfying; but I suppose we must just *do* our work, and leave results to God."[57]

Gordy Pryor's self-doubt might have stemmed from her guilt surrounding her "intellectual decadence" and champagne tastes, including her love of opera, art museums, and reading clubs enjoyed by the New York bourgeoisie.[58] In an another letter to Lena from 1878, Pryor admitted: "I must either devote all my hours, when free from school, to music and study, and be of no use to anybody in the world; or I must "fling away ambition," give up my dreams of high culture, and do what little I could for other people." Although she chose the latter (at least while she was still single), she confessed that "the disappointment of selfish aspirations does shoot through me sometimes with a painful pang."[59] Gordy Pryor likely shared this dilemma with many of her bourgeois contemporaries who had devoted themselves to mission work but who identified so strongly with their own class. Nevertheless, time, her spiritual and intellectual maturation, changed location, and marital status as well as her occupation with responsibilities as a housewife and mother to four did not appear to alter Gordy Pryor Rice's sense of Christian duty and excitement for the improvements that faith-based organizations could bring to disadvantaged Americans.

If anything, Gordy Rice grew increasingly frustrated with life on her Charlotte County, Virginia, plantation, finding that opportunities in mission work there were very limited compared to New York. According to Gordy, Southside Virginia, like many areas in the New South, struggled to prosper as it had before the war and thus had few religious outlets in the 1880s.[60] For her, missionary work had been such a major component of her identity prior to moving back to the South, and she had difficulty accepting that she could not undertake such challenges in faith-based work, namely her teaching career, while serving as the matron of a large farm with four young children. At this time in her life, she could not imagine why some women did not find more fulfillment in such opportunities. Writing to Lena in November 1891, she alluded to a mutual friend's expressed ingratitude regarding mission activities: "Little does Mathilde know of the rewards of missionary work! It is all the more "blessed."[61] Earlier that year, Mrs. Rice wrote to Lena of her jealousy surrounding mission work that the former was engaging in out in California: "I cannot help envying you all your opportunity—and rare ability—for good work. And how catholic you are in your sympathies, embracing our poor white people, the Mexicans, the Chinese, the Negroes!"[62]

By the early 1890s, opportunities in mission work were expanding in impoverished south central Virginia. In 1891, Gordy Rice praised the ecumenical expansion of Sunday Schools for African Americans and poor whites, all organized by southerners, many of whom were women, and all "working faithfully without a cent of salary." According to Rice, "across the river" from them, "a good woman, Mrs. Lester, has a school of very poor white people—a labor of love." In an "adjoining county, Dr. and Mrs. Jaeger, Episcopalians, have a large coloured Sunday School, have had a church built for the negroes, and are planning an orphanage."[63] The insightful Mrs. Rice acknowledged that faith-based efforts to uplift both the area's Black and white populations were not entirely random but helped to preserve race relations. According to her, "when the negroes alone are helped, the equally poor whites are naturally embittered, and the antagonistic feeling between the races is greatly increased."[64]

In addition to her responsibilities with a Sunday School in the early 1890s, Gordy Rice also served a prominent role in assembling Christmas bundles—450 alone in December 1892—and school supplies for the area's Black and poor white populations; writing articles on such topics as "The Negro's Greatest Need" in such publications as the *Home Mission Monthly*; distributing religious publications and raising money for Blacks to attend "respectable" seminaries at which they could be exposed to a "more intelligent Christianity."[65] Feeling a bit more enthused about her growing mission work, she concluded one epistle with the following sentiment: "I do not yet know what I can become in life, but, whatever I am, I want to do good work for Christ. I hope never to forget. Freely ye have received, freely give! I want to pass on to others all that has been done for me, and so let your work keep on."[66]

Regardless of their location, women like Susan Smedes, Sara Rice Pryor, and Gordy Pryor Rice revealed that they could simultaneously embody and defend femininity—an attribute that many within their region continued to prize for the "fairer sex" after the Civil War—along with intellectual and public aspirations. Particular to Gordy Pryor Rice, her voluminous correspondence with Franklina Bartlett, which spanned over twenty years, reveals an interest in such topics as old beaux, trousseaus, evening gowns, needlework skill, and motherhood, all alongside such more serious subjects as theological debate, ancient literature, and community activism. To adopt a life of service and hard work did not mean that such a woman had to discard her identity as a "southern lady" and all that it entailed.

Five

HOME MISSION WORK MEETS
CONSERVATIVE PROGRESSIVISM

The Social Gospel movement was a nationwide religious and social reform movement that spanned the late nineteenth and early twentieth centuries. It sought to apply Christian values to social problems, particularly issues of social justice and economic inequality that had been spawned by industrialization. This chapter contributes to the emerging scholarship on the Social Gospel movement in the South.[1] It acknowledges that progressive reform was not as far-reaching in the South as it was in other regions of the country.[2] Consequently, white southern women engaged in mission work filled a vital void in their attempts to address such societal problems as poverty, child labor, education, housing, and public health and sanitation. Alternately, while such women did not bring about social reform through a network of well-developed secular professional organizations, as did their counterparts in the North, they did engender widespread societal change through a collection of evangelical Protestant denominations and allied faith-based organizations. Quite simply, they served as the religious, albeit small-scale, predecessors to the modern welfare state that played a significant role in uplifting, even modernizing, American society from Theodore Roosevelt's brand of Progressivism in the 1900s to Franklin Roosevelt's New Deal of the 1930s to Lyndon Johnson's Great Society of the 1960s. Similarly, according to historian Anastatia Sims, women involved in secular organizations in turn-of-the-twentieth-century North Carolina served in such positions of influence as the state's "public housekeepers." Crusaders for a host of issues ranging from prohibition to the establishment of public libraries to calls for the enactment of food safety laws, these women translated "private domesticity into public housekeeping" and, in so doing, "contributed to a redefinition of the proper role of government."[3]

Whether or not southern females in mission work chose to adopt such modern labels as "progressive," they did understand, at least on some levels, that their religious-based community and social work extended beyond their home congregations. They sensed that they possessed the power, influence, commitment, and perceived moral superiority to bring about significant change. For them, God was watching them and encouraging them in their efforts. Referring to the promising advancements among female Southern Baptists, Eliza Y. Hyde wrote a friend in 1891, "Every year we are making progress, in our mission work, and before long S. Carolina will indeed be an army trained, and marching inward to noble deeds for the Master."[4]

There were literally thousands of southern women who did not entirely live the lives outlined by historian Jean E. Friedman, who argued that southern women inhabited a socially, politically, intellectually, and religiously "enclosed garden" in which the rural evangelical kinship system "resisted women's reform" and women's opportunity in the public sphere "even into the twentieth century."[5] Indeed, the rural nature of much of the South, along with the influence of kin and evangelical Christianity, did limit southern women's success in developing female networks of reform as early as northern women did in the nineteenth century. However, Friedman likely exaggerates the extent to which the "enclosed garden" controlled or suppressed such women's aspirations and efforts by the latter part of the century. Rather, as argued by John Patrick McDowell and Anne Firor Scott, southern religion—between 1880 and 1920—manifested significant concern with social reform, and southern women were a large part of such efforts.[6]

This chapter highlights southern female mission workers' politics and worldviews, particularly those related to race, class, and gender, of the postbellum South. Southern women who represented miscellaneous Protestant churches, societies, and organizations were not radical, at least by the definitions of the late nineteenth and early twentieth centuries. They were only magnifying their traditional female roles and applying them to environments beyond their households. Such values align with those of the nineteenth-century-woman movement which supported women's right to initiate measures of social welfare, charitable benevolence, and temperance.[7] Southern female mission workers did not self-identify as feminists as that would jeopardize their prized role as a "lady." As religious historian Gregory Vickers has written, during the late nineteenth century, "mother and homemaker were made functions of the more inclusive worker and were redefined as world mother and community homemaker."[8]

Exemplifying this role of "community homemaker" was Virginian Mollie Apperson, the first woman to serve in the officially appointed position of missionary to Richmond. Named in 1892 by the Baptist General Association "to serve on a full-time, salaried basis," Apperson spent many years engaging in "house-to-house visitation work" in poor Richmond neighborhoods before moving on to similar positions in Newport News and the mining town of Pocahontas. In each, she sought to ensure that working-class and immigrant Virginians possessed the domestic knowledge, skills, and Christian values to maintain healthy and functioning households.[9] Perhaps akin to the much more recent Phyllis Schlafly, a well-educated constitutional attorney and conservative activist, southern evangelical women between 1880 and 1920 sought to use their emerging cultural influence to uplift segments of southern society while reinforcing conservative social mores that aligned with those promoted by many southern Democrats. Most visibly, this included their insistence on the continuing deference of poor white, working-class, and Black communities to the southern elite. Maternalism—with a healthy dose of paternalism mixed in—structured the thoughts and actions of those southern women engaged in home mission work.

These southern evangelical women demonstrated particular concern for poor whites, Blacks, and immigrants in a number of urban locations throughout the South, including New Orleans, Nashville, Charleston, and Atlanta.[10] Denominations expanded efforts to serve the South's foreign-born. That said, little more than 2 percent of the South's population was foreign-born during the peak decade of immigration into the region (1900–1910). As a result, there was only a modest need for home missionaries who could assist such people. For example, in 1899, seventeen missionaries representing the MEC, South, worked with immigrants in ten southern cities.[11] In such missions, southern women typically exuded an attitude of concern that, although often mixed with enforced deference and condescension, conveyed their interest in education, health care, and improved living and social conditions among the South's poor and underserved. Likewise, elite southern women preferred to serve in communities where they could help eradicate conditions, notably divorce and alcoholism, that they considered detrimental to family stability. Their emphasis was simply on a higher morality, especially a brand of morality that reinforced middle-class and elite values and did not conflict with well-established southern viewpoints on race and gender. In support of this contention, these female mission workers did not leave behind personal sources, such as letters and diaries, that suggest they had any desire to radically alter the social and/ or racial structure of southern society.

✝

Illustrative of an interest in uplifting—not revolutionizing—poorer mountain populations religiously and socially are Caryetta Davis and Ora Harrison and their mission work in southwestern Virginia. Two single women, one from central Virginia and one from Rocky Mount, Virginia, Davis and Harrison served Episcopal mission schools and led church services as well as recreational and adult education classes in Franklin County, Virginia, during the 1910s. Affectionately known by their pupils and their greater communities as Miss Etta and Miss Ora, one local historian described them as "two women ... who were inspired by God to go alone into these communities to bring the people the best of a more progressive society in the most Christian way while maintaining the best of their present life."[12]

Appalachia attracted as many, perhaps even more, northern missionaries as southern ones. Northern missionaries considered southern mountaineers more worthy of their religious, educational, and social uplift due to the fact that many had remained loyal to the Union during the Civil War.[13] Reflecting their own racism, northern missionaries also believed that the very few Blacks living there made the mountain South a more attractive region in which to offer their beneficence.[14]

These two Episcopal women and their few dozen contemporaries, the majority of them single, typically targeted "the un-churched, some Brethren, and children of reluctant Primitive Baptists" and sought to enrich their primitive and isolated lives through a combination of religious and educational pursuits, including practical, "home economics" ones. In particular, Davis, Harrison, and their fellow missionaries in an underserved Appalachian county taught at two Episcopal-founded schools, St. John's and St. Peter's (later known as the Phoebe Needles Memorial School). By the early 1920s, these served between

75 and 125 students each in first grade through two years of high school. St. John's School was located in Endicott, while St. Peter's School was in Callaway, both in Franklin County. Davis, Harrison, and Appalachian mission workers representing other denominations played an influential role in the lives of those they served. The women working at both schools kept large households, attached to their respective schools, where many of their students boarded during the winter months. As remembered by many former pupils, these educators were not only their instructors and/or principals but their religious mentors, Sunday School teachers, nurses, and surrogate parents.[15]

No evidence suggests that missionaries at St. John's and St. Peter's ever attempted to alter the basic customs or culture of these Appalachian children. In fact, another missionary, Lucy Calista Morgan, who started her career in 1920 at the Episcopal Appalachian School outside Asheville, North Carolina, opened the Penland School of Handicrafts (now Penland School of Crafts) in Spruce Pine, North Carolina, in 1923. Weaving and pottery making were Penland's initial foci. By establishing trade and industrial education, Morgan ensured that southern mountaineers could preserve their artistic talents while, at the same time, creating a means to achieve greater economic stability through sale of crafts.[16]

Notably, the aims of Episcopal missionaries like Morgan, Harrison, and Davis contrast with David E. Whisnant's characterization of female Progressive era reformers in Appalachia. In his eyes, such missionaries, nurses, and teachers actually threatened mountain culture through their close-minded and elitist, albeit well-meaning, efforts at uplift and modernization.[17] Similarly, Henry D. Shapiro has noted that faith-based and social workers were partly responsible for promoting the mythical image of Appalachia as a "strange land and peculiar people" as a means to justify missionary pursuits in the southern mountains.[18]

Women representing other Protestant denominations, particularly the Methodists, Presbyterians, and Baptists, engaged in similar progressive projects in other parts of the South and used similar tactics, namely uplift through a combination of religious and industrial education. While serving in the Thomasville area of south Georgia at the turn of the twentieth century, Annie Heath, a Methodist deaconess, recognized a need for a home, spiritual guidance, and education for "orphan, needy and dependent girls."[19] A local family donated its nine-room home to Heath's cause. The building was subsequently named the Vashti Industrial School for Girls.[20] The combination school and home grew quickly. By 1907, the Vashti School had outgrown its nine-room building. In response, the Women's Home Missionary Society of the MEC, South, purchased a former cigar factory and sixty-five acres. The next year, seventy girls moved into Vashti.[21]

Southern women engaged in home mission work hoped to be influential figures who would personally direct less fortunate southerners on paths toward economic and familial stability along with establishing an enriched relationship with God. At the same time, female mission workers typically held narrow theological and social views regarding the viable paths that would bring those whom they served material and spiritual benefits. What most laborers for Christ seemed to want—if not specifically stated—was for poor whites, Blacks, and immigrants to adopt behaviors, mindsets, and religious expressions that paralleled those held by white middle and elite classes. Some disapproved of Black forms of worship. Sudie Furman, who was long involved with the Mary Hanley Society of Bethel, a Baptist women's mission society located at Society Hill, South Carolina, habitually commented upon this reality in her correspondence with society members, friends, and family.[22] In 1890, Furman's aunt replied: "There is certainly no lack of enthusiasm among them. Many of them, have yet to learn, that religion is not a thing of mere emotion. There is a great deal yet to be done for those people, and in doing it, we must be governed by the law of Christian love."[23]

Similarly, mountain missionary Caryetta Davis alluded to excessive emotional expression as it related to poor whites in Appalachia. Although not explicitly acknowledged, Miss Davis, with familial ties to some elite and well-educated Virginia families, likely exuded cultural superiority over those whom she served.[24] This contrasted with her close colleague, Ora Harrison, who came from a family of more modest means.[25] Often, mountaineers, particularly Primitive Baptists, rejected Episcopal mission work, especially its ideas that emanated from an educated clergy and mission workers. According to Esther Maxey's *Miss Ora and Miss Etta,* in their minds "some were God's elect, some were not," and the haughty Episcopalians were simply "in defiance of God's will."[26] Such sentiments, as observed by female mission workers like Caryetta Davis, became less commonplace after those whom they served (and perhaps indoctrinated) gained literacy. As told by Maxey, "with the ability to read, the children grew to love the 'Book of Common Prayer,'" and "their parents were soon interested and learned to read with them."[27]

Despite the best of intentions of those such as Caryetta Davis, condescension and formal and informal enforcement of deference were elements in elite southern women's relationships toward Blacks and poor whites. This particularly applied to so-called society women who held administrative positions within their respective denominations' ladies' auxiliaries but who experienced limited day-to-day contact with nonelite southerners.[28] Some southern women may have been perturbed, for example, by deteriorating race relations at the end of the nineteenth century, and may have believed that Christianity could serve as a bridge between the two communities. During the last two decades of the nineteenth century, Black and white southerners watched state and local legislative bodies enforce de jure subordination, while local communities underpinned de facto subordination of Blacks. The former included a barrage of restrictions written into law, so-called Jim Crow laws, while the latter included informal, yet oppressive, codes of behavior or etiquette. At the turn of the twentieth century, Blacks faced disfranchisement, a repressive penal system, and an increase in extralegal violence, particularly lynching.[29] A combination of factors led to these declining race relations. They included a severe economic depression in the 1890s that engendered competition between poor whites and Blacks for jobs, housing, and public services; white fear surrounding the rise of a professional class of Blacks in southern cities like Atlanta and Charleston; the acceptability and perceived legitimacy of scientific racism especially as it applied to the United States' imperial aspirations; and an inactive, laissez-faire federal government that kept out of southern affairs.

Isa Beall Williams Neel, a widow in Cartersville, Georgia, and president of the state's Woman's Missionary Union between 1911 and 1932, wrote that "the leaven of Christianity is responsible for this new and effectively organized movement on behalf of better relations between the Negro and the white races of the South."[30] A highly accomplished woman, Neel was a graduate of Mary Sharp College in Winchester, Tennessee, organizer of the Floyd County, Georgia, Associational WMU, and, upon her retirement from the WMU presidency, a member of the faculty at Bessie Tift College. A well-known orator in Baptist circles, Neel was elected vice president of the Georgia Baptist Convention, the first woman to serve in that capacity.[31] Neel authored a pamphlet in the 1910s entitled "W.M.U. Interest in Inter-Racial Relations," which was dispersed to WMU societies (also known as associations) throughout the South in an effort to convince Southern Baptists, particularly women, that their efforts to uplift and mold thousands of Blacks were essential.[32] Referring to a platform adopted at a recent WMU Convention in Kansas City, Missouri, the WMU would "reach the oppressed and unsaved in our immediate localities," in an effort to secure "more sympathetic and equitable relations between the races."[33]

Neel and her contemporaries wanted to assume roles in which they could ameliorate conditions within their own communities, yet they often interacted with such individuals in condescending ways that reinforced Black and poor white dependence on elite society.[34] For them, there was a fine line between the introduction of some change or progress to disadvantaged communities and the imposition of modern or progressive values that challenged the racial and class hierarchy that continued to structure the postbellum South.[35] Women like Neel may have opposed convict leasing and felt disturbed by lynching, but they were perfectly comfortable with legal segregation. Despite the wording of the WMU pamphlet, in no way did such women desire "equitable relations between the races."[36]

The Southern Baptist Woman's Missionary Union (WMU) epitomized this dual reality of social uplift and deference. According to Isa Beall Williams Neel, "with the largest group of Negroes resident within Southern Baptist Convention territory, more than three million of whom are Baptists, the great responsibility is on Southern Baptists and the larger active interest in the inter-racial movement should be shared by them."[37] Female Southern Baptists could reach their respective Black populations through a three-fold program "of survey and service through the home, the school and the church." Some institutions through which WMU women in Georgia would impact race relations included a "state institution for delinquent Negro boys," a "school for delinquent Negro girls," and "daily vacation Bible schools for Negro children." At the time of the pamphlet's publication, all such institutions were in existence. In addition to these, Neel acknowledged that the WMU had recently established different programs, including summer schools, that would "properly train" white women as teachers and administrators of community centers.

While Neel outlined a number of ways the WMU could ameliorate relations between whites and Blacks, her pamphlet consistently reinforced Black subservience, pliability, and acceptance of white-directed religion. This publication was replete with such phrases as "Negro life is to be reached with immediate and beneficent influences," "to lift and mold the ideals and morals of the Negro race," "the Negro is easily influenced for good," and that the "Negro" was "grateful for sympathetic attention."[38] Such phrases exuded both condescension and expectation of deference while celebrating the efforts of WMU women. Specific to the latter, the pamphlet characterized the "personal service" provided by female mission workers as "Christ-like." The WMU pamphlet likewise implicitly reinforced disapproval of Black forms of worship. It was not an anomaly. Other women expressed more direct objection to Black religious practices. For example, in an article published in 1900 in the *Home Mission Monthly,* a Presbyterian magazine, Marie Gordon Pryor Rice wrote: "With the Negro, however, religion seems to be peculiarly dissociated from ethics; and therefore it is that he needs line upon line, precept upon precept, in the direction of ethical culture."[39]

White southern women's reasons for engaging in mission work to support African Americans and poor whites varied across a wide spectrum. Some elite and educated white women truly believed they could help eradicate poverty and suffering in some of the poorest communities. Perhaps a few sincerely felt guilty about their or their families' role in fighting a war to perpetuate slavery. Others simply wanted to exercise authority or influence in a public or professional setting, and mission work was a respectable and accepted arena in which they could exert some command. However, at least a minority of southern white women wished to use home mission societies and organizations as institutions through which they could continue to control their actual (and perceived) inferiors. Particular to mission work intended to benefit African Americans in the post-Reconstruction South, some white women viewed it—if only privately—as updated, repackaged versions of the religious instruction and guidance that many antebellum plantation mistresses had provided.

Isa Beall Williams Neel's pamphlet alludes to this latter assertion. Otherwise, it is unlikely she would have highlighted Blacks' malleability and vast numbers and have praised the establishment of institutions aimed at reforming "delinquent boys" and "delinquent girls." Just as many slaveholding women believed that enslaved people, who might outnumber the white members of a plantation by ten to one, were a population in need of control by their overseer, master, or mistress, many white southerners in the late nineteenth and early twentieth centuries (and beyond) saw Blacks as a threatening menace or, as asserted by Neel, an "acute problem."[40] Especially in communities located in the Black Belt, a region stretching across parts of South Carolina, Georgia, Alabama, and Mississippi and named for its dark, fertile soil well-suited for cotton cultivation, whites were often well in the minority. As a result, they found ways to keep Blacks poor and politically silenced, yet dependent on whites.

The most basic "service" provided to Blacks by home missionaries was literacy, which could give them the tools to advance in southern society. However, on the other extreme, one might identify similarities between home mission work and sharecropping and political restrictions such as grandfather clauses, poll taxes, and literacy tests in that the former could reinforce Black dependence and inferiority, all with a seemingly innocuous and maternal touch. In other words, mission work could distance itself from other forms of blatant control and exploitation by masquerading as Christian benevolence. Neel, and indirectly other members of the Woman's Missionary Union, suggested a discomfort with Blacks' proximity to whites, literally and figuratively. In particular, she proclaimed that "the Negro's nearness constitutes a first challenge." Neel did not say that Blacks' closeness presented a great opportunity for fellowship. Rather she added that "no barrier of distance ... separating us ... in the nursery, in the kitchen and the laundry, in the closest and most intimate relations of the home life is enough."[41] White-directed Christian guidance was thus one means to ameliorate uneasy feelings—if only those tinged with guilt—about racial nearness.

The Woman's Missionary Union reinforced racial and class hierarchy and deference through means other than pamphlets. For example, one WMU "Year Book" from 1914-15 featured a striking visual that upheld middle-class and elite women's agency and ability to shape society via a number of pathways.[42] The visual entitled "The Aim of Personal Service: By All Means Save Some" expressly conveys that southern women—through their "friendly visiting," "consecrated leadership," "Christian ministration," "open church building," "Christ-like living," and "helpful association"—will mold their neighbors of all ages, including those in prison, factories, hospitals, or on the playground. For some white southern women, "personal service" was perhaps interchangeable with social engineering.

†

Analysis of their thoughts and actions reinforces that southern women involved in faith-based organizations typically held moderate to conservative
political views. Most accepted women's place in the public sphere, especially
women's right to be publicly vocal on issues that were natural extensions
of women's domestic responsibilities. However, most wanted to preserve or
repackage the societal values of the Old South. Illustrative of this mindset,
and concurrent with their religious pursuits, these same evangelical women
helped found and perpetuate "heritage" organizations that celebrated elite
white southern culture. Writer and Christian community activist Virginian
Sara Agnes Rice Pryor, for example, served as a founder, administrator, and
fundraiser to Virginia Antiquities, Daughters of the American Revolution,
Mary Washington Memorial Association, and the National Society of the Colonial Dames of America.[43] The United Daughters of the Confederacy, in fact,
recommended Pryor's first memoir, *Reminiscences of Peace and War,* to its
members, specifically citing its admirable defense of the southern cause.[44]
Staunchly pro-southern before, during, and after the Civil War, Pryor was
nonetheless more pragmatic and open-minded than many of her contemporaries. For example, she characterized Lincoln as a virtuous man, as evidenced
by "his spirit of forgiveness and forbearance" toward the South and described
his assassination as "tragic." In contrast, Pryor despised Radical Reconstruction
and believed that the South suffered such "shame and sorrow" under it.[45] In
her memoir, she likewise recalled how she and her husband were chastised
by family and friends for leaving Virginia for a new life in New York City and
for accepting "that the salvation of the South could only be assured by acqui-
escence in the inevitable, and in the full exercise of justice to the negro."[46]
Despite the move, Pryor's southern identity was, and continued to be, a deep
source of pride.

Mary Ellen "Nellie" Peters Black of Atlanta was another southern woman
involved both in home mission work and heritage organizations like the Colonial Dames and the United Daughters of the Confederacy. She helped establish
Holy Innocents, Atlanta's first Episcopal mission. Later, Black served as secretary of the Atlanta Archdeaconry, which was set up upon the formation of the
Woman's Auxiliary to the all-male Board of Missions. At the age of thirty-five,
Black became a widow and became even more immersed in religious and civic
work. Best known for her work in the Atlanta Free Kindergarten Association,
Black believed that kindergartens would provide both a moral compass and

instill a sense of order and discipline into white and Black students from poor and working-class families. In Nellie Peters Black's opinion, kindergarten education would buttress the moral sensibilities to which poorer whites and Blacks had been exposed through female mission work. The City of Atlanta introduced kindergartens in 1919, much to the credit of Nellie Peters Black's lobbying efforts. A staunch supporter of public education, Black ardently campaigned for state compulsory education laws as well as the admittance of women to the University of Georgia. However, her influence was not as strong with members of the Georgia state legislature as it was with those in the Atlanta City Council. Black was largely silent on such polarizing and volatile issues as Jim Crow laws, lynching, and even women's suffrage. Both Pryor and Black embraced progressivism that reached beyond that of the more "typical" southern mission worker while they concurrently celebrated the Old South.[47]

These daughters of Dixie often assumed positions, within their heritage organizations, as recorders of their region's or church's history.[48] It should not be surprising that there was a correlation between well-to-do southern women's involvement in associations that celebrated their ancestry and region's history and participation in religious work and societies. Members of both types of organizations typically shared similarities with Sara Agnes Rice Pryor. They were privileged women who possessed the luxury of time and financial security. These women did not engage in paid labor outside the home—unless they desired to do so for their personal fulfillment, which was not commonplace during this era—nor were many of them expected to perform household chores. In fact, most likely benefited from the assistance of domestic servants. Both mission work and participation in heritage organizations offered elite, educated southern women "respectable" arenas in which to exert power and influence informally and honorably, while, at the same time, sustaining their class's fierce hold on the South.

While there was a strong correlation between home mission work and participation in heritage organizations, there was also a connection between southern women's activity in faith-based organizations and their interest in writing for politically and socially conservative audiences who read and promoted the growing collection of Lost Cause texts. These texts romanticized the Confederate cause and elevated the institution of slavery as a humanitarian endeavor. During the late nineteenth and early twentieth centuries, white women of the South boldly entered the world of publishing to an extent never seen before. Historian Sarah Gardner traces the evolution of such women's "distinctly southern story of the war" between the 1860s and the 1930s, in the progress arguing that they fought for a white supremacist, patriarchal, political order. She argues that such women participated with men in creating a discourse about the South that promoted, among many issues, the transformation of racism into philanthropy.[49] And it is in this regard that Gardner's analysis relates to the story of southern missionaries. Heritage organizations in which female missionaries assumed active roles took shape and/or gained popularity and cultural influence by the very late nineteenth century. The United Daughters of the Confederacy (UDC), in fact, was established in 1894.

Such societies, particularly the UDC, encouraged members to combat northern interpretations of the antebellum South and the Civil War by writing novels, biographies, histories, and memoirs that emphasized the benevolent nature of slavery. Presaging the arguments of historian U. B. Phillips, these women characterized plantations as institutions where slaveholders culturally and especially morally uplifted the enslaved.[50] These female authors, many of whom participated in mission work, sought to convince generations of southerners (and northerners) that the slaveholder-enslaved relationship was one based upon love and humanity, even philanthropy.

Oft-cited Letitia M. Burwell, Victoria V. Clayton, Nancy Bostwick DeSaussure, Elizabeth W. Allston Pringle, Sara Agnes Rice Pryor, and Susan Dabney Smedes were all involved in faith-based work after the Civil War and published at least one pro-Southern memoir.[51] Lesser-known Mary W. C. Early, described in her obituary as "a woman of a deeply religious nature" who "always contributed to [the church's] various needs," also promoted this myth of an altruistic, moralistic institution of slavery.[52] Early, a life-long resident of western Virginia, wrote numerous newspaper articles between the end of the Civil War and the early twentieth century. In one from 1892, "Old Virginia," Early referred to the benevolent nature of slavery and underscored the value of white women's religious guidance: "Not only were the temporal wants of the negroes well supplied, but the mistress of the plantation generally undertook their religious instruction also, and would gather them around her on Sunday afternoons, and read them plain, practical portions of the Holy Word, such as the ten commandments, the sermon on the mount, the parable of the ten virgins, the prodigal son, etc., and this would be followed by singing and prayer." While Early admitted that "it was very much like the old patriarchal life, and even if it had some elements of wrong," she resolutely believed that "Old Virginia" offered "some admirable features, as for instance the protective kindness and care that humane slaveholders showed toward their negroes, and the faithful and child-like attachment that the latter evinced to their owners."[53] In her ardent defense of "Old Virginia," Early upheld the notion that women, in their mission work with Blacks in the postbellum South, could emulate the patriarchal methods used by plantation mistresses to religiously instruct the enslaved and, in return, could expect deference.

The question thus arises why elite and educated southern women felt comfortable in, and accepted by, those who inhabited the generally conservative South between the end of Reconstruction and the end of World War I. Gendered analysis provides one explanation. These earnest and enterprising Protestant southern women, through opportunities in religious circles as well as heritage organizations and publishing, felt welcome to adopt more public, and ultimately more fulfilling, personas because they did not reject their femininity. And femininity, at least as southern society defined it, was a characteristic that white men strongly equated with dependence.[54] In other words, women who engaged in religious activities and careers posed far less of a threat to the long-standing gendered (and even racial) hierarchies of the South than did some suffragists and feminists in the North. Through their faith-based work, southern women directly and indirectly upheld the institution of marriage (i.e., shunned divorce), the antebellum South and the Confederacy, and a subordinated Black population.

Similarly, fathers and husbands generally approved of their daughters' or wives' involvement in mission work. However, some societies, notably the Woman's Missionary Union, required that top-level administrators have "the cooperation of [their] family." Particular to the WMU, it stipulated that "unless the husband and children also feel a sense of dedication and are willing to share the wife and mother with the Baptist women and youth of the state, she could never accept the challenge" of assuming the position of state WMU president.[55] More generally, men may not have rejected their wives' or daughters' participation because such women and their religious work were not directly contributing to southern men's delicate sense of masculinity, maimed most prominently by a Confederate defeat, in the postbellum years ... and beyond. Seemingly, what elite white men and women had mutually agreed upon was women's *independence* to promote sexual, class, and racial *dependence* upon the patriarchal remnants of the Old South in the New South.

White southern women did have the opportunity to forge religious organizations that were established, developed, and even governed by fellow women, yet many accepted the limits to their and their societies' independence.[56] On a basic level, southern women understood that the very existence of their religious organizations and home and foreign societies had been approved, funded, and dictated by men at their denominations' convention, general assembly, or synod.[57] Likewise, some women explicitly desired to use their religious organizations to reinforce their dependence upon men. The concept of female independence must have been a foreign and even uncomfortable concept for many women of the postbellum South. The WMU, for example, accepted its "natural" place as only an auxiliary to the all-male Southern Baptist Convention (SBC). In their words, they were "not independent" from the SBC and aimed to promote a "close and cordial" relationship, presumably one with significant male oversight.[58]

White women's participation in these burgeoning Protestant societies of the 1880s, 1890s, and beyond did not threaten man's position as head of household, head of the church, or head of southern society nor did it imperil the institution of marriage. Specific to the latter, as long as southern women were involved in faith-based activities and organizations, through which much work completed was done gratis, they were financially dependent on their denomination and/or spouse. Not only did southern women in mission work, including those occupying the highest administrative positions within their respective religious societies and organizations, indirectly uphold marriage via their financial dependence on men, but they also vocalized their disapproval of divorce and divorced women. Kentuckian Belle Bennett, an officer within the Methodist Woman's Board of Home Missions, wrote in 1908 that "no woman who is divorced from her husband, or who has been so unfortunate as to have had her name dragged in the mire of public scandal, should be elected to any office in a Conference or district, and certainly such a one ought not to occupy a place on this Board."[59] The Board's Organization's Committee on Sociology and Philanthropy agreed with Bennett, and, in 1914 voiced its support for "a strict interpretation of the disciplinary regulations against marrying divorced people."[60] Admittedly, this Methodist woman did not directly assign blame to the woman for the dissolution of her marriage, yet the message is clear that divorced women were undesirable and second-rate. Such a sentiment differed from that of many northern feminists like Elizabeth Cady Stanton, who supported divorce over a continued unhappy marriage that likely spawned suffering and immorality.[61] Southern female mission workers' negativity toward divorce suggests women did present highly gendered arguments in upholding their organizations' dependence on men.

✝

Most of these women appeared content to embrace their simultaneous roles as faith-based community workers and perpetuators of traditional southern values. Little evidence suggests that women resented their gendered limits. Nonetheless, a disproportionate number of leaders in faith-based organizations were single. It is plausible some believed that, as single women, their mission work would afford them greater professional and intellectual development than as mere wives with limited participation in church work.[62] Among the mass of southern women there were undoubtedly a few who did, if only privately, voice irritation or anger over the gendered expectations or status quo.

Marie Gordon "Gordy" Pryor, who married her cousin Henry Crenshaw Rice at age twenty-eight, conveyed some of these seemingly rare frustrations. Describing herself in 1893, at a time when she was deeply involved in mission work, Rice wrote: "I think I am more like George Eliot's "Mr. Casaubon" [in *Middlemarch*] than any other character in fiction, with ambitions and aspirations, but denied the power of fulfilment."[63] Despite these rumblings, Rice also understood that one would be unsuccessful, particularly in fundraising efforts through the churches and religious organizations where men's support was crucial, if one did not commit to "practical" goals and approaches, meaning the southern status quo. In other words, most southern women accepted, at least publicly, the gendered realities of the late nineteenth and early twentieth centuries and responded accordingly. Some influence and power were preferable to having no clout. Communicating with close friend Franklina Gray Bartlett regarding her suitability to speak on behalf of their religious organization, Rice wrote: "Tell Mr. Bartlett [Franklina's husband] to let me see every one of your published words. You are just the woman to be a public speaker, so gentle, so refined through and through, that the most conservative could find no fault." Gordy Rice, who regretted her limited opportunities for mission work in rural Virginia, concluded: "I want you to go on in the path for which you have such a fitness."[64] Further attesting to the value that southern society, including women, placed on "feminine leadership" is Miss Alma Hunt and, more specifically, her words about Martha McIntosh, first president of the South Carolina Woman's Missionary Union (Baptist), during the 1890s. In Hunt's memory, "the gentle, yet firm, spirit of Miss McIntosh guided the young missionary organization for four years with wisdom and harmony."[65]

While white southern women occupied a society in which dependence on males dominated, evidence also suggests that a few southern men, including clerics, were growing more comfortable with women who expanded their religious influence beyond the household. In fact, they were among those who helped redefine women's stature within southern churches and beyond during the Progressive era. Methodist minister J. William McCain of Baltimore wrote in 1891 to Gordy Rice that he not only accepted, but promoted, activist southern women and their Christian work. "A conservative naturally," McCain acknowledged that, in the past, he had held "very Southern ideas ... of women being shielded from the public view, ruling supremely at home and in the ball room" but who were "modestly silent in all forms of meetings." However, he admitted that he had "been converted, and [found] that women [could] speak in public without being immodest or anti-scriptural either." He convinced himself that scripture provided strong evidence for such views. McCain referred to one recently delivered sermon in which he upheld women's religious contributions: "I preached upon the text from Joel, which Peter quoted at Pentecost, by which he explains the strange conduct of the disciples in speaking with tongues. There as you will remember he says the Spirit will be poured out on the daughters as well as the sons, and upon the handmaids as well as the servants. Now says the apostle the prophecy is fulfilled, and how could it be fulfilled, if the women did not speak as well as the men?"[66]

Reverend McCain's confident words suggest that perhaps a few men sought to convince others that southern society—both on social and scriptural grounds—should be more accepting of women's work in the Social Gospel. Thus, some southern clerics opened their ears and minds to women's ideas regarding education, community outreach, and even scriptural analysis. The exclusively male clergy likewise played a significant role in shaping the conceptions, perceptions, and interpretations, religious and otherwise, of such women. In other words, notable southern clerics, especially more cosmopolitan ones like Reverend McCain, did transcend their conservative, gendered biases. However, this does not mean that a majority of such men followed McCain's line of thinking. Rather, many used the pulpit to reinforce gender and racial hierarchies. Citing the Apostle Paul, Southern Baptist Convention leader John Broadus opposed women who spoke before mixed public assemblies.[67] Mission societies throughout the South referred to their guest speaker clerics. Many such men lectured upon such topics as women's role in southern society or women's role in the church, or "woman's work for woman."[68] One may presume that these men, directly and indirectly, sought to indoctrinate women in ways which would underscore contemporary southern politics and gender hierarchies.

The period between the end of Reconstruction and the early twentieth century offered educated, elite white women of the South a wealth of opportunities to engage in religious work that was fully ensconced in the public sphere. Indeed, evangelical Protestant Christianity was not the *entirely* confining institution for middle-class and elite southern women that some scholars, most notably Jean Friedman, have painted it to be. Rather, involvement with home mission work presented women options to simultaneously embrace their individual ambitions alongside the politics of their race and class. While a few women voiced discontent with their society's conservative views regarding gender, most would have said that their involvement in faith-based organizations permitted them to have their cake and eat it too.

Six

RECRUITMENT

The religious environment of white southern women was markedly changing in the late nineteenth and early twentieth centuries. To an unprecedented degree, these women could express their religious faith in ways that took them into the public sphere, as foreign missionaries, members and leaders of religious organizations, and home missionaries, where they labored in educational, administrative, and social work pursuits. A veritable female-focused, Christian-based crusade was in progress, and its promoters accepted that the movement's continued success depended upon careful and consistent marketing campaigns. In particular, they understood that it was necessary to recruit increasing numbers of compatible southern women into their faith-based, reform-driven community. To do so, they needed to escalate their efforts in advertising and promotion.

This chapter complements and builds on the earlier discussion of the large-scale changes transpiring in the public religious landscape of white southern women between the late nineteenth and early twentieth centuries. More specifically, it examines white women (and to a minimal extent men) in the New South who contributed to the "selling" and "marketing" of mission work to other southern women between 1890 and 1930.[1] This forty-year span is not a randomly chosen period. Rather, it marked the time when religious organizations and mission work reached their peak in popularity and cultural influence. To interest more women in faith-based opportunities, recruiters exercised three broad methods, methods that structure this chapter. They helped organize and sustain mission training colleges, denomination-specific institutions of higher learning whose aims were to rigorously prepare white southern women for home and mission work. Others delivered speeches to churches or regional and statewide denominational meetings about opportunities in home and foreign missions. And finally, recruiters sought to entice potential female workers for Christ through their published and unpublished writings, some of which found their place in religious magazines and newspapers with large circulations. Through these three means, white southern women furthered their advancement within the public sphere and, in so doing, honed their analytical, composition, editing, oratorical, interpersonal, management, bookkeeping, nursing, accounting, and teaching skills. As a consequence of their marketing of faith-based work, they indirectly, and sometimes consciously, reinforced their conservative, patriarchal, and racist southern society.

While white women of the New South deserve credit for recruiting and promoting female participation in Protestant churches, organizations, orphanages, and schools, they always remained at the mercy of white men. At the local level, men controlled the politics and pocketbooks of their churches and denominations and could dictate the goals or agendas of any such female mission worker or organization. At the state or regional level, white men determined the parameters of acceptable female identity and mobility in the New South. While many southern men accepted and even advocated women's founding of, and participation in, religious auxiliary organizations, many other men fiercely rejected missionary women as public figures, particularly those who spoke in mixed public assemblies. Not until 1918, for example, did Southern Baptist women gain the right to vote at Southern Baptist Convention (SBC) meetings. Before then, they could neither attend the convention nor serve on the SBC's boards (Foreign Missions, Home Missions, Sunday school).[2] Nonetheless, between 1890 and 1930, these religious women often successfully maneuvered this generally conservative gendered environment and emerged as individuals primed to embrace even greater public roles that held more at stake—socially, economically, and politically—for them and southern society. Alternately phrased, these women's interface with religion in the public sphere occupied an intermediary position between an existence defined entirely by domesticity and dependence versus one characterized by career development and independence.

✝

As earlier chapters have shown, women in the antebellum and Civil War South were introduced to religious ideas, concepts, forms of worship, and opportunities through a number of modes. These included reprinted sermons in newspapers and other religious publications as well as personal contacts with family members, educators, and clerics, a majority of whom were men.[3] These so-called marketing techniques did not disappear in the post-Reconstruction South. In fact, southern women continued to absorb religious content through such means as religious publications, especially newspapers, magazines, journals, and pamphlets. These works, the majority of which had national as opposed to regional readerships, blossomed in the late nineteenth century. The relative paucity of southern-based publications, however, did not deter southern women from perusing them. Rather, they referred in their diaries and letters to their avid reading of *Heathen Woman's Friend,* the *Baptist Missionary Magazine,* the *Presbyterian Standard, Missionary Herald at Home and Abroad,* and many others.[4] *Heathen Woman's Friend,* to cite just one publication, boasted a readership of nearly 25,000 during the early twentieth century.[5]

By the turn of the twentieth century, some of these exclusively male-directed religious publications welcomed female authors. For example, the *Baptist Courier* permitted women to contribute articles beginning in 1898.[6] The Woman's Missionary Union (Baptist) began publishing *Our Mission Fields* in 1906 and *Royal Service* in 1914, ushering in a new wave of written expression conceptualized and developed by and for women. Nonetheless, according to historian Melody Maxwell, authors for such magazines "stressed female missionaries' unique roles in ministering to women on mission fields," through education, health care, and evangelism, while, at the same time, urging women "to expand through work that was acceptable to and generally endorsed by male SBC leaders."[7] Building onto these advancements, white southern women seized the opportunity to work as key figures, either augmenting or replacing men, in the selling and marketing of the opportunities available within their evangelical Protestant churches and religious societies, most significantly mission work.

Notably, this shift coincided with a growth in the number of college-educated southern women. The New South experienced the founding of all institutions included in the Seven Sisters of the South, all normal schools south of the Ohio River, and all southern mission training colleges. The original "Seven Sisters of the South" institutions, the southern counterpart to the Seven Sisters of the northeast (Barnard, Bryn Mawr, Mount Holyoke, Radcliffe, Smith, Vassar, and Wellesley), were Agnes Scott, Hollins, Mary Washington, Queen's, Randolph-Macon Woman's, Sophie Newcomb, and Sweet Briar. The first normal school to open south of the Ohio River was Florence Normal School (now the University of North Alabama). Originally founded as LaGrange College in 1830 (and then as Florence Wesleyan University in 1854), the then crippled Methodist institution was reestablished by the Alabama state legislature as Florence Normal School in 1872. Finally, the first female mission training college, the Mission Training College for Inner and Foreign Missions in Clinton, South Carolina, opened its doors in 1892.

Female leaders within the Baptist, Methodist, Presbyterian, and Episcopalian churches ardently encouraged educational pursuits for women at their respective denomination colleges. They appreciated that the younger women would one day assume leadership roles and that a college education would offer a strong foundation. For example, in her 1910 presidential address to the Georgia Woman's Missionary Union, Mrs. E. G. Willingham highlighted the great opportunity for the church in the "College Girl." Willingham implored her audience to ponder whether the WMU was "doing for her what [it] should." Recognizing that "mighty forces reside in the College Girl," Willingham made it clear that it was the responsibility of the WMU to nurture young women's intellectual penchants and to encourage their attendance at Baptist institutions of higher education. Should the WMU not reach these women, Willingham suggested, the organization would lose valuable talent to other religious outlets including the Young Women's Christian Association and Philathea, both interdenominational entities.[8]

MISSION TRAINING COLLEGES

Women's mission training colleges, affiliated with denominational institutions of higher learning, were an important starting point for those serious about opportunities in home and foreign mission work.[9] Many white women enrolled at southern mission training colleges had previously been accepted into foreign mission programs. The only three mission training colleges in the New South were the Mission Training College for Inner and Foreign Missions, the

Scarritt Bible Training School, and the Women's Missionary Union (WMU) Training School. Founded in 1882, the Mission Training College for Inner and Foreign Missions, a Presbyterian institution, was attached to Presbyterian College (1880) and Thornwell Orphanage (1875) and was located in Clinton, South Carolina. The Scarritt Bible Training College, later Scarritt College and the Scarritt Training School for Christian Workers, founded in 1892 in Nashville, Tennessee, was a Methodist institution that benefited from a partnership with the George Peabody College for Teachers. Finally, the Woman's Missionary Union (WMU) Training School, founded in 1901 in Louisville, Kentucky, was a Baptist institution attached to the Southern Theological Seminary. Technically, the Woman's Missionary Union Training School did not become its own entity until 1907. The Southern Theological Seminary first permitted women to take classes there in the 1901–2 academic year, but it was not until 1907 that the WMU Training School assumed its status as a coordinate of the seminary.[10] These three mission training colleges prepared women to enter into home and foreign mission work. However, just as many engaged in such pursuits as graduates of one of the many southern women's denominational colleges.[11]

These schools opened their doors, in part, because denominations realized that women sent into home and overseas mission work environments arrived unprepared, both practically and even theologically. According to Thelma Stevens, an alumna of Scarritt in the 1920s, the Woman's Home Missionary Society and the Woman's Foreign Missionary Society of the MEC, South, back in the early 1890s, "wanted a training school for the missionaries that they were going to send overseas and that they were going to use for the deaconesses … and [that] there was no place that they felt was adequate for that kind of training."[12] Likewise, Fannie Heck, the first president of the Woman's Missionary Union Training School in Louisville, stated that it "offers the advantages of the highest and most thorough Theological Training, coupled with all that fits a woman for the practical, everyday life of a trained worker in her own home church, a missionary to any part of our country or to some far heathen land."[13] The typical length of the mission training college programs was two years, although the Presbyterian institution permitted college graduates to complete the curriculum in one year.

These three schools prepared students for faith-based careers well-ensconced in the public sphere, yet they did not directly challenge the widely accepted view that women's primary place remained in the home. Women

Woman's Missionary Union Training School group photo, c. 1909.
Courtesy Archives, Special Collections, and Digital Initiatives, Jack Tarver Library, Mercer University.

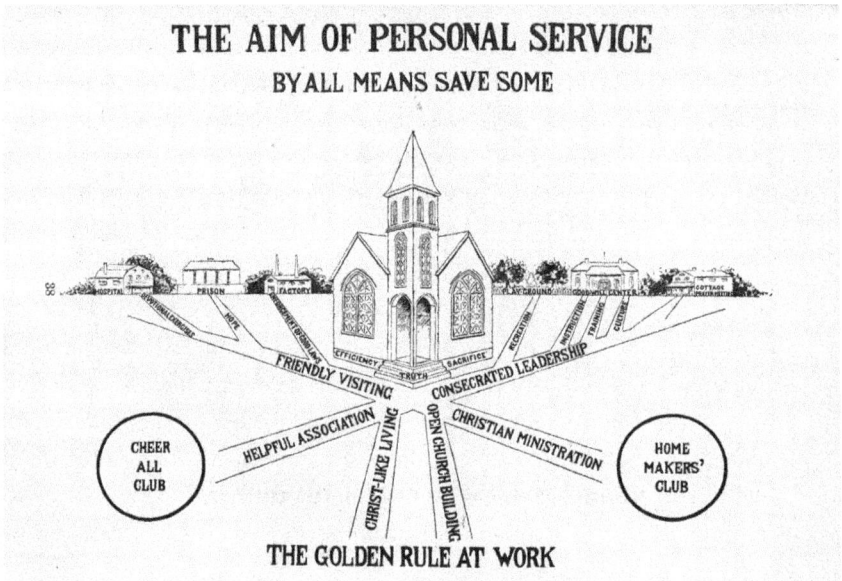

Page from Woman's Missionary Union yearbook, 1914–15.
Courtesy Archives, Special Collection, and Digital Initiatives, Jack Tarver Library, Mercer University.

realized that they could use their talents and skills from the domestic sphere and simply apply them toward the improvement of American society and international cultures. In their eyes, they should meld their femininity and evangelical values to address problems created by a modernizing and industrializing world. In historian Barbara Miller Solomon's words, "educated women may not have been consciously trying to redefine womanhood; yet all along their actions did extend its definitions."[14] Students at such schools occupied an environment where they could, if only subtly, challenge definitions of womanhood.

The denominational leadership had no intention of equalizing opportunities between the sexes by the opening of these colleges. According to religious historian Glenn Miller, the WMU Training School faced significant opposition from the Southern Baptist Convention. For years its president, Fannie Heck, struggled to recruit a man who would agree to read its official reports to the SBC. During the 1900s and 1910s, the convention forbade any woman from addressing the all-male organization.[15] Perhaps this slight was a blessing in disguise. If the SBC seemingly cared so little about the women's institution, it translated into less direct oversight of the school's curriculum and guidelines. Nonetheless, at the forefront of the Louisville institution, and likely its Methodist and Presbyterian counterparts, was an emphasis on reinforcing southern women's generally conservative identities as evangelical Christians and southerners.

While men were slow to acknowledge the value of the education offered by the WMU Training School, female leaders within the WMU were ardent supporters both of the institution and of prospective students. To entice appropriate young women, the WMU offered various scholarships for those in attendance. For example, the WMU of Georgia offered three such scholarships beginning in the early 1910s. Mrs. H. A. Etheridge of Atlanta voiced at the annual Georgia WMU meeting that members could "not rest upon [their] laurels" until the organization had recruited more young women from Georgia to the WMU Training School. Etheridge likewise prodded members to establish relationships with young women in which they could convey "the necessary words of encouragement" and to contribute liberally to the three scholarship funds.[16]

A gender and class hierarchy undergirded the mission training colleges, WMU Training School in particular. Men assumed responsibility for virtually all legal and financial matters. Elite southern women, many of whom had ties to the leading families of their respective denominations, took care of most day-to-day administrative issues. Meanwhile, white women of more humble backgrounds served as teachers. A large number of female administrators and teachers were single. The WMU, which oversaw the Woman's Missionary Union Training School in Louisville, consciously placed in administrative positions educated and respectable women leaders like Heck who "were models of ideal Southern Baptist womanhood for the rest of the denomination."[17] Women who were "earnest," "highly cultivated," "sympathetic," "fertile in resources," and "with a warm heart" were just those kinds of administrators whom the WMU Training School aimed to attract.

On a broader level, these female administrators viewed mission training schools as a means to keep nonelite southerners subordinate to, and, at best, supportive of, the elite's interests, while they also aimed to bring culture and higher-level education to those whom they instructed. The hierarchy at the WMU Training School mirrored that of the denomination at large: founders and/or administrators were members of the economic elite, while the majority of students were Baptists of more modest means. The WMU Training School acknowledged five founders: Eliza Broadus, Fannie Heck, Anna Eager, Emma Woody, and Maude McClure. Born between 1851 and 1863, each woman had grown up in an affluent southern family, was a recipient of an academy and/or college education, and defined herself by her Baptist faith. Collectively, these school founders had previously held administrative positions in such national and local Baptist organizations as the WMU and the Southern Baptist Women of Louisville.[18] The WMU Training School, however, may have minimized these class disparities between leadership and students, both real and perceived. Students who completed their studies at the WMU Training School gained not only an education but social capital. In support of this, several alumnae in this category ultimately held leadership positions in their respective state WMU organizations.[19]

The Mission Training College for Inner and Foreign Missions in Clinton, South Carolina, graduated its first class in 1894. It presents an appropriate institution through which to examine how men and women enticed other southern women—for example, through printed institutional annual announcements—to consider careers in home and foreign mission work. This

Presbyterian school offered its pupils attractive conditions and accommodations. The "course of study," which included "special Biblical and medical instruction," was "wholly gratuitous." Instead of tuition, students offset any expenses through their gratis mission work at the school and out in the community at such locales as orphanages and schools.[20] The same basic conditions, at least as they appertained to tuition and supplies, applied to students at Scarritt.[21] Another bonus was students' ready access to classes at Presbyterian College as well as professional classes at the Thornwell College for Orphans. Classes at these two institutions, both in Clinton, were free of charge except for an annual matriculation fee of five dollars.[22] The Mission Training College sought to provide a high-quality, affordable, Christian-based, practical, yet intellectually stimulating, education to white southern women who desired a missionary career or at least several years' experience in professional work, leading to employment as teachers, secretaries, bookkeepers, stenographers, and librarians. It is thus not surprising that it and other mission training schools attracted young southern women of moderate means from devout households.[23]

The Mission Training College's annual college "announcements," akin to today's college brochures, marketed this institution in enticing ways.[24] The first page of the booklet highlighted successful and diverse outcomes of its alumnae. Graduates held positions as teachers, principals, administrators for religious organizations, and foreign missionaries. In so advertising, administrators underscored the idea that the Clinton, South Carolina institution, was not an inessential "finishing school," but a place at which one prepared for distinction, at least by the standards of the turn-of-the-century South. After all, the success of home and foreign mission work was contingent upon the healthy recruitment of well-prepared female workers. At the same time, administrators, as did former, current, and future female mission workers through their speeches and published writings, emphasized that the educational experience at mission training colleges would be intellectually, physically, and professionally rigorous.

Admission standards included "a good common school education," a satisfactory grade on entrance examinations in arithmetic, geography, grammar, and "kindred studies," membership in the Presbyterian Church, as well as a recommendation from the applicant's "Pastor and Session" which attested to her "piety, intelligence and fitness for the work."[25] While the Mission Training College conveyed class inclusiveness, by virtue of its affordability, it also sought to exclude those who lacked "respectability" and a long-standing relationship with the Presbyterian Church.[26]

Specific to students' academic credentials, it is likely that many of those who matriculated at Mission Training College possessed far more than "a good common school education." According to T. Laine Scales, a scholar who studies the intersection of gender and religion, in a foreign missions sample of 106 former Woman's Missionary Union Training School students, only nine women had not attended some type of institution of higher education. These nonmissionary institutions of higher education would have been either non-Baptist affiliated schools, either state-supported or private, or colleges affiliated with the Southern Baptist Convention.[27]

According to Mission Training College's promotional literature, enrolled students entered a challenging and theologically stimulating two-year curriculum. Pupils took a "Biblical course," the same course given at Presbyterian College; a "pastoral course," which incorporated classes and readings on the "exegetical study" of the Old and New Testaments, history of missions, "City Missions, Infirmary, Sunday-School and Orphanage work"; a "hygienic course," which included instruction in physiology, anatomy, chemistry, therapeutics, and nursing; a "course of reading in Medical Literature," as well as instruction in English, Latin, Greek, French, German, and mathematics.[28] Similarly, Scarritt Bible Training College assembled a three-year course that included classes in Old and New Testament, Sunday school pedagogy, personal work, domestic science, music and public speaking, systematic theology, church history, comparative religion, missions, and ecclesiology.[29]

The required biblical course, previously open only to men at Presbyterian College, recognized southern women's intellectual capacity to engage in theological study. It signified the continuing breakdown in the belief of the clergy as a purely masculine profession, let alone pursuit. Similarly, female students at Woman's Missionary Union Training School were permitted to take electives at the Southern Baptist Theological Seminary. As historian Charity R. Carney argues, in the decades leading up to the Civil War southern evangelical clerics had "developed their own version of masculinity and formed new standards for relationships based on melding together southern norms and doc-

trinal standards."[30] This conservative conception of masculinity defined southern clerics long after the Civil War, yet southern female mission workers subtly identified viable paths to navigate around it. This reality of religious courses
that were identical in content for men enrolled at Presbyterian College versus
women enrolled at Mission Training College—in addition to the opportunities
in pre-med type coursework—may have been a major selling point for these
female religious institutions, and it certainly set them apart from the higher
education offered at the burgeoning normal schools.

Beyond these academic requirements, Mission Training College prescribed
that its students work a certain number of hours per week at neighboring
Thornwell Orphanage. There, they labored as nurses, teachers, religious mentors, and Sunday School instructors.[31] Other students devoted time to "pastoral
visiting in the town." Not only did the women offset expenses for which the
school took responsibility, but they gained valuable experience and confidence
in environments that were more public, more independent, and perhaps even
more reform-minded.[32] Similar requirements existed at other mission training schools. For example, at the Woman's Missionary Union Training School,
students completed "field work" in churches, missions, and social work agencies in Louisville. Later, by the 1910s, the institution had established its own
settlement house.[33]

College administrators sought to lure southern women by highlighting
wide-ranging successes of their alumnae, nearly all of which fell in the public
sphere. According to the 1902–1903 MTC college announcement, they served
as matrons of orphanages; teachers at mission schools; school principals;
public school teachers in North Carolina, South Carolina, and West Virginia;
stenographers; administrators of hospitals, orphanages, and seminaries as well
as in the headquarters of the Y.W.C.A.; a home missionary in Waco, Texas;
and foreign missionaries in Soochow, China; Sochi, Japan; and Lavras Minas,
Brazil.[34]

Institutions like the Mission Training College offered southern women
great opportunities to embark on a path far different than the insular and
domestic options to which they were accustomed. That said, promotional literature still exuded the values of middle-class respectability and paternalism.
Students likely felt that their parental-like administrators and instructors—of
both sexes—were always keeping a watchful eye on them. For example, MTC

staff stressed to prospective and current students that they were "not permitted to receive gentleman visitors except on one evening each week" and "were not permitted to spend the night outside their own cottage, except in dutiful attendance upon the sick."[35] Even the president of MTC, Reverend William P. Jacobs, D.D., made it a priority to meet with the pupils three times per week so he might instill paternalistic values through lecture and tested their comprehension and acceptance of the material through graded recitations.

These three southern mission training colleges subtly challenged the traditional place of southern women in religious life. Not only did such schools supply the Protestant denominations with women workers but they also established the standards with regard to culture and values for evangelical women serving worldwide. Alumnae and female supporters of these institutions promoted the religious education and training that women received at denominational mission training colleges. In particular, such women wrote letters to influential leaders within their respective denominations, and they delivered speeches to groups of women (and some men) at numerous venues, in attempts not only to recognize female talent and potential but to broaden conceptions of southern femininity. Specific to the latter, alumnae and female supporters of mission training colleges hoped that these expanded conceptions would be more universally accepted by southern society at large.

Mission training colleges operated, at least in their own original purposes, for some thirty to sixty years. Upon its move from Kansas City to Nashville, Tennessee, Scarritt began accepting males into its missionary classes during the 1920s.[36] Alumna Thelma Stevens recalled that during her time there in the 1920s, "there were Vanderbilt students who took classes there, but no full time men in those early days." Although Scarritt evolved from its exclusively female roots in the 1920s, Stevens stressed that the "Women's Division" of the "National division" of the Methodist Church continued to play a strong role for many decades: "But Scarritt was a child of the women."[37] The WMU Training School at Louisville remained an exclusively women's institution for nearly a generation longer than did Scarritt. Not until 1945 did the school begin admitting men and subsequently it renamed itself the Carver School of Missions.[38] And finally, the Mission Training College for Inner and Foreign Missions in Clinton, South Carolina, suffered a slow demise. Nearby Thornwell Orphanage absorbed the physical remnants of MTC throughout the 1910s and 1920s. MTC, as a separate entity, closed sometime after 1925.[39]

SPEECHES

Oratorical marketing of evangelical Protestant faiths marked a second public outlet for white southern women during the late nineteenth- and early twentieth-century South. Typically, these women delivered speeches to churches and regional and statewide denominational meetings, as well as to local communities. As did those who promoted southern mission training schools, women lecturers highlighted the benefits of mission work for the woman who provided the Christian-based services as well as for those whom she assisted, educated, or mentored. However, they also stressed the obstacles, loneliness, and criticism that those who entered the field habitually faced. While the marketing atmosphere of mission work was socioeconomically inclusive, promoters of Christian service only sought women who would represent their churches dutifully, yet zealously, at home and abroad. Overtly, missionaries wanted to recruit ambitious, competent, organized, and industrious workers, but covertly they sought women who would exude the values of a conservative, patriarchal South. In other words, such women did not want to jeopardize their growing faith-based opportunities in the public sphere or their increasing acceptance among southern men by behaving in ways that forcefully challenged, or contradicted conceptions of, traditional gender roles. Much was at stake for these pioneering mission women in the turn-of-the-century South: not only funding of their auxiliary religious organizations but also professional respect and expanded opportunities in higher education, in the emerging workplace, and in their communities.

Beginning in the late nineteenth century, white female mission workers embraced opportunities to make their voices heard—literally—by women across the South about the bountiful opportunities for them in faith-based work. Such missionary women were aware of southern male clerics' sermons that reinforced the position of the more "moral" or "fairer" sex and their natural inclination for religious work. Perhaps their own, or visiting, ministers had delivered sermons to that effect or perhaps they had read published sermons and texts by influential clerics at their mission training institutions.

Southern clerics helped establish related beliefs much earlier. Presbyterian minister Thomas Verner Moore published a well-circulated address in 1852 entitled, "Adaptation of Religion to Female Character: A Discourse to Young Ladies," and in 1860 Episcopalian Reverend Philip Slaughter published *Man and Woman; or, The Law of Honor Applied to the Solution of the Problem, Why Are So Many More Women Than Men Christians?* Both offer examples of what educated southern women—both Moore and Slaughter were Virginians—may have read and/or accepted regarding the relationship between gendered expectations and religion on the eve of the Civil War and beyond.[40] While both were patriarchal in tone, each encouraged white women to embrace roles in which they could carry their Protestant faiths to those beyond the domestic sphere. Moore and Slaughter thus afforded women a degree of moral authority and agency at the same time that such southern women grappled with scripture that reinforced restrictive and subordinate roles for women. For example, they read Genesis 3:16: "Unto the woman he said, I will greatly multiply the sorrow and thy conception; in sorrow thou shalt bring forth children; and thy desire shall be to thy husband, and he shall rule over thee." Other southern women took to heart 1 Timothy 2:12: "But I suffer not a woman to teach, nor to usurp authority over the man, but to be in silence." Southern women felt more reassured in their roles as public evangelizers when they received strong support from male clerics.

It was only during the last two decades of the nineteenth century that southern clerics beyond those very few like Moore and Slaughter began encouraging white women of the middle and elite classes to apply their unique gendered attributes in domestic *and* societal environments.[41] Changing opinions among denominational leadership would be a slow process. Corroborating this reluctance among ministers to promote women's mission work was Margaret Moore Douglas, a Presbyterian who served in Brazil as a single woman for thirty-five years. At various churches throughout North and South Carolina, Douglas informed prospective missionaries that she had "never heard a missionary sermon [that addressed female mission work] till I was twenty one years of age [in 1895], that was preached by Dr. Alexander Sprunt."[42] Until female mission workers could convince more clerics to overtly promote women's contributions in religious work, southern women accepted that they were going to have to be their own mouthpieces.

Publicizing mission work by (and for) such women affords an appropriate example for extended analysis. Through extant speeches, one sees how white southern women cast mission work: for the dedicated, well-trained, and ambitious few. This contrasts with the evangelical Protestant message of spiritual equality disseminated since the Second Great Awakening. As Christine

Leigh Heyrman and others have maintained, southern evangelicalism offered "a stark alternative" to the region's traditional culture, which had centered around competition during the eighteenth century.[43] Yet those women who recruited mission workers at the turn of the twentieth century reintroduced an emphasis on competition by marketing faith-based opportunities for a very select subpopulation of southern women.

Missionary administrator Emma Lenore Amos delivered a speech to the Women's Baptist Missionary Society in Athens, Georgia, during the first decade of the twentieth century on the merits and challenges of mission work and its leadership. The speech's title was "Difficulties of Leadership and Its Compensations." Amos, born in 1857 in Dalton, Georgia, to a middle-class family, never married and spent much of her adult life in faith-based pursuits. She died in 1914 in Forsyth, Georgia. Amos attended, and presumably graduated from, the Monroe Female College (also in Forsyth) in 1875, a Baptist-affiliated institution.[44] Founded in 1849 as the Forsyth Female College Institute, the school was renamed the Monroe Female College in 1857 and then later renamed Bessie Tift College in 1907 after an alumna. In 1900, Amos organized a chapter of the Woman's Missionary Society at the Forsyth Baptist Church. Shortly thereafter, she emerged as a leader not only in her home church but among the Baptist Woman's Missionary Union of Georgia, an auxiliary to the Georgia Baptist Convention. Amos particularly relished her role as mentor to young Baptist women in part because she had not benefited from the same kind of guidance in her youth. In fulfilling such a role, she promoted educational training opportunities as well as leadership development for younger Baptist women. To achieve this, Amos organized the Young Woman's Auxiliary in 1906 at her church in Forsyth. Concurrent with this, Amos served as librarian at her alma mater, where she also edited the "College Monthly." At the end of her life, Amos held the title of Secretary for the Georgia Conference of the Woman's Missionary Union, whose office was in Atlanta. She identified herself "as the pioneer of the [Baptist] Woman's Mission Work of the Central Association."[45]

Amos was assigned by her superintendent to give this presentation on the challenges and benefits of missionary work to Baptist churches and female audiences, especially local WMU organizations, throughout Georgia and South Carolina. The Woman's Missionary Union was particularly focused in its efforts to send out women, particularly those in leadership positions, to speak to other Baptist women. Such women were not welcome to speak at the all-male Southern Baptist Convention, and thus they did not rely on church leaders to spread their recruitment message. Rather, Baptist women felt compelled to share their message on their own. This particular speech was not one in which Amos directly, or even indirectly, campaigned for financial contributions to miscellaneous Baptist missionary funds and societies. Rather, she simply desired to spur white southern women, independently of any male cleric, into action.

Amos refused to trivialize mission work or condescend to her largely female audiences. Referring to the words of nineteenth-century Anglican (and later Catholic) theologian William Frederick Faber, Amos described service opportunities within the religious sphere as acts of humility and compassion: "There is no line of glory emblazoned on the earth's surface, but a line of suffering runs paralleled with it, and he who reads the glowing letters of the one, without stooping to decipher the blurred characters of the other, gets the least half of the story earth has to give." In her own words, she characterized mission work as more fulfilling than other pursuits in "scientific, literary or commercial" fields. This latter comment suggests that Amos did not necessarily disapprove of women's participation in more public, intellectual, or professional areas. Rather, for her, there was nothing that could surpass the sense of sacrifice and satisfaction one received from "Christian service."[46]

Amos praised white southern women for their passion for home and foreign mission work, particularly recognizing the efforts of individual female missionary pioneers who "*always* meet with obstacles in opening a way for others to follow." However, she wanted southern women to internalize that a religious organization's overall strength was tied to the efficacy of its leadership. Citing scripture, Amos acknowledged particular weakness in the leadership of southern women's religious societies and organizations: "So in the gradual development of mission zeal and enthusiasm among our women, Leaders have been necessary and organizations imperative to insure success. The reason that Leaders are so essential is easily found in the sad lament of one of the prophets of old speaking as Jehovah's mouthpiece: 'Israel doth not know, my people doth not consider.'" Amos maintained that passion, or being "alive with interest," was only one important ingredient for success in mission work and that those who were considering such careers needed to focus on developing tangible skills that would foster the mission's effectiveness. Not only were female mission workers to be well-trained and credentialed, but they should possess "full information as to conditions in distant lands and the needs of our people."[47]

Amos carefully outlined necessary prerequisites for service. They included ownership of theological, academic, and administrative expertise, a substantial knowledge and understanding of the physical, economic, political, and cultural attributes of the country to which a missionary served, as well as the physical and psychological strength to persevere during discouraging times. Building upon this latter characteristic, she identified a number of challenges that women missionaries needed to overcome. One obstacle was indifference or resistance exhibited by male clerics. Amos cited times when she and her colleagues had encountered pastors who had entirely "opposed Woman's Work" in the religious sphere and who had "refuse[d] the [missionary] organizations in their churches." Pastors ignored their letters written from distant fields asking for "the names of some prominent women in their churches" to whom "mission literature might be sent for distribution." Amos likewise cited pastors who had "criticized unkindly, misunderstood, misrepresented and falsly accused" mission workers of negligence, lack of progress, and failure to abide by church policy.[48]

Men, however, were not always to blame for female missionary setbacks in Amos's eyes. Rather, she recognized that women needed to take more initiative and be more assertive as mission workers. For Amos, just because women missionaries were transferring their domestic talents and skills to the public sphere did not mean that they should adopt a meek, subordinate, or complacent demeanor. She singled out southern women who "decline[d] to either lead a devotional service or prepare a paper" at annual conference meetings as well as women who lacked courtesy and initiative, having "fail[ed] to present at meeting without notifying [a] Leader so someone else could serve instead."[49]

Other identified problems stemmed from women's laziness, incompetence, or petty, internal disagreements.[50] Amos chastised southern female mission administrators who prepared "financial reports so confused that nothing intelligible [could] be made of the figures."[51] But perhaps above all, Amos could not stand "to see women complacently satisfied with their religious attainments, so completely at ease in Zion" that they saw "no necessity for Christian activity or spiritual development in themselves." Displaying her talent for imagery and knowledge of the Old Testament, Emma Amos wove scripture into her admonition to mission workers. "At ease in Zion" comes from Amos 6:1.[52] In that passage, Amos, a Hebrew prophet, berates the leaders of Israel and Judah against their false confidence of security, and he implores them to learn from what happened to three nearby city-states—Calneh, Hamath the great, and Gath.

Emma Amos certainly did not sell mission work through encouragement or saccharine rhetoric, but rather she characterized careers in the religious sphere as a great challenge in which every step "wound through a trackless forest" and in which each advance was "a venture uncertain and beset with thorns of disappointment and of pain." Finally, in an attempt not to place herself above those other southern women (or male clerics) in mission work, Amos acknowledged her own flaws in leadership. On one occasion, she admitted, "Probably if I had realized my responsibility as a Leader more fully the success of our Union [the Woman's Missionary Union] had far exceeded its present achievement." In other instances, Amos referred to "her own feeble efforts" and used such adjectives as "weak" and "difficult[ies]" when describing her deficiencies in Christian service. Amos had little patience for female mission workers who lacked humility, who could not stand correction, and who shunned continual spiritual and professional growth.[53]

Emma Amos's message likely deterred many southern women from entering mission work and faith-based careers. Apparent throughout her lecture was her strong belief that women who were not wholly committed to a heavy workload, who could not overcome setbacks, or who were unwilling to make personal sacrifices for God were not welcome in the field, especially as leaders. That said, although Amos's rhetoric was stern and resolute—perhaps reminiscent of the self-conscious Victorian career woman who was trying to earn professional respect—she could also sell Christian service in gentler and less off-putting ways. For example, although Amos chastised white southern women for their ineptitude in leadership and administrative positions, she habitually gave her audiences reason to think that improvement in that category was possible. Similarly, she tried to convince prospective mission workers that disappointment was a simple reality of mission work but that the benefits of service to God always outweighed the setbacks. In Amos's words, "the joys the Leader find amid the struggle and stress and pain fully compensate for all the sacrifice, the toils, the anxious cares and bitter disappointments she meets along the arduous way." Ultimately, this veteran missionary's message was clear. For the ambitious, educated, and earnest woman, mission work proved fulfilling. In fact, Amos considered her career in the religious sphere "to be the best of my life," one that she would not have traded for "any earthly fame or achievement."[54] Although one cannot determine the effect Amos's speech had on her audiences, one may presume that—collectively—she and other officers within the Woman's Missionary Union who delivered speeches reached many thousands of Baptist women through their ambitious efforts at promoting faith-based opportunities.

Presbyterian foreign missionary Margaret Moore Douglas and her speech on her career as an instructor at Erskine Evangelical College in Pernambuco, Brazil, affords another opportunity to explore the ways by which southern women sold mission work to others.[55] Douglas led a devout and successful life before the Executive Committee of Foreign Missions of the Presbyterian Church in the United States (Southern) appointed her as a missionary in 1905. She was the daughter of a notable Presbyterian minister and educator, John Douglas, who had served as president of Yorkville Female College in York, South Carolina. Upon Margaret's birth in 1875, the Douglases moved to White Oak, South Carolina, where they occupied a modest cotton farm and John served as the minister of Mount Olivet Presbyterian Church. Margaret Moore Douglas graduated from Winthrop College in 1898 and then enrolled in graduate courses in mathematics at the University of Chicago. Upon completion of her studies, she returned to upstate South Carolina, where she taught mathematics at Ebenezer Academy and Winthrop College. Douglas, like so many of her counterparts in mission work, never married.[56]

In a manner similar to that of Emma Amos, Douglas—who delivered her lecture to audiences at Presbyterian churches throughout North and South Carolina in 1925 when she was home on furlough—characterized missionary careers as for the select few. In contrast to Amos's speech to all-female audiences, one may assume, Douglas delivered hers to mixed-sex groups, probably campaigning for financial support of Presbyterian foreign missions. As a result of this reality, Douglas tended to be laudatory, consistently highlighting successes over setbacks. Her address, which was more descriptive of mission work and definitely less impassioned than Amos's, nonetheless complements the latter's contention that missionary organizations were not seeking ordinary women. That said, and agreeing with Emma Amos, Douglas implied that opportunities abounded, especially for single women, who were willing to make a professional and religious commitment. She embodied these lofty aspirations, serving in a myriad of roles. These included teacher of Latin, of mathematics, of English, of physical education, of the Bible, and of drawing; administrator; curriculum planner; financial officer; and supervisor of student teachers at the Brazilian girls' boarding institution, the Colegio Americano de Pernambuco (later Colegio Evangelico Agnes Erskine or Erskine Evangelical College) from 1905 until her death in 1940.[57]

After some brief pleasantries and cursory introduction of life in Pernambuco, Brazil, Douglas described the challenges that missionary women—including herself—faced on a daily basis. She asserted that "the missionaries who live in [the Brazilian cities] have to accommodate themselves to a great many inconveniences."[58] She proclaimed that missionaries had to assume many duties that transcended their official ones. For example, Douglas acknowledged that there was little separation in responsibilities between instructional and janitorial staff, adding that although she was an administrator at Erskine Evangelical College, she was also its "housekeeper." Other quotidian responsibilities included maintaining the school grounds, nursing sick boarding students, and shopping for food and supplies for two hundred pupils. In mentioning these duties, it is conceivable, Douglas may have been implying that elite southern women, those who had been accustomed to household servants, ought not to enter into the mission field.

Douglas focused her speech on religious obstacles that missionaries in Brazil would face but could overcome with the grace of God. For her, the religious barrier was Roman Catholicism and its "immoral influence" on natives. Citing the "immorality of the priests" and "the lack of the Bible" in Catholic education as well as mocking the excessive "idolatry" and "imagery" in cathedrals, this decidedly Calvinist mission worker revealed her prejudices. Just as Protestant evangelicals had conveyed for several generations, Douglas felt comfortable deriding Roman Catholics for their emphasis on ceremonialism as superficial theater while she condemned their elaborate rituals, holy day observances, and rigid hierarchy. However, she also injected enthusiasm in emphasizing the crucial role that "devout" and "pure" Protestant mission workers could play in response to Roman Catholicism's leverage. In her words, "a great responsibility rests on us to give them just now in the time of their awakening the true gospel as it is taught in God's word."[59] In Douglas's opinion, a "true gospel" was one devoid of Roman Catholic influences.

Margaret Douglas's niece described her aunt as "a person of intense, not to say fierce, quietness," and thus it is possible that the speech exhibited a more restrained tone than one delivered by an extrovert. Likewise, it is possible that, as a female speaking to mixed-sex audiences in churches in the Carolinas, she felt uncomfortable giving high-stakes lectures. In such settings, Douglas was not only selling faith-based opportunities to devout local women but to the more influential churchmen who determined the expansion—or contraction—of particular mission projects. One, however, cannot deny that Douglas committed herself to a life of sacrifice and service and that she cared about her career to the extent that she vigorously campaigned for others to follow in her steps. Women in religious organizations across the South heeded Douglas's example and became more publicly vocal about mission work. Others delivered frequent lectures on such topics as "Finance in Missions," "Our State's Part in the Campaign for Denominational Education," and "The Call to China for Me" in an effort to generate interest and financial contributions.[60] In instances when women's religious organizations could not recruit well-known or accomplished female speakers like Douglas to lecture on opportunities in home and foreign mission work, some appear to have appointed their own members to identify and deliver appropriate readings or lead open discussions at future meetings. For example, according to a minute book from the Ladies Benevolent and Missionary Society of the Presbyterian Church of Athens, Georgia, "the president appointed the seven directresses to select some suitable paper on missions to be read at the next monthly meeting (which will occur the first Wednesday in July) and someone to read the paper designated."[61]

PUBLISHED WRITINGS

Finally, published writings—including previously delivered speeches, articles, histories, and biographies of prominent church and mission leadership—written by white missionary women in the New South offer an opportunity to more closely examine some of the ways by which such women promoted their professional lives and Christian service to like women. Some such materials were authored by one woman, while others appeared under an organization's name, such as the Woman's Missionary Union. Through their published documents, histories, and lectures—materials which would, in theory, reach a variety of readers—white southern women reinforced the acceptability of southern women assuming jobs, volunteer work, or even careers ensconced in the public sphere.

Perhaps the most basic writing endeavors were those in which they chronicled the histories and traditions of their churches, religious academies, or prominent denominational leaders. The publication or completion dates for such materials fell close in time to those of the turn-of-the-century biographies, memoirs, and histories produced by women in heritage organizations like the United Daughters of the Confederacy that sought to place the Old South, slavery, and the Civil War in a positive light. Similarly, female-authored sources on churches, religious academies, and denominational leadership employ self-celebratory rhetoric. Although small in scope, these sources were another means by which white southern women controlled the master narrative of the South. For example, one distinguished Georgia family, the Northens, spawned several women who authored biographies and institutional histories on such topics as the Mt. Zion Academy, a Presbyterian institution in Hancock County.[62] These histories generated pride and greater interest in the work of particular churches and/or denominations and thus might have gotten the attention of prospective benefactors. Although not specifically acknowledged, southern women composed these publications for reasons largely related to marketing and promotion of mission work.

Beyond histories, southern women prepared localized publications for their religious auxiliaries in which they balanced information unique to their organization with material related to women's mission work more broadly. One group, the Ladies of the First Presbyterian Church of Augusta, Georgia, for example, assembled a regular publication—*Missionary Circles*—for its members and other interested parties. According to women who produced it, *Missionary Circles* "contains helpful suggestions how to conduct meetings, the Missionary Creed and twelve programs—one for each month. Each program is made up of papers, readings, music, children's exercises, etc. to be assigned to different members of the church and congregation."[63] Such materials offered advice to women on how they could lead more professional and perhaps even more enticing meetings, both of which would lure increasing numbers of women into the field of mission work.

At least in the case of *Missionary Circles*, denominational and regional origin of religious materials appeared to play little role. Rather, *Missionary Circles,* whose ties were with the Presbyterian Church, incorporated portions of previously published leaflets from the Methodist Episcopal Church and Baptist Church written by both southern and northern women.[64] Thus, at least on some occasions, southern women displayed ecumenicalism and downplayed interdenominational and interregional competition in favor of advancing their shared evangelical mission. Included were short pieces that educated women on the sometimes harsh realities of missionary life in foreign nations in inclusive and lighthearted ways. One female-authored booklet, for example, suggested that women's religious auxiliaries "assign a country or a missionary station to each lady and ask for a three-minute item concerning it at the next monthly meeting; or write up and distribute a question box, the answers involving a little research, and direct to the Reports for information."[65] Leaflets like *Missionary Circles* pulled speeches, administrative reports, and religious teaching tools from annual denomination-wide publications. One such example is the "Report of Woman's Missionary Society, 1897" from the Fayetteville, North Carolina, presbytery. This one edition included observations from a female missionary serving in China; a reprinted speech written by another female mission worker entitled "What the Church Expects of Her Young Women in Christianizing the World"; a letter from a Presbyterian minister and his mission work in the Belgian Congo; full-length papers on women's leadership and work in philanthropy; and a report from the president of the Woman's Missionary Society summarizing all other papers given by members. Although most members were unable to attend state and regional conferences for their respective religious auxiliaries, by the last decade of the nineteenth century publications like *Missionary Circles* were accessible, disseminating important information about, and inspirational pieces regarding, mission work, many of which women had authored.[66]

Southern women found other means to reach like-minded women beyond their organizations and communities. North Carolinian Kate Hamilton produced religious instructional materials, such as the teaching pamphlet, "Talks About Christian Giving, Thanksgiving Ann," that indoctrinated generations of young Presbyterians.[67] The fictional Thanksgiving Ann was a "grandmotherly" Black woman who imparted Christian advice to the children of the Allyn home, where she worked as a cook and housekeeper. Thanksgiving Ann, who the family regarded with "a curious mixture of patronage and veneration," stressed the concept of Christian giving by contributing as much money—in this case, $3.00—to the traveling Bible Society agent as did Mr. Allyn, the "master" of the house.

By the end of the parable, each member of the Allyn family had imbibed the teaching of their domestic worker. Mrs. Allyn, in particular, concluded that Thanksgiving Ann was "right" that "all [their] hopes for the world to come are in Him." Taking further instruction from Thanksgiving Ann, Mrs. Allyn chastised those who "provide lavishly for [their] own appareling, entertainment and ease," yet "apportion nothing for the interests of His kingdom, or the forwarding of His work."[68] It is a bit ironic that a white southern woman conceptualized a religious pamphlet that mocked the cheapness of the affluent Allyn family, while the poor Black woman arose as the hero—the Christian paragon. As we have seen, sources authored by white southern women routinely stressed Black ignorance and dependence. In the eyes of southern whites, they were individuals who benefited from white generosity and moral uplift. In "Talks About Christian Giving, Thanksgiving Ann" the roles are reversed. Perhaps this pamphlet spurred many more white southerners into action. After all, a wealthy white family would not want to be surpassed in any religious virtue by their Black hired help. A shaming leaflet like "Talks About Christian Giving, Thanksgiving Ann" might well have served as an effective weapon within the female worker's arsenal of religious tools.

Baptist Isa Beall Williams Neel of Cartersville, Georgia, and her published pamphlet, "W.M.U. Interest in Inter-Racial Relations," affords a very different example of how white women sold mission work to others using race as a motivator. It reveals how "workers for Christ" addressed race relations in the New South.[69] According to Neel, the WMU had presented their interracial "Plan of Work" at a recent Baptist convention. There they adopted the following resolution: "Knowing that personal service is Christ-like living in one's own community, we will, to reach the oppressed and unsaved in our immediate localities, particularly encourage efforts including cooperation in the promotion of local inter-racial communities for the securing of more sympathetic and equitable relations between the races."[70] This treatise identified a number of tangible areas in which the WMU had ameliorated race relations, citing its crucial role in the community's founding of a "state institution for delinquent Negro boys," a "school for delinquent Negro girls," and "daily vacation Bible schools for Negro children." In doing so, Neel's essay stressed problems that would result should southern women not do their Christian duty, which meant their responsibilities correcting delinquency through faith-based outreach and reinforcing racial subordination.

Neel thus drew in her readers, and their interest, by playing on their emotions. Referring to the poor state of interracial relations, Neel opined, "the highest Christian impulse is seeking to solve an acute national problem, which if neglected or left to self-seeking un-Christian agencies, will bring immeasurable hurt and loss to both races involved."[71] Similar to the speech given by Presbyterian missionary Margaret Douglas in which she promoted Christian service in Brazil as a great opportunity to combat the supposed impure influences of Roman Catholicism, Neel offered mission work toward southern Blacks as a privilege and a necessity. Attempting to instill a touch of fear in her readers, Neel wrote, "God will not hold us guiltless if we fail through these every day channels of contact to express, individually and in more effective organized capacity, the spirit of the Master through practical and constructive program of helpfulness."[72]

To draw white southern women into interracial mission work, Neel included a poem stressing white superiority and the pliability of Blacks. She portrayed mission work as a reasonable responsibility for southern white women and asserted that those whom they served were obedient, child-like, and appreciative beings who resembled southern enslaved people as described by then contemporary proslavery historian U. B. Phillips.[73] In contrast to the somber tone of the article as a whole, the acrostic exudes an uplifting and encouraging timbre while making it clear what white southern society thought of the Black community.

Nearest us for Christian ministries
Easily influenced for good
Grateful for sympathetic interest
Religious by nature
Our opportunity and our obligation

Whether or not they were fully conscious of it at the time, white southern women like Neel and Hamilton were using their religiously themed writings to defend, and in some cases, fight for a white supremacist, patriarchal political order that they probably believed should be the national—if not international—

model. Historian Sarah E. Gardner has argued that after 1865, white southern women participated "equally with their male peers in creating a discourse about the South and the Civil War that had its hallmarks the transformation of racism into philanthropy and of defeat into victory." Indeed, this reality crossed over into religious territory where southern women gave lectures and published pamphlets, articles, and instructional materials in attempts to entice others into faith-based opportunities. These included those that reinforced the racial hierarchy from a white perspective while celebrating Caucasian religious achievements and progress. Significantly, the composite narrative advanced by female mission workers gradually transformed into the national story of racial turmoil, violence, and tension, although such women tried to package it as racial uplift, reconciliation, and philanthropy.[74]

Seven

FOREIGN MISSION WORK AT HOME AND IN THE FIELD

Concurrent with home mission work during the late nineteenth and early twentieth centuries was white southern women's continuing involvement, often in the form of dedicated careers, as foreign missionaries. While opportunities in home mission work did not typically arise for women until after the Civil War, meaningful outlets in foreign mission work had existed for the devoted few for several decades. A majority of these early female foreign missionaries had followed their husbands to distant lands as helpmates rather than intentionally entering such faith-based work on their own. Nonetheless, Georgian Martha Jane Williford Payne, the case study of chapter 3, confirms that there were a few southern women who committed themselves to foreign missionary careers before 1860. Payne, who served a Liberian community between 1850 and 1870, was one of the first American women, and definitely one of the first single southern women, to answer God's call to spread His Word throughout the "heathen lands" of the world. Martha Jane Williford Payne, however, would not be an anomaly among southern women for long. When southern Methodists, Baptists, and Presbyterians split from their northern peers in 1844, 1845, and 1861 respectively, they immediately entered into foreign mission work. Until the beginning of the Civil War, they established foreign mission boards, the main administrative units overseeing such work, and collectively dispatched a few hundred missionaries across the globe.[1] Southern women participated in this steady expansion of foreign missions, though, as had been the case before their denominations' respective schisms, nearly all were married.[2] Careers and outlets in foreign mission work, however, quickly dried up after the Confederate bombing of Fort Sumter in 1861.

✝

This chapter resumes with the period immediately following the Civil War and Reconstruction eras when women's participation in foreign mission work, both at home and as proselytizers abroad, proliferated. It seeks to expose the diversity in backgrounds, denominational affiliations, religious and sociopolitical beliefs, and field experiences among white female foreign missionaries between 1875 and 1930. At the same time, this chapter emphasizes the similarities shared by this category of women. Specifically, such women, more often than not, were single and well educated for their time and place. As were their sisters in home mission work, female foreign missionaries tended to be ambitious and career-minded individuals who held more progressive views on issues of gender, notably women's role in, and penchant for, religious work.[3] Most women in this category held at least a bachelor's degree, and a disproportionate number held graduate or professional degrees. Many, in fact, had been (or would become) instructors at southern women's colleges.

While they may not have received the recognition that those pioneering northern women in education, social work, medicine, and journalism have, these female foreign missionaries belong in a special, underappreciated category of southern women. They challenge many common negative characterizations of middle-class and elite white southern women in the late nineteenth and early twentieth centuries. In contrast to the popular image, female foreign missionaries were not anti-intellectual, vapid, romantic, impractical, vain, indolent, or anachronistic, nor were they (entirely) restrained by domesticity and patriarchy. At the same time, southern female mission workers embodied long-standing traits idealized in southern society. As a group, they were maternal, feminine, and devout. The female missionaries further reinforce, as do so many of their peers in other faith-based projects, that evangelical Protestant Christianity was not the entirely confining institution that scholars and laypeople alike have characterized it to be. Careers in foreign mission work offered to southern women one of very few satisfying and challenging professional outlets not only within religious circles but in public environments more broadly. Such a woman publicly achieved far more than her mother or grandmothers had, but she never transgressed the delicate equilibrium of any man's masculinity and authority. Foreign mission work, in particular, welcomed the highly competent and ambitious, yet ladylike, woman.

Nevertheless, white southern women who served as foreign missionaries, while aspiring, zealous, and supportive of women's influence in the public sphere, strongly identified with the South and its generally elitist and racist principles. One often detects such manifestations of women missionaries' "southernness" through their assessments, particularly in their private writings, of those Asians, Africans, and Latinos whom they served. Those of African descent received more direct discrimination from their southern missionaries than did Asian and Latinos. For example, Presbyterian missionary Margaret Douglas refused to admit any "negroes" to her Brazilian school despite the mission's vigorous recruitment efforts seeking additional students.[4] Douglas omitted from her journal virtually any discussion of Brazilians of African descent, as though she were sweeping an unpleasant or unimportant topic under the rug. Likewise, Frances Worth, a missionary in the Belgian Congo during the mid-1920s, repeatedly revealed her racial biases in correspondence with family and friends. In one letter, she compared her "native assistant," Kabongo, to the "faithful [Black] servant at home" who deserved occasional recognition for his obedience. Worth asked her mother to buy Kabongo "a *very cheap, gaudy, figured bandana*," concluding that it was "useless to pay anything much for it because he won't even know that it's nice. All they want is big and gaudy bandanas."[5]

There are dangers in overgeneralizing racism among white southern female missionaries. Many of these women did, on occasion, exhibit glimmers of racial moderation that one would not associate with white southern women of this period as a whole. Nevertheless, such women were in the minority even among those southern white women working for their denominations.[6] Foreign mission workers recorded their southern-shaped thoughts and opinions on issues of gender, race, and evangelism in a variety of sources. Some left candid evaluations in their private journals; some shared their perspectives with friends, family, and denominational administrators through correspondence; while still others sought highly public venues, namely published books through which they documented and promoted their careers and viewpoints. Many sources paint a highly idealized picture of southern women's missionary activities and must be treated with caution in order to avoid accepting, at face value, excessively laudatory or romanticized portrayals of such workers.

FOREIGN MISSION SOCIETIES AT HOME

Faith-based organizations and auxiliaries administered and participated in by southern women at home spawned and supported their greater, typically long-term, service abroad. Not only essential to a nuanced appreciation for women's foreign missionary careers, these organizations, auxiliaries, and activities at home shed light on conceptions of southern womanhood, both within and outside of religious circles, during the late nineteenth and early twentieth centuries. In such venues, southern women found themselves grappling with the confines of patriarchy as well as their own religious expression and authority. Simultaneously, they may have participated in redefining and promoting an idealized southern woman, one who combined values of the Old South with the New South.

Men dominated Protestant foreign mission boards.[7] For example, the SBC Foreign Mission Board, organized in 1845, included a president, editorial secretary, recording secretary, corresponding secretary, educational secretary, treasurer, and auditor.[8] Similar organizations or boards for other southern Protestant churches include the Board of Missions, Methodist Episcopal Church, South (organized in 1846); the Executive Committee of Foreign Missions, Presbyterian Church of the United States (organized in 1861); and the Board of Missions and Church Extension, United Synod, Evangelical Lutheran, South (organized in 1886). Men on such foreign mission boards held disproportionate authority and influence relative to all matters concerning foreign missions, including women's role in them. In particular, men determined which women were best suited for foreign mission work as well as the location and nature of their assignment.[9] They also served as an official conduit between female missionaries and their families.[10] Yet southern women exhibited interest in faith-based projects abroad and wielded some influence with the male-led foreign mission boards.

In reaction to men's hegemony over foreign mission boards, southern women explored their options on how best to spread God's Word. This came in the form of furthering foreign mission projects among themselves, specifically through organizations and auxiliaries that they administered largely independently of any men. During the late nineteenth century, women representing each of the major Protestant denominations established foreign and joint foreign-home mission societies. Technically, male leaders in each of the denominations granted women permission to forge such societies. In the case of the Methodist Episcopal Church, South, men at the 1878 General Convention in Atlanta authorized women "to organize for connectional missionary work."[11] The General Convention deemed that "the operations of this [women's] Society should be conducted in connection with the Board of Missions and subject to its advice and approval."[12] Baptist and Presbyterian women faced similar top-down control.[13]

The three major foreign (or joint foreign-home) missionary societies organized by women in the South were the Woman's Foreign Missionary Society of the Methodist Episcopal Church, South (1878); the Woman's Missionary Union of the Southern Baptist Convention (1888); and the Women of the Church of the Presbyterian Church of the United States (1898). In 1872, Episcopal women established the Woman's Auxiliary to the much older Domestic and Foreign Missionary Society (1821). Unlike its Baptist, Methodist, and Presbyterian counterparts, the Episcopal Church never officially split over the issue of slavery. In 1861, southern Episcopalians had formed the Protestant Episcopal Church in the Confederate States of America, a schism not recognized by the Episcopal Church of the United States. Regional animosities were quickly jettisoned after the Civil War, and, in 1866, southern dioceses rejoined the national church. Consequently, the Woman's Auxiliary was not a purely southern organization, although southern females served in it.[14]

While women in the South were late to create distinct administrative entities, they assembled their own foreign missionary organizations in the decades before the 1870s, 1880s, and 1890s.[15] In some cases women from individual churches, such as the Presbyterian Church in Athens, Georgia, convened to forge a missionary society, while, in others, women from a collection of regional churches did the same. This latter method applied to Baptist women in Virginia who established the Rappahannock Baptist Association in 1843. The WMU absorbed this and other organizations throughout the South upon its formation in the late 1880s.[16] The Rappahannock Baptist Association resembled mite societies in the antebellum South that focused upon fundraising pursuits. This association, in the years before the Civil War, reinforced male authority and dependence, for example, by welcoming men's guidance and public presentations. According to one member who produced a history of the organization in the early twentieth century, "no woman [then] would have dared stand in [a missionary] meeting and be recognized."[17]

Southern women, like their northern and European counterparts, withstood a fair degree of gender discrimination in these mission circles.[18] They encountered apathy, discomfort, skepticism, and distrust from some men and even other women in their churches. Such doubters of women's religious voice included theologians, members of church foreign mission boards, and women who served in religious organizations. In a speech delivered to the Baptist Missionary Society of Athens, Georgia, mission leader Emma Amos enumerated several instances of gender discrimination encountered by her colleagues. "To hark pastors who oppose Woman's Work and to refuse the organizations in their churches" was a fundamental problem. According to Amos, women encountered significant discrimination by clerics who "criticized, unkindly misunderstood, misrepresented and falsly [sic] accused . . . the pioneer Leader in our W.W. [Womans Work]." Likewise, Amos cited women leaders who earnestly begged for pastors' cooperation, "asking [for] the name of some prominent women in their churches [to whom] mission literature might be sent for distribution," only to "fail utterly to receive a reply."[19]

As a consequence of such vexation, these women found themselves in defensive mode and vigorously shielded their female peers in mission work. Laura Askew Haygood, a graduate of Wesleyan College, founder of an industrial high school in Atlanta and a Methodist missionary in China, addressed this in a speech she delivered to a group of female mission workers in August 1884. Her sentiments more than hint at her frustrations while promoting women's rights in faith-based pursuits:

> To her as well as to man was the Comforter promised; to her as well as to him was given the great commission to teach and to testify to the risen Christ; upon her as well as upon him came the Pentecostal gift of tongues; to her as well as to him was allowed the precious privilege of ministering of her substance to the dear Lord's physical wants when He walked among men, and to her in a very peculiar sense was given a part in the sweet assurance that in the persons of the weak brothers and sisters "for whom Christ died" this blessed ministry may go on through the ages.[20]

Southern women like Haygood incorporated strong scriptural evidence into their discourse. This suggests that they consciously attempted to obtain greater acceptance, authority, and recognition within religious circles by remaining true to God's Word. They sounded more like legalistic theologians than impassioned feminists.

While southern women cited gender discrimination in their foreign mission work, others lauded prospective missionaries' spiritual penchant and professional accomplishments. It is a gross overstatement to suggest that all southern clerics and elders within particular sects were opposed to women's "missionary expressions." Some key figures acknowledged the crucial role that women played in furthering missionary aims and the role that women's auxiliaries could play. In the late 1880s, Methodist bishop Holland Nimmons McTyeire praised women's efforts in a letter to the General Secretary of the Woman's Foreign Missionary Society: "Let me congratulate you and your coworkers and the whole Church on the results of the first decade of the Woman's Board. You have shown practical wisdom in the location of the fields to be occupied and in the selection of the laborers."[21] McTyeire continued with more specific comments of approbation: "You have shown enterprise in raising funds and economy in spending them. You have shown excellent administrative ability in the management of your affairs at home and abroad. Your periodicals and leaflet literature have informed and quickened the whole Church on the subject of missions."[22] Likewise, according to an officer of the Woman's Foreign Missionary Society of Cherokee Corner in Oglethorpe County, Georgia, "Brother [Miles Hill] Dillard encouraged us by adding that while enthusiasm and numbers made missionary work easy there [in China], that he thought we of Cherokee Corner Church deserved more praise in that we were laboring on, few in number and under the chilling influence of unsympathizing observers. He promised to give us a little help in his next visit which would be sometime in December."[23] Finally, some men praised women who sought foreign mission careers. In 1907, Stuart McGuire, a Richmond, Virginia, physician, described aspiring medical missionary Dr. Emily Runyan as "a woman of high Christian character and a physician of unusual ability."[24]

By the turn of the century, foreign missionary societies experienced substantial growth in membership and had amassed significant budgets. In 1900, membership in the MEC, South, organization, for example, had surpassed 75,000 and worked with a budget in excess of $93,000.[25] Southern Baptist women substantially increased their efforts in foreign mission work between the 1880s and the 1910s. During that time, the WMU raised under $20,000 each year for foreign missions with a fledgling membership, but by the early 1910s, the Baptist organization—which, by then, was the largest Protestant missions organization for women in the world with over 100,000 members—had amassed more than $168,000 in a single year.[26] In the late 1880s and early 1890s, Southern Presbyterian women, still officially unorganized throughout most of the 1890s, collected between $20,000 and $25,000 for foreign mission projects in a given year.[27] By the 1910s, there were nearly half a million southern women involved in organizations like the WMU.

To better gauge the general interest among southern women in pursuits related to foreign missions, one must place them within a national context. According to one scholar, by 1915, "there were more than three million [American] women on the membership rolls of some forty denominational female missionary societies."[28] Considering the reality of the South's much smaller, more rural population, and general lack of religious diversity, one can conclude that the three main missionary organizations in the South were very successful in their recruitment of women. They offered intellectual engagement, celebrated female contributions, and provided frequent opportunity for socialization. Denomination societies like the WMU typically met once a month within individual parishes. Often such monthly meetings centered around a theme, for example "Supremacy of Love" or "Social Evangelism in Korea."[29]

Such societies were under the leadership of a president, one or more vice presidents, one or more secretaries, and a treasurer.[30] Significantly, leadership at the local level was dominated by married women, although disproportionate numbers of female foreign missionaries were single. While southern women engaged in mission work sought to expand conceptions of femininity, the choice to install married women in leadership positions suggests that missionary societies sought to reinforce more traditional gendered norms, including marriage.

While these three missionary societies proffered ample support to women serving in foreign countries, they also offered a wealth of professional opportunities to women who remained in the United States. The Woman's Foreign Missionary Society of the MEC, South, of Cherokee Corner, Georgia, boasted of the many skills possessed and responsibilities held among its officers and general members. Records from the 1880s revealed that some members researched and purchased foreign property as to expand mission activities.

Some solicited subscriptions for missionary publications. Some gave lectures on their past experiences as foreign missionaries or on such topics as the challenges of female leadership. Some led Bible study or group readings on leaflets, articles, or books on foreign mission work. Some wrote letters and prepared supply bundles for those serving abroad. Some submitted pieces to, or took on editorial positions with, the *Woman's Missionary Advocate.* Some corresponded with organization-wide officers about matters pertaining to the four major committees: Extension of Work, Finance, Literature, and Juvenile Societies. And, many helped organize fundraising drives for foreign missions and for the Scarritt Bible and Training School of Kansas City, Missouri.[31] While they catered to different audiences, women who participated in foreign mission work at home engaged in similar jobs and activities and exercised the same set of skills as did those who focused on home mission work.

More broadly, southern women attended missionary conferences held throughout the South as delegates from their particular parishes. These were anticipated events and sources of inspiration and celebration. Referring to her attendance at the MEC, South, Missionary Conference in Decatur, Georgia, in May 1882, an officer of the Cherokee Corner auxiliary wrote: "With very few exceptions these reports were hopeful, evidencing a growing interest in foreign missions among the women of the church. I wish that in every instance a delegate instead of a letter had been sent. I am sure that the earnestness and consecration breathing forth in the words and faces of many of the women present would have quickened the faith and hope of others and sent them back to their societies imbued with a more earnest desire to labor in this blessed field."[32] Southern women from other Protestant denominations were presented with similar outlets.[33] For example, the WMU offered southern Baptist women opportunities to involve themselves in conferences and to serve on executive boards on the city, associational, state, and South-wide levels. While the WMU operated as a single administrative unit at the national level, it also functioned at smaller city, associational, and state levels.

Foreign mission societies certainly bestowed women with formal and professional opportunities to labor for Christ but also engendered friendship and light-hearted entertainment. Olive Bagby, a Virginia native who served as a teacher and Baptist missionary in Shanghai during the 1910s, recorded the "pet names" for nearly sixty members of her local WMU. These included such names as "Dainty Little Coquette," "Most Sensible Housewife," "Laughing Little Flirt," and "Intellectual Modern Thinker." These collectively attested to the value women placed on a more multidimensional southern lady. It was perhaps a given that southern women who devoted themselves to mission work were expected to be intelligent, practical, and earnest. Bagby, however, attests that southern women also valued those who were witty, maternal, domestic, and feminine.[34] Some of the pet names added a touch of self-deprecation—with such adjectives as "naughty," "bossy," and "vain." Mission work was a serious pursuit, yet it was no place for perfectionists. Taken together, these pet names underscored the positive features and manners that women of this class, time, and place consciously offered.

FOREIGN MISSION WORK ABROAD

While southern women pursued fulfilling work through their foreign missionary societies at home, the ultimate goal among such organizations was to extend women's Christian influence—quite literally—around the world. The three largest Protestant denominations in the South—Baptist, Presbyterian, and Methodist—each dispatched many hundred to a couple thousand women abroad between 1880 and 1930. Baptists and Presbyterians developed more of a focus in foreign mission work compared to Methodists, who concentrated greater efforts on home mission projects. In any given year, the MEC, South, typically had forty missionaries in active foreign service. In contrast, the SBC or the PCUS might have more than three times that number in some years.[35] For example, in 1913 Southern Baptists boasted 156 women missionaries serving seven nations.[36] Many foreign missionaries—either as single women or as helpmate wives—entered such work believing that they were committed to a long-term career and to their faith.[37]

Southern women served as missionaries around the globe, yet one may make generalizations relative to particular locations or peoples of interest per religious denomination. The MEC, South, dispatched women to China (Nanking, Shanghai, and Soochow); to Mexico (Mexico City, Saltillo, San Luis Potosi, Chihuahua, and Guadalajara); to Brazil (Piracicaba); to Korea (Seoul, Songdo, and Wonsan) and to Cuba. The SBC sent female missionaries to the Yoruba Mission in present-day Nigeria, China, Italy, Mexico, Brazil, Japan, and Argentina. Missionaries representing Southern Presbyterians established missions in Greece, China, Japan, Korea, Congo, Cuba, Mexico, and Brazil.[38] All three denominations thus expressed marked interest in establishing missions in China, Mexico, and Brazil, yet there was little evident discord. Almost all respected and supported the efforts of their peers affiliated with other churches, even male and female missionaries from the American North. Indeed, the foreign mission field—at least as defined by Protestant denominations—appeared to be an ecumenical environment.

✝

By virtue of their relatively small numbers in, and substantial professional and spiritual commitment toward, foreign mission work, these women were exceptional, embodying "otherness." Ambitious and well-educated women faced few professional outlets in the South. Mission work was one of few places where they could apply their college and graduate-level educations, skills, and knowledge. At the turn of the twentieth century, lifetime mission work as a teacher and especially physician was one of the most innovative career paths for women. Three of the first southern females who earned a medical degree were Drs. Mildred Philips of Texas, Emily Earl Chenault Runyon of Richmond, Virginia, and Martha "Mattie" Ingold of Caldwell County, North Carolina.[39] By 1900, there were over seven thousand female physicians in the United States, but only a small fraction of those were of southern origin.[40] Southern female physicians faced insurmountable discrimination in their communities and opted to practice outside the South or serve as medical missionaries. Mildred Philips graduated from Philadelphia's Woman's Medical College of Pennsylvania in 1884 and spent her career as a medical missionary in Soochow, China, for the MEC, South. Emily Runyon graduated from the Woman's Medical College of Chicago, affiliated with Northwestern University Medical School, practiced medicine in Virginia for nine years and planned on a lifetime career as a Methodist medical missionary in Soochow, China. Her dreams quickly vanished soon after her arrival in China. The MEC, South, Foreign Mission Board accused her of drug addiction and released her.[41] Similarly, Mattie Ingold graduated from Woman's Medical College of Baltimore in 1896 and served as a Presbyterian medical missionary in Korea.

Female foreign missionaries were not simply breaking through the proverbial glass ceiling. Rather, they were filling crucial roles—for both the churches and countries they served—and they did so at bargain rates.[42] Protestant churches provided women with low or nonexistent salaries. Until the 1960s, female missionaries who were married almost always received no salary, while single women typically earned between from 10 to 50 percent less than single men. These often-indispensable professional positions and careers that were done gratis or for a reduced salary included those in teaching at traditional, normal, and industrial schools as well as at religious institutions that trained native missionaries; day and boarding school administration; medicine and nursing; and social work. For example, and specific to women's opportunities in medicine, the Southern Presbyterians constructed twenty-one hospitals between 1898 and 1925: ten in China, five in Korea, five in Zaire, and one in Mexico.[43]

The rapid establishment of foreign missions in which women could actively participate is a testament to the demonstrated acceptance of, if not only desperation for, southern women in the public sphere. Only five years after the formation of the Woman's Missionary Society, MEC, South, women were already at the forefront of a number of projects. In China, they were administering the Bible Woman's Institute in Soochow as well as boarding and day schools in Nanking, Shanghai, and Soochow. Female Methodist missionaries occupied similar positions in Latin America. In the Brazilian centers of Piracicaba and Rio de Janeiro, they operated boarding schools and were on the verge of opening two orphanages. In Mexico, women had opened boarding schools, one on the United States border near Laredo and one in Central Mexico.[44]

FOREIGN MISSIONARY CASE STUDIES

Up until this point, this chapter has presented, using broad strokes, the collective experience of southern women engaged in organizations, auxiliaries, activities, and careers pertaining to foreign mission service. While such background and analysis are crucial to understanding these women's place within southern society, there is also benefit to closer exploration of a few representative—and one unrepresentative—missionaries. In so doing, one gains a better sense of female proselytizers' sociopolitical views toward "otherness," defined broadly as different peoples and cultural landscapes, as well as of their thoughts and conceptions of southern culture and southern womanhood. Three single women who committed to a long-term career in foreign mission fields have left detailed accounts of their missionary experiences. They provide insight into their lives, beliefs, and identities, at least how they wanted to be cast and remembered. Lula F. Whilden, a Baptist served in Canton, China, from 1872 until her death in 1914. Laura Askew Haygood, a Methodist, committed herself to a missionary career in Shanghai, China, between 1884 and 1900. Margaret Moore Douglas, a Presbyterian, labored in Recife, Brazil, from 1906 until her death in 1940. In contrast to these three women, Frances McBryde Worth, a Presbyterian, left her mission in Luebo in the Belgian Congo in 1927 after only three years' service, and offers an appropriate counterpoint.

Collectively, these missionaries with lengthy careers in their respective foreign environments—namely Haygood, Whilden, and Douglas—displayed values associated with the more multidimensional conceptions of idealized white southern womanhood that educated, middle-class and elite southern women had crafted between the end of the nineteenth and early twentieth centuries. They were highly feminine, devout, and cultured, yet they possessed intellectual curiosity, initiative, and leadership skills. They achieved far more than most of their female forebears had ever dreamed of, yet they never (consciously) thought about seriously challenging man's masculinity and authority as were many American feminists in the North.[45] Such southern women reinforced their feminine, often maternal, identities in their daily actions in the mission fields, and that is how southerners remembered and even celebrated them. The Reverend Egbert W. Smith, D.D., field secretary of the Executive Committee of Foreign Missions for the PCUS, memorialized Margaret Douglas in a manner that harkened to the Old South. In 1940, Smith wrote:

> Continually she reminded me of what my Virginia-born mother told me was often said to her when she was a girl by her old black mammy, "Be still, my child, and learn composure." In an unusual degree [Douglas] had that habitual serenity and poise that not only "Stamps the caste of Vere de Vere," but stamps also, in a far higher and purer form, that inner circle of God's children who reached the spiritual attainment of a mind at leisure from itself, a heart so centered on Christ, so satisfied in Him,

so filled with His Spirit, that the daily worries and trials of life have no power to reach or ruffle that central calm, that inner peace of God that passes all understanding.[46]

Although Reverend Smith's words are reflective of just one man's thoughts on one woman, they are representative of many southerners' conceptions—and boundaries—of modern womanhood.

Whilden, Haygood, Douglas, and Worth assumed professional positions in their respective foreign missions that complemented southerners' conceptions of acceptable gender roles, and they subtly expanded and redefined southern female identity. Reverend Smith may not have acknowledged such women as "modern" or "progressive," yet collectively these four women encouraged innumerable women of the South to consider the merits of, and satisfaction received from, higher education and faith-based careers. In this regard, southern women in foreign mission work resembled their counterparts in professions falling under the home mission label. These four women all worked in education but also demonstrated their penchant for management and enterprise, characteristics assigned to successful men. For example, Margaret Douglas, who became director of the Agnes Erskine School in Recife, Brazil, in 1913 and held that title until her death nearly thirty years later, embodied such traits. In that position Douglas nearly doubled the school enrollment; oversaw thousands of boarder and day students; managed the school's finances; continually developed and tweaked the school's curriculum; participated in recruitment and outreach projects in the Recife community; and participated in discussions with the PCUS.

Whilden, Haygood, Douglas, and Worth were well prepared for the unknown worlds that awaited them. All had earned college degrees and immersed themselves in home mission societies and projects. Baptist Lula Whilden, born in 1846 in Camden, South Carolina, lived in China between the ages of two and nine with her missionary parents.[47] The Whilden family returned to the South in 1855, and Lula entered and graduated from the Greenville Woman's College years later. Upon her graduation in 1870, Whilden remained in upstate South Carolina to teach at her alma mater, while she occupied a prominent place within the Woman's Missionary Union.[48]

Methodist Laura Askew Haygood, born in 1845 in Watkinsville, Georgia, also exhibited potential for religious work. Laura spent much of her childhood in Atlanta where she was a member of a devout yet progressive household. Her father was an attorney by training and a long-time superintendent of the Sunday school at Trinity Church. Her mother, the daughter of a Methodist minister, taught religion and Bible to pupils enrolled at the school she established at her Atlanta residence. The Haygoods strongly supported women's education, and there was no question that Laura and her sister would attend college. Both Haygood daughters continued their studies at Wesleyan Female College. Upon her graduation, Laura Haygood established a private school for girls in Atlanta that later merged with Girls High School, where Haygood served as a teacher and principal. Educator, author, and United Daughters of the Confederacy officer, Mildred Lewis Rutherford, who worked at the school under Haygood's direction, fondly remembered Haygood and her amiable and maternal presence: "She was so loving and kind to me when I was thrown under her at the High School. I needed a kind and sympathetic heart in those early days, and Miss Haygood proved be all that was needed. No one will ever know how she encouraged me in my crude work. From being my principal she soon became my friend."[49]

Laura Haygood was also at the forefront of organizing home mission societies that provided food and shelter to Atlanta's impoverished population during the 1870s and 1880s. Her mission work further included the establishment of an industrial school intended to help the city's uneducated and unskilled denizens transcend poverty. Prior to her service in Shanghai, China, Miss Haygood served as a frequent speaker, delivering speeches, such as "Relation of Female Education to Home Mission Work," at Methodist churches and home mission auxiliaries. She also taught two Sunday school classes, led the Sunday school normal class, and was president of Trinity Home Mission.[50]

Presbyterians Margaret Moore Douglas and Frances McBryde Worth also lived up to the precedent of well-prepared, well-educated, and accomplished missionaries set by Whilden, Haygood, and their contemporaries. Born in White Oak, South Carolina, in 1875, Douglas also grew up in a devout household that emphasized female education. Her father was minister of Mount Olivet Presbyterian Church and served as president of Yorkville Female College in York, South Carolina. In 1898, Douglas graduated from Winthrop College and afterward enrolled in graduate courses in mathematics at the University of Chicago. Upon completion of her studies, Douglas returned to upstate

South Carolina where she taught mathematics at both Ebenezer Academy and Winthrop College until 1905. That year, the Executive Committee of Foreign Missions of the PCUS appointed her as a missionary.[51] Frances Worth, a Wilmington, North Carolina native born in 1896, boasted a fine education and adventuresome spirit. Raised by her widowed mother, Worth attended prep schools in Switzerland, the Moravian-founded Salem College (North Carolina), an early leader in southern female education, and Columbia University.[52]

Despite their training, including language training, each woman felt less useful to their missions until improving communication with their respective native populations. For example, in March 1885, a few months after her arrival in Shanghai, Laura Haygood wrote to a friend in Georgia: "I am gaining a little every day with the language, but it will be months before I can converse readily, and two years before I shall be able to teach Bible classes in Chinese."[53] Similarly, the others confided to their family, friends, and journals that language remained the greatest barrier to fulfilling their goals, at least in the first months and couple of years.

Skills and experience were certainly assets, but these women also possessed passion for—perhaps at times a healthy dose of self-righteousness—fulfilling God's plan for them. One Methodist woman described Laura Haygood on the eve of her departure for China: "there was an eagerness in her heart to fill up the measure of all she had done or might do in Atlanta for Christ."[54] Similarly, Margaret Douglas wrote that she was "thankful the Lord gave me strength to do what seemed to me to be right." Douglas's niece, Mary Douglas Stauffer, who assembled her aunt's journal in the 1980s, praised her "selfless dedication" and demonstrated perseverance when faced with stark cultural differences. Stauffer cited Brazilian poet Mauro Mota, who wrote about Margaret Douglas and other founders of the girls' school in Recife: "it took remarkable individuals to confront as women a sexist culture, as North Americans a foreign culture, as Protestants a Catholic culture."[55] One Methodist administrator remembered Lula Whilden during those years when she was back in the United States and too ill to return to her foreign mission work: "For Miss Whilden there followed weeks, months, and even years of weakness, weariness and pain with the ever-present heartache for China."[56] These three women exhibited genuine passion and commitment toward their missionary careers. Nevertheless, scholars must approach the recorded memories and impressions of these missionaries with a degree of caution. The laudatory language is as much a reflection of the idealized rhetoric with which elite and middle-class white southern women were associated as it is of reality. Southern female missionaries found themselves on rhetorical pedestals just as had their plantation mistress ancestors.

A GENDERED TERRAIN

As foreign missionaries in China, Brazil, and the Belgian Congo, Lula Whilden, Laura Haygood, Margaret Douglas, and Frances Worth faced new gendered landscapes, many of which they considered to be backward and confining. In response, they sought to make them more modern, progressive, and western. Alternately, many female missionaries measured their success by the extent to which indigenous peoples emulated them. In this regard, these women may have resembled their forebears who provided religious instruction to their enslaved people as well as their contemporaries in home mission work. At the same time, they exhibited varying levels of respect for, and acceptance of, indigenous cultural practices, even though many would reject Christianity. This suggests that at least some southern missionary women, with their more worldly educational and professional life experiences, may have been more open to diversity and contrast. Methodist Laura Haygood, for example, wrote in 1886, "we dare not hope that all of the children who are to-day enrolled in our day schools will become Christians, but may we not remember that when ten lepers were healed only one returned to give thanks?"[57] Her words may have been those of a realist who did not expect immediate transformation, but to others her remark connoted a toleration of difference.

✝

Methodist Laura Haygood and Baptist Lula Whilden faced similar conditions in late Qing Dynasty China, despite the fact that the former was an educator, administrator, and religious mentor while the latter focused her missionary efforts on religious education through home visits, traveling door to door as an evangelist. Haygood left a bevy of letters written to Methodist leaders, family, and friends. Whilden produced reminiscences of her Chinese experiences shortly before her death, reminiscences that women from the South Carolina

WMU ultimately published in 1916. In contrast to Haygood's correspondence, which reflected her day-to-day obstacles alongside her triumphs, Whilden's remembrances were a carefully crafted text. Whilden intended her collection of recorded experiences to function as promotional literature for continued missionary efforts by Southern Baptists in China. Despite these differences, both women offered insight into issues of Chinese gender and their roles in shaping it.

Haygood viewed herself as a reformer who would culturally and spiritually uplift Chinese girls and young women. As a supervisor of educational institutions in the Shanghai district, Haygood oversaw four schools, both all-girl and coed, with staffs largely composed of Methodist women from the American South.[58] Throughout her career, she combated not only indifference among the Chinese parents to everything concerning the betterment of their daughters' condition but also their strong distrust of a foreigner. At the time that the southern Methodists established a mission in Shanghai in the 1850s, many Chinese girls and women were bound, quite literally, by gendered traditions. Uneasy with creeping modern influences, many Chinese wanted to reinforce feudal patriarchy during the late Qing Dynasty. Women lived with bound feet, which kept them at home and out of the public sphere. Foot binding, along with polygyny, were two such practices that kept powerless members of society, namely women, subordinate.[59] Haygood likewise referred several times to overworked and exploited girls and women in households. One activity engaged in by many females was the creation of "ghost money" or counterfeit money.[60] Education was not a typical component of female childhood. According to Haygood, few schools for Chinese girls existed, even by the mid-1880s. Only wealthy families hired private tutors to teach their daughters reading and writing at home. One of Haygood's schools, the Clopton School, established by the MEC, South, in the mid-1850s, offered them educational and advancement opportunities that had never before been available.[61] Haygood resolved to make education her number one priority in China.

Throughout her career in Shanghai, Laura Haygood believed education assumed a vital role, perhaps as indispensable as exposure to Christian enlightenment, in the work of southern Methodist missionaries. There were opponents back in the United States who were uneasy about Haygood's missionary focus. They worried that day schools were introducing too many "secular" influences. In March 1886, Haygood wrote to the General Secretary of the Woman's Foreign Missionary Society, trying to allay any such fears with scriptural backing:

> To some of you it will seem that we are giving undue prominence to school work, or, as others have thought, that we are magnifying the work of education and neglecting the work of evangelization. Some would sorrowfully remind us that Christ and His apostles did not open schools in Judea for Hebrew children. Very true; but He did commission the disciples to go forth as teachers, and charged Peter to feed His lambs, and gave to the world a gospel for all times and all men and all wants.... He would never have excluded the children of the kingdom from the work of missionaries.

Within the same letter, Haygood reminded her opponents back home that even Jesus Christ had few followers at the end of His life but that that should not mean that His works and teachings were wasted efforts: "And who of use would dare to say that His work was in vain, because at the close of His life among men only a few hundreds of all the multitude were numbered among His followers?"[62]

Laura Haygood saw children—both boys and girls, but particularly girls—as the future bearers of greater societal change and schools as the instruments through which southern Methodists could bring such a change. Experience was teaching missionaries like Haygood that in "no other way could they reach mothers and homes so effectually as through the children." Schools that taught "arithmetic and geography and kindred studies and music," in Haygood's view, would enlighten generations of Chinese, or, in her words, "awaken the sleeping mind, deepen interest and quicken thought."[63] This, however, is not to say that Christian instruction was not a significant part of the Methodist curriculum. At the Trinity Schools, students congregated every morning in church for a short service of song and prayer, and on every afternoon they assembled for a meeting with the native pastor for a Bible lesson and singing.[64]

In 1886, Haygood reported that there were approximately 150 children enrolled in Methodist day schools in Shanghai. More than two-thirds of the attendees were girls. Haygood admitted that they gave preference to females in spite of the fact that "the parents are still more anxious to send their boys to school, if we had place for all." She hoped the MEC, South, would dispatch twenty-five missionary-educators over the next five years. With their efforts, the mission "would have a hundred schools in Shanghai, and access through them to a thousand homes."[65] Haygood's lofty goals reflected commitment, vision, organization, and leadership.

Among Haygood's aims was to expand the Clopton School's influence in Chinese life, transforming the institution into a normal school to train native teachers. Indeed, Haygood envisioned a Chinese society where women took on influential roles. In her 1891 report to the Foreign Mission Board, Haygood wrote: "I have seen some of the [Chinese] little girls grow into earnest, faithful women, and take their places in the rank and file of Christian women in China who are helping to bring in the kingdom of our Lord and of His Christ." She continued, acknowledging the role southern Methodists, and specifically the Clopton School, played in bringing about this gendered transformation: "I feel that there is no department of our work in Shanghai that is more important than this training school for teachers and helpers."[66] Two years later, in 1893, Haygood praised the increasing support for female education among the Chinese. She reported that all graduates of the Clopton School had found employment in schools and that "the demand for such teachers [was] in excess of [their] supply."[67]

The Clopton School was only one component of Laura Haygood's ambitious plan to reshape Chinese society. Unfortunately, however, she struggled with poor health for over a decade before her death. She found herself relegated to her bed all too often, and, in 1889, out of desperation, spent several months "resting" in Japan. This limited her actions. Nonetheless, among her bigger accomplishments during these painful years was the establishment of, and administration over, the McTyeire Home and School in 1892. McTyeire, "a school for higher learning," educated a number of prominent Chinese women, including the second wife of President Sun Yat-sen, Kaoru Otsuki. Haygood assumed a primary role in the conception, promotion of, and fundraising for this women's institution. Extant letters confirm that she was a tireless correspondent with several auxiliaries within the Woman's Foreign Missionary Society of the MEC, South, trying to raise financial support for the Chinese school as well as to attract more Methodist women to church and mission work. Although administrative responsibilities occupied much of her time, Haygood sought to make the school one with a warm, welcoming environment for both her teachers, American and Chinese, and her students. One Methodist couple who served with Haygood in China claimed "she was not only the founder and head but the big, all-loving heart."[68] This adulation suggested that it would be difficult for many missionaries to match Laura Askew Haygood, her efforts, results, and devotion to her faith. What rings true is that southern women could and did succeed in administrative positions, effectively combining a professional and a maternal persona.

✝

Lula Whilden sought to reach, educate, and enlighten Chinese women and girls through work with the Southern Baptist mission in Canton between 1872 and 1914. Unlike Laura Haygood, Whilden never assumed oversight of any school. In fact, Whilden never taught at a Baptist mission school in China despite the fact that she had served as an instructor at her Greenville, South Carolina, alma mater for several years. Rather, Whilden remained committed to *the* fundamental aim among missionaries: introducing "heathens" to the teachings of Jesus Christ. Although Whilden did not operate as a teacher in Canton, Baptist female missionaries readily served in such positions. In fact, the SBC placed its female missionaries in one or more of three categories: "evangelistic," "educational," and "medical." While Whilden appeared under the "evangelistic" label, as many female Baptist missionaries were engaged in educational pursuits as in evangelistic ones. In contrast, a small percentage worked as medical missionaries.[69] Like her Methodist counterpart, Whilden believed that societal change would come through contact with children and women. For nearly thirty years, with one long interruption in the 1880s and early 1890s, this Baptist missionary visited innumerable "heathen homes" through which she shared the Gospel with thousands of women.

Yet even during this hiatus, Whilden remained committed to missionary work. In 1882, after ten years of service, she returned to the United States in order to rest and improve her health and to generate increased interest in mission activities in China. She admirably succeeded in the latter but could never fully address the former. Whilden first traveled to Greenville to the Southern Baptist Convention headquarters, where she delivered several speeches on her personal experiences in Canton. These were intended both to raise money for existing missions and to recruit more women into the foreign field. After her presentations at the SBC, she was in high demand across the South as a "motivational" speaker. According to Fannie Heck, Whilden "held seventy-one missionary meetings during the first year, with only two months of entire rest." Whilden intended to return to Canton after a year and a half, but poor health kept her in her home country. Despite this limitation, Whilden continued to labor on behalf of her church. In 1886, after a lengthy period of confinement in bed, she relocated to Baltimore, where she ministered to a local Chinese community. Until 1892, when, at age forty-six, she was finally healthy enough to return to China, Whilden focused her proselytizing efforts on women who worked in laundries. During these years between 1886 and 1892, Whilden also established a Sunday school and Monday afternoon class in Baltimore's Chinatown.[70]

When Whilden first arrived in China, in the early 1870s, there were only 120 Chinese whom the Southern Baptists had converted in the Canton Mission District. By the end of her career in, 1914, over 5,500 had accepted Christ.[71] She played a significant role in this transformation both through her direct contact with Chinese households and through her training of several dozen Southern Baptist women engaged in evangelistic work in Canton. Echoing sentiments expressed by Laura Haygood, Whilden presented herself as a level-headed woman who accepted that many would not adopt Christianity and would only think of Christ as "the foreigner's God, who could never be anything to them."[72]

Although this is not stated in her memoirs, Whilden sought to change the gendered environment in China and reveal that, in God's kingdom, all souls, regardless of sex, were spiritual equals. As Laura Haygood bemoaned the girls and women who suffered from foot binding, Whilden lamented the common practice of child selling. In this sexist culture, girls, especially disabled ones, were of little use to Chinese families and were often sold as "singing girls."[73] Exploitative men who purchased such impaired girls first trained them to sing and play the guitar and then later dispatched them to the seedy nocturnal streets, dressed in elaborate costume, with painted and powdered faces, where they performed for hours. At daybreak, the handicapped singing girls, most of whom were blind, returned to their owners and relinquished any money they earned. In Whilden's words, "they are the miserable outcasts from society, and yet they have become so from no fault or through no wish of their own."[74]

During the 1890s, the maternal Whilden literally purchased six of these blind Chinese girls and cared for and educated each at her own expense. Too many unwanted young girls suffered a worse fate. In one chapter of her memoir, Whilden recounted tales of abandoned female children. Referring to one particular child left on the pavement, Lula remembered: "it was sick, too weak to walk, but the mother (thinking it would die soon) had put it there." Throughout her remembrances, Whilden recorded her deep disgust for such women, who she labeled "monster" mothers. Perhaps naively, she concluded that she could help end such inhumane practices by spreading the Gospel to as many households as possible. In her eyes, "monster" mothers were "heathens" who "did not see things in the light of Christianity" and were "without under-standing." Over her career, she claimed that she had heard "many a heathen mother" defend the abandoning of female children: "Better that one should suffer than that all should."[75] In this instance and others, Lula Whilden's neg-ative descriptions of the Chinese related more to their status (or lack of it) as Christians—and specifically as Christian mothers—than to their racial or ethnic identification.

This Baptist missionary exhibited deep sympathy for a number of physi-cally, mentally, and financially disadvantaged women. In addition to the blind and abandoned children, Lula Whilden portrayed herself as a tender-hearted friend and mentor to mutes, beggars, hunchbacks, and "boat women," those who literally spent their entire lives on small boats, subsisting on scraps. In-deed, her memoir paints a woman who could rival any northern torchbearer of the Social Gospel movement. It further presents a missionary who exhib-ited deep sympathy and compassion toward those she served, showcasing a woman who did not outwardly exhibit any racial or ethnic biases.[76] Despite this, Whilden never appeared to possess a particularly nuanced comprehen-sion of the challenges that Chinese people faced during the late Qing Dynasty. Such contemporary issues included recurring drought and famines alongside a fast-growing population and ineffectual governance. All these realities might provide insight into, though not condone, the inhumane treatment received by undesirable young girls.[77]

COMBATING CATHOLICISM AND
MAKING CHRISTIAN WOMEN

Half a world away, in Recife, a large city in northeastern Brazil, Presbyterian Margaret Moore Douglas began an ambitious missionary career that spanned more than thirty years. Margaret Moore Douglas kept a journal in which she recorded her experiences, observations, and views between 1906 and 1915. Unfortunately, the journal abruptly ends in 1915, over twenty-five years before her death. Her niece, who transcribed Margaret's journal, surmised that, by the mid-1910s, her aunt simply had too many responsibilities to keep up with journal writing. Nonetheless, Douglas suspected that someone, someday, might read her journal: "What I write in this journal is only scattering and disconnected fact, but they may be of interest to some one to read some time, any may help them realize what a great work and great struggle it is to bring Brazil to the light of the gospel."[78]

In August 1906, Margaret Moore Douglas arrived at her South American destination ready to assist with the fledgling American College of Pernambuco, a Presbyterian school that Miss Eliza Reed, another female missionary from the South, had established just two years before.[79] A long-time fixture at the school, Douglas worked, at varying times, as teacher, administrator, curriculum planner, financial officer, supervisor of student teachers, and even housekeeper. During her tenure, the all-girl institution evolved from a school of a couple dozen pupils to a school of a couple hundred. Throughout the years, Douglas was also a frequent contributor to religious publications such as "The Missionary." She attended religious conferences, such as the Christian Association Convention in Rio de Janeiro in 1909. And she kept fully apprised of developments within the PCUS back home as well as within her Brazilian presbytery. This South Carolina native's ultimate objective was to shape young girls and adolescents into Christian women, which for her exclusively meant Protestant women, who would serve as leaders in their respective communities and as exemplary examples of Christian womanhood.[80] While it was "not the custom of this country for the girls to make themselves so public," Douglas firmly believed that an educated, well-trained Christian woman was an asset to society and one who would contribute to the remaking of the religious landscape of Brazil.[81]

Working in an overwhelmingly Catholic nation, Douglas aggressively labored to bring Protestant influences into the country one girl at a time both through formal instruction and her maternal, nurturing ways. A school like the American College of Pernambuco could "help to break down the opposition to the gospel."[82] The school offered a balanced array of classes meant to produce a well-rounded lady who was competent, feminine, and devout. These included courses in Portuguese, French, English, Latin, mathematics, Bible and catechism, history, geography, elocution, calisthenics, drawing, embroidery, and music. With the exception of Portuguese, the official language of Brazil, these classes were the same ones taught in leading female academies across the South.

In contrast to a few teachers at the school, Margaret Moore Douglas understood that it was essential to take a more intimate approach than mere course work to truly mold Brazilian girls. Responding to the early advice of Eliza Reed, who said that she ought not take school girls into her home, Douglas confided in her journal: "I can do *so* much more with the girls if I have them in home with me."[83] Douglas, who strove to exude a strict yet nurturing persona and "always set a Christ-like example," aimed to serve as a mentor who would address theological and social issues relative to the adoption of a new faith. Perhaps most commonly, she provided advice and support to girls whose families did not approve of Protestant teachings. Douglas accompanied her Brazilian pupils to all church services and activities, taught a Sunday school class, and instilled in them ideas about responsibility, sacrifice, and womanhood.[84] On a more quotidian level, Douglas took motherly initiative by inoculating her girls against smallpox and shielding them from the robbers and other seedy characters who lingered around the school property. Instructor Eliza Reed kept a pistol to deter such individuals.

In addition, Margaret Moore Douglas wrote parables, such as "Corinna's Dolls," as a means to educate the young Brazilians on inappropriate religious practices, such as burning incense, and behaviors, such as stealing, that were common among Catholics, at least according to Douglas.[85] In this particular allegory, Corinna was a little girl who enjoyed her grandmother's "sanctuary" that included "images," "incense," and "ribbons." One day, Corinna decided that she would like to use some of these "images" when she played with her dolls. She removed them from the sanctuary in spite of the fact her grandmother had instructed her not to touch the images. Although Corinna had been a naughty child, she rehabilitated her reputation through her acceptance of the Protestant faith. In the words of Douglas's parable, Corinna, who later "heard the gospel preached," "learned that she must not take what does not belong to her, and neither must she or her dolls kneel down before an image."[86]

Douglas's journal reflected many instances of her personal satisfaction when such girls had made progress in appreciating "Christian truth." She prayed earnestly for her Catholic students and boarders who, by virtue of their religious affiliation, had not accepted the Gospel, at least in her definition. In October 1910, she wrote about one such student, Beatriz: "I pray constantly that she may be converted, she was saying today after she came from church, that since she has been here at school, and been studying the Bible, she has realized how far she was from Christ."[87] Although no journal entry explained her theological objections to Catholicism, Douglas commonly described Catholics as dishonest, two-faced, disingenuous, ignorant about the Bible's teachings, sexist, melodramatic, and obsessed with imagery. She particularly disapproved of Catholic services and expressed her dislike for their ritualism and the role assigned to the Virgin Mary. Referring to Englishman John Ruskin, a leading social and art critic in the nineteenth century and his book *The Stones of Venice,* Douglas criticized Catholic culture in Brazil ("It matters literally nothing to a Romanist what the image he worships is like"), and she described "the Papacy [as] being entirely heathen in all its principles."[88] While she was highly critical of the Catholic faith, likely more so in her journal than in conversation with Brazilians, Douglas often cited Protestant figures and intellects who had shaped and legitimized her religious views. In addition to John Ruskin, she referred to the writings of Englishman Richard Baxter, a seventeenth-century Puritan leader. While an ardent anti-Catholic, Margaret Douglas revealed intellectual curiosity and a penchant for debate, unlike many women of her generation.

In 1913, Margaret Douglas accepted the position of directress of her institution. Her responsibilities were far more administrative than anything else. As a result, she had considerably less time to develop close relationships with the growing student body than she had had as a teacher. Her attention fixated on school finances, fundraising, the religious and academic curriculum, official correspondence, and teacher training. Between 1913 and the early 1930s, the American College of Pernambuco significantly increased the number of its boarding students; expanded curriculum offerings to include more practical and feminine subjects like "domestic science"; hired more instructors; introduced more opportunities in athletics; purchased adjacent buildings and land; erected an auditorium and dining hall; installed gas lights and a modern sewage system; and renovated much of the original campus.[89] By the early 1920s, the institution educated approximately 175 students in grades one through high school each year. Thirty to forty of those were boarding students. Several unmarried female missionaries from the American South plus ten Brazilians constituted the school's staff.[90]

Despite her faults, this modern southern woman demonstrated intellect, ambition, and competence alongside her femininity and religious passions. If one is to accept the assessment produced by Mrs. C. Darby Fulton, the executive director of the Executive Committee of Foreign Missions of the Southern Presbyterian Church in Nashville, Margaret Douglas left an indelible print on innumerable Brazilian girls. In 1935, Mrs. Fulton took a cross-country tour of Brazil to visit with American College of Pernambuco (then named Agnes Erskine Presbyterian College) alumnae.[91] She was thoroughly impressed with the women who had benefited from this "superior" Christian education. Referring to some of those whom she met, Mrs. Fulton wrote: "In every case we found these women occupying places of responsibility and leadership in the life of their churches. They were far above the average level in intelligence and training and showed the unmistakable impress of this splendid school." She concluded that the school was "not a provincial affair but is an institution whose fine Christian character is making itself felt through this whole north section of Brazil."[92] Douglas remained in her administrative position until her death in 1940. The renamed Agnes Erskine Presbyterian College remains committed to its founding mission to this day.

FALLING SHORT OF THE IDEALIZED IMAGE?

Laura Haygood, Lula Whilden, and Margaret Douglas were three committed workers who labored for their missions and for God right up until their deaths. Despite their faults, often tied to some naivete and religious intolerance, they were devout, refined, maternal, and feminine professionals who sincerely believed that their efforts would benefit women worldwide as well as bring personal and professional satisfaction to countless southern women who were either inspired by them to enter missionary work or even served alongside them. If one is to compare them to their southern Protestant peers for whom sources exist, Haygood, Whilden, and Douglas were typical southern women engaged in faith-based pursuits during the late nineteenth and early twentieth centuries.[93] However, a few missionaries fell outside of this norm. These women did not live up to the idealized image of the southern lady as crafted by those like Haygood, Whilden, and Douglas and their respective denominations.

One example was Frances McBryde Worth of Wilmington, North Carolina, who briefly served with the PCUS in the Belgian Congo during the mid-1920s. Worth may have had the good breeding and sound education, but she fell short as a missionary who exuded a maternal, humble, and patient as well as competent and enterprising persona. Her primary role was to educate and train native teachers at a newly established PCUS mission school in the village of Bulape in the Belgian Congo. It remained under the strong influence of the Roman Catholic Church. Nonetheless, Presbyterians had made some progress in the ten years they had been sending missionaries there. At the Annual Conference of Evangelists in 1925, Worth reported that the number of PCUS missionaries had grown from just seven to "about a hundred people."[94]

The mission school, at which Worth would "be monarch of all I survey," included "over five hundred brats and 35 teachers."[95] Worth taught multiple Sunday school classes each week and assisted with church services. In her correspondence, Worth portrayed herself as a busy worker for Christ. Yet all too often she dwelled on gossip in North Carolina; complained about how her students exasperated her; expressed jealousy over female missionaries to whom their families had sent cars; or brooded over trivial matters, such as her inability to locate a bathing costume. In fact, Worth's correspondence reveals her as a woman who was whiny, short-tempered, and self-centered. If one is to accept the typicality of Haygood, Whilden, and Douglas, it is difficult to comprehend why the PCUS selected her as a missionary. Worth's private writings certainly tainted the image of female foreign missionaries that those like the PCUS advertised.

Frances Worth's many letters to her mother and sister further reveal that she harshly reinforced southern gender and racial customs among the native Congolese, those "at the bottom rung of primitiveness."[96] This included altering Congolese women's conceptions of marriage and motherhood in ways that more closely resembled those of southern white women. With regard to the former, she aimed to make "natives" look upon marriage in the "right way" by convincing them that their Christian marriage ceremonies were inappropriate. Perhaps Worth believed that such a primitive people was not worthy of an ostentatious display, one she may have associated with the elite southern wedding celebrations that sometimes lasted for a few days. Regardless of her reasoning, she informed her family that they were "inclined to make too much show and public parading."[97] On occasion, Worth resorted to corporal punishment, a practice not supported by her PCUS colleague Emma Larson, to ensure that her students had fully adopted her instruction and advice. In one letter, she recorded: "I took great pleasure the other day in lining up seven girls and slapping them all in front of the whole school! Since then they have behaved much better."[98] Although she was acting sixty years after the end of slavery, this North Carolina native treated natives with the same degree of condescension, disgust, and even violence that her female forebears had employed with their enslaved people.

Frances Worth left her African mission work after only two years of service and spent most of her future life in New York City, where she retired as an executive secretary for the Manhattan Ear, Nose & Throat Clinic.[99] Ever the lady obsessed with hierarchy, prestige, and her own self-importance, Worth's February 1989 obituary fittingly referred to her as an "honorary princess" in the Belgian Congo as well as mentioning her heritage, which included her direct descendance from King Edward I of England and King Malcolm II of Scotland.[100]

One must exercise a degree of caution with the sources with which these four southern missionary women left and be careful not to deify them as have their communities, churches, and heritage organizations. There is no denying that these women consciously and unconsciously helped craft an image of the lady of the New South that may have been overly idealized. Through their example, they unveiled their conceptions and models of southern womanhood to which elite and educated women could aspire in the years after Reconstruction. Unable to completely free themselves from the Old South, particularly notions pertaining to hierarchy and deference, decorum, and conceptions of femininity, they nonetheless promoted and defended their increasingly independent and professional lifestyles by, in part, laboring to liberate those women they served abroad.

EPILOGUE

FROM PEDESTAL TO PULPIT

Daughters of Divinity has explored dozens of white southern women and their faith-based experiences, pursuits, and careers over the course of a turbulent one hundred years in southern history. Between 1830 and 1930, the white South grappled, sometimes painfully and sometimes optimistically, with its identity as it applied to the past, present, and future. During this time, it lived through the latter years of the Second Great Awakening, an ever-evolving institution of slavery, an acrimonious relationship with the North, secession and the Civil War, reunion and Reconstruction, Redemption, redefined race relations and Jim Crow, modernity, urbanization, industrialization, Populism, progressivism, and more. The South witnessed more change, and at a faster pace, than in any other period since the English settlement of Jamestown, Virginia, in 1607. While the South sometimes embraced such development and moderation with vigor, in just as many instances, its privileged members longed for—after 1865—the perceived comforts of the past, namely those tied to racial, class, and gender hierarchies.

Elite, educated white southern women experienced this region-wide strife and confusion, and this work has placed them at the center of this struggle in southern identity. However, it has expanded the confines of southern identity from those of mere regional markers. Rather, by featuring gender as a category of analysis, this study has delved into women's debates concerning evolving concepts of southern womanhood. Indeed, female mission workers exemplified ambition and agency, yet did not appreciably challenge the comfortable and even conservative confines of Protestant culture. They assumed a vital role in delineating and at times expanding the bounds of gendered acceptability because they did not embody radical or feminist ideologies or practices. White southern men, while dynamic shapers of southern culture, did not entirely dictate definitions of gender.

Particularly in the years after 1880, with the creation of faith-based organizations and publications, missionary women assumed more influential, public-minded roles in which they gave speeches, wrote essays and articles, and took on administrative and leadership positions. In so doing, they offered their audiences what they believed to be a worthy archetype of southern womanhood. These women consciously set out to place their faith-based work in a favorable light in an attempt to recruit more individuals to, and encourage financial support for, their causes and projects. However, it is not as readily apparent whether they *intentionally* aimed to outline the feminine paragon of the South.

White southern female mission workers, along with their colleagues, their churches, and their families, left a veritable treasure trove of sources that provide insight into their professional lives. However, such records tend to paint an idealized history of their actions, beliefs, and identities. These sources include individual parish histories; denominational and organizational histories, newspapers, journals, and pamphlets; local histories; memoirs; obituaries; as well as institutional histories of mission training and denominational liberal arts colleges.[1] Significantly, they share one key component: all were intended to be read, at the time and in the future, by a larger public. Collectively, these records, most of which were mass produced, portray feminine, competent, well-educated, well-trained, well-bred, tireless, patient, modest, and devout southern women who had achieved success as professionals and as Christians. These sources, particularly pamphlet propaganda, identify female mission workers as sympathetic and committed workers for Christ who tried to uplift Blacks and poor whites in the South as well as Africans, Asians, and Latin Americans throughout the world.[2]

Although problematic, such sources are highly significant because they mark one of the first concerted efforts by white southern women to record— or perhaps make—their own histories for those beyond their extended families and communities. Such women took great initiative in constructing their own identities as well as those of their cherished colleagues. For example, and specific to the latter, several Woman's Missionary Union leaders assembled a booklet to be distributed at the August 1914 memorial service for Emma L.

Amos, dynamic Baptist activist, educator, and leader. The memorial booklet included a biography that highlighted Amos's academic and professional
accomplishments; various reminiscences and tributes; essays on her lasting
impact on the WMU and the broader Baptist community; information on a
church building fund established in Amos's honor; and even a twelve-stanza
poem reminiscent of the one penned by Anna, the antebellum classmate of
Sallie Didd Beck at Griffin Synodical Female College and discussed in the introduction. The former poem, written by a fellow female mission worker and
simply titled "Miss Emma L. Amos," underscored Amos's delicate, feminine
nature alongside her passion, Christian convictions, commitment, intelligence,
and fortitude. One representative stanza reads:

> And with the spirit of her Lord,
> She touched humanity for good,
> She left her impress on the world,
> Because for God and right she stood.[3]

Emma Amos's memorial booklet is a testament not only to her far-reaching
contributions and unwavering faith but to the supportive and sentimental sis-
terhood of mission workers. It also reinforces the idea that women, in particular, exercised moral authority and served as commanding, yet compassionate,
evangelizers. Quite simply, Amos's peers contributed to the construction of
an idealized form of white southern womanhood.

Male church ministers and those who held leadership positions within their
respective denominations corroborated these southern female mission workers. For example, Reverend Egbert W. Smith, field secretary of the Executive
Committee of Foreign Missions in the southern Presbyterian church, memorialized long-time missionary Margaret Douglas with excessively laudatory
words. Published in the September 1940 issue of the *Presbyterian Survey*, Smith
hyperbolized: "The effect of this Christlike serenity and sweetness of spirit
upon the thousands of girls who passed under her care, eternity alone can
measure. No wonder they admired and loved her. No wonder they tried to be
like her. For, however excellent our teaching may be, it is our daily example
that makes the deepest and most lasting impression."[4]

Smith identified Douglas as a skilled teacher and a woman worthy of emulation, yet, in referring to the latter's "Christlike serenity" and "sweetness of

spirit," the Presbyterian cleric stressed that female mission workers of the early twentieth century still exhibited feminine and nonthreatening traits that had been associated with antebellum southern ladies. The role such a woman played in southern society may have functioned as an informal compromise between middle-class and elite men and women. Alternately, men and women afforded southern female mission workers a degree of authority and influence so long as they preserved tradition and only tentatively embraced modernity. In the process, such women forged an unofficial coalition with southern men by which they preserved race and class dynamics, all in "honorable" ways.

By her very book title—*The Southern Lady: From Pedestal to Politics, 1830–1930*—Anne Firor Scott implied that, by the start of the fourth decade of the twentieth century, elite southern women had finally stepped down from that highly conspicuous and idealized pillar on which they had stood in the years before the Civil War and, many might argue, beyond. This book, however, concludes that privileged southern women who engaged in faith-based work and careers may not have wanted to jettison their idolized place on the pedestal after all. Rather, white female mission workers sought to redefine that pedestal on their own terms, one that simultaneously celebrated their Old South identities, traditions, and politics and endorsed their New South lives in the public sphere.

NEW RELIGIOUS ROLES

Redefinition of that pedestal continued in the decades after 1930. Mission activity among white southern women did not evaporate in those years, although their religious institutions and their roles within those institutions experienced profound change. Specific to the former, some Protestant denominations in the South questioned their viability to remain separate from their northern branches. This book has recounted those years leading up to the Civil War, when the Methodist Episcopal, Baptist, Presbyterian, and Episcopal churches all experienced schism due to different stances on the institution of slavery. The Episcopal Church's split—which created the Episcopal Church in the Confederate States but was never officially recognized by the northern wing—was briefest of all. It lasted a mere five years from 1861 to 1866. In contrast, the southern branches of the Methodist Episcopal, Baptist, and

Presbyterian churches remained separate from their northern counterparts for many generations.

Of these three denominations, Methodists were the first to broker reunification of the Methodist Episcopal Church with the Methodist Episcopal Church, South (MEC, South).[5] The topic of reunification had been broached by clerics immediately after the Civil War as well as during the 1910s.[6] However, during the 1930s leaders from both branches expressed a renewed desire for reunion. As a testament to this commitment, representatives from both regional branches, along with those from the much smaller Methodist Protestant Church, formed the Joint Committee on Unification. Racial divides, however, threatened the success of the merger. Influential bishops and laymen within the MEC, South did not support reunion should it be contingent upon acceptance of Black church members. Stretching back to those first immediate years after the Civil War, the MEC, South, had essentially operated as an institution for whites only. Desiring a religious environment entirely apart from that of whites, large numbers of Blacks had joined the African Methodist Episcopal Church, the African Methodist Episcopal Zion Church, and the (Northern) Methodist Episcopal Church. However, those who remained in the MEC, South, felt increasingly alien and uncomfortable, splitting from their white peers in 1870 to form the Colored Methodist Episcopal Church. A merger would thus incorporate those Blacks who had joined the (Northern) Methodist Episcopal Church, the result of which would be a denomination with nearly 326,000 Black members. After some compromise between the northern and southern factions, reunification occurred on December 5, 1939, at which time the branches merged to form the Methodist Church. Although the merger was a step toward interregional reconciliation, it did not resolve the issue of racial segregation within the church. In fact, and as a concession to southern Methodists, the new church assigned autonomy to individual congregations to address race issues, particularly as they pertained to membership, as they saw fit. The Methodist Church did not meaningfully confront racial divides until it merged with the Evangelical United Brethren Church to form the United Methodist Church in 1968.

Scholars have given scant attention to the role that women played in the 1939 Methodist merger. While women's contributions were overshadowed by the more public roles of male church leaders, their involvement was essential to the merger's success. Women from the South did contribute to discussions and decisions that shaped the unification process. Their involvement ranged from advocacy for inclusivity and equality to practical contributions in organizing and implementing the merger. The latter marks an occasion when some white southern women diverged from their typically conservative racial politics. For example, Louise Young, a Tennessee native and professor of sociology at Scarritt College for Christian Workers in Nashville, Tennessee, served as a liaison between the Woman's Missionary Council and the Black community. Young listened to dissatisfied Black Methodist leaders and their concerns for representation, leadership, and fair treatment in the proposed new church. In 1936, Young chaired the Woman's Missionary Council's Committee on Interracial Co-operation, whose purpose was to study the "effect of the proposed plan of Methodist unification on the Negro membership." The next year, Young assumed leadership of the Study Group on Unification and Race Relations, a subgroup of the Committee on Interracial Co-operation.[7]

After the 1939 merger, Methodist women faced a multitude of new and exciting opportunities in the church. Some roles were natural extensions of those that southern female mission workers had filled in the nineteenth and early twentieth centuries, while others were radically different. Specific to the former, southern women continued to seek opportunities in mission work, both domestically and internationally. As their mothers, grandmothers, and great-grandmothers had before them, southern Methodist women of the mid-twentieth century played key roles in establishing and administering missions, schools, and hospitals, and, in the process, leveraged their positions to advance social causes and outreach programs. Similarly, southern women assumed substantial roles as lay leaders. They served on church boards, committees, and various church organizations where they led efforts in such "feminine" areas as education, youth work, and community service.

However, other Methodist women in the South yearned for greater influence and positions of authority, and, like their long-ago female forebears, pushed for expanded educational and professional opportunities in religious work. In so doing, this generation of mid-to-late twentieth century Methodist women helped expand the boundaries of southern womanhood ... yet again. While lauded by feminists for their bold and modern views, these women were, ironically, using the same arguments for advancement as had been employed by southern women generations before. They believed that their stereotypically feminine strengths, for example, empathy, communication, and multitasking abilities, would be assets. They also maintained that, compared to men, they prioritized collaboration and inclusivity as well as added a uniquely female perspective on theological matters. Methodist women from the South served as district superintendents and conference leaders, but, most transformative of all, they found themselves leading from the pulpit. In 1956, the General Conference of the Methodist Church approved full clergy rights for women, although opposition remained strong for many years to come. In wake of that 1956 decision, seminaries began admitting women, and, in due time, female theologians and scholars emerged who contributed to the development of Methodist thought.

Southern Presbyterians reunited with their northern peers much later than did the Methodists. In 1983, the United Presbyterian Church in the United States of America (also known as the Northern Presbyterian Church) came together with the Presbyterian Church of the United States (PCUS) to form the Presbyterian Church (USA). However, southern Presbyterian women pursued the clergy many years before the 1983 merger. The PCUS ordained its first woman, Rachel Henderlite, in 1965. A Henderson, North Carolina, native, Henderlite was ordained at All Souls Presbyterian Church in Richmond, a predominantly Black congregation that she helped establish. She also earned the distinction of being the first full-time female faculty member at a PCUS seminary. As had her Methodist counterparts, Henderlite faced opposition from both men and women, receiving numerous letters that condemned her ordination as unscriptural. She was a participant in the famous March on Washington in 1963 as well as the Selma-Montgomery March in 1965, and her values did not align with those of the majority of southern female Presbyterians.[8]

In 2024, the Southern Baptist Convention (SBC) remains wholly separate from the American Baptist Churches USA (formerly the Northern Baptist Convention). The SBC, generally more theologically and socially conservative than its Methodist, Presbyterian, and Episcopalian counterparts, has been reticent to embrace expanded leadership roles for women. However, the liberal Watts Street Church in Durham, North Carolina, ordained Addie Davis to the gospel ministry in 1964.[9] A graduate of Meredith College and Southeastern Baptist Theological Seminary, Davis held progressive views on race similar to those of Henderlite. After her ordination, Davis searched long for a church in the South to whom she could pastor but did not find a Southern Baptist Church open to her leadership. Instead, Davis found a new professional home at the First Baptist Church in Readsboro, Vermont. The SBC has remained closed to female pastors. It holds to a complementarian view of gender roles, which asserts that men and women have distinct roles that complement each other. According to this perspective, which is grounded in scripture, pastoral leadership is a role reserved for men.[10]

In contrast to those southern women who have pursued positions as ministers and pastors, other southern women—whose politics may more closely align with those of their female ancestors that have been covered in this book—have found community in conservative national (and even international) evangelical organizations. These organizations spawned in response to discomfort with the social and political upheaval engendered in the 1960s. Some southern women, for example, have found a spiritual outlet in Women's Aglow Fellowship International. Incorporated in 1972, Aglow seeks to reclaim traditional roles for men and women that reinforce male authority and female subservience. It attracts primarily white, middle-class women who live in the suburbs in the Sun Belt.[11] Still other southern women have found idols worthy of emulation in such charismatic Christian Rights women's leaders as Tammy Faye Bakker, cohost of the PTL ("Praise the Lord") Club, and Anita Bryant, popular singer turned born-again Christian and antihomosexual crusader.[12] Together, these more conservative female activists have ardently rejected feminism, replacing it with a womanhood defined by submission and domesticity.

Modern-day white, southern women engaged in religious pursuits continue to celebrate, copy, expand, or adjust stances and tactics advanced by southern female mission workers of yesteryear. While ideologically and theologically diverse, such women share an enduring commitment to shaping and reshaping *their* conceptions of womanhood.

NOTES

INTRODUCTION

1. Corley, "The Presbyterian Quest," 89.

2. Ibid., 89–90.

3. Sallie Didd Beck Johnson Commonplace Book, 1860–81.

4. Wesley, *The Politics of Faith*, 3.

5. See Boles, *The Great Revival*; Carney, *Ministers and Masters*; Harlow, *Religion, Race, and the Making of Confederate Kentucky*; and Noll, *Civil War as a Theological Crisis*.

6. Higginbotham, *Righteous Discontent*.

7. For a sampling of newer scholarship on this topic, see Bettye Collier-Thomas, *Jesus, Jobs, and Justice* (Temple University Press, 2013); Marla Frederick, *Between Sundays* (University of California Press, 2003); Cheryl Townsend Gilkes, *If It Wasn't for the Women* (Orbis Books, 2001); and Demetrius Williams, *An End to This Strife* (Fortress, 2004).

8. Scott, *The Southern Lady*.

9. Historian Christine Leigh Heyrman takes a similar approach in her book *American Apostles: When American Evangelicals Entered the World of Islam*. A study of failed missionary activity in the Islamic world by Americans during the early republic era, *American Apostles* analyzes how such failures galvanized values and ideas among American evangelicals while stoking curiosity about exotic people and lands.

10. See Elder, *Love and Duty*; Fredette, *Marriage on the Border*; and Molloy, *Single, White, Slaveholding Women*.

11. Olmsted, *Journey in the Seaboard Slave States*.

12. Farnham, *Education of the Southern Belle*, 30.

13. Faust, *Mothers of Invention*, 85.

14. Whites, *Civil War as a Crisis in Gender*.

15. Gardner, *Blood & Irony*.

16. Janney, *Burying the Dead but Not the Past*.

17. Cox, *Dixie's Daughters*.

18. Cash, *The Mind of the South*.

19. Robert, ed., *Gospel Bearers*.

1. THE FORMATIVE YEARS

1. Heyrman, *Southern Cross*, 5, appendix, 264–65.

2. Ibid., 160. See also Carney, *Ministers and Masters* and Friedman, *Enclosed Garden*.

3. As quoted in Lyerly, *Methodism and the Southern Mind*, 109. See also Morgan, "Grow We Must," 1–5.

4. Stephan, *Redeeming the Southern Family*. See also Stephan, "Reconsidering the Boundaries of Maternal Authority in the Evangelical Household."

5. Elizabeth Willis Gloster Anderson Memoranda, 1822–1862, "Description of Contents," Folder 1, p. 1, University of North Carolina Southern Historical Collection.

6. Biographical information about the Anderson family, including Elizabeth Willis Gloster Anderson, can be found in Elizabeth Willis Gloster Anderson Memoranda, "History," Folder 1, pp. 1–15 and "Penny Nichols Family Tree" on Ancestry.com, accessed April 23, 2024. See https://www.ancestry.com/family-tree/person/tree/108467607/person/352488831172/facts.

7. The term "college," particularly "ladies' college," had a different meaning during much of the nineteenth century and should not be compared to popular use of the term "college" in the contemporary era. Specific to the early and mid-nineteenth century, "college" was used interchangeably with "seminary" or "academy." Female colleges of the antebellum era did not grant degrees, nor did they prepare students to enter a degree-granting institution. However, I use the term "college" to mimic the terminology used by educators of the day as well as modern-day scholars who study early women's education.

8. Farnham, *Education of the Southern Belle*, 37, 50, 103.

9. The date of Annie Belle Northen's history of Mt. Zion Academy is unknown. However, it likely dates to the early twentieth century. See "Mt. Zion Academy" in Northen Family Papers, 1832–1944.

10. Clinton, "Equally Their Due."

11. Farnham cites North Carolina governor John Ellis's 1860 data on female higher education in the South. According to Ellis, the state of North Carolina boasted thirteen female colleges, Georgia had at least ten female colleges, Tennessee had five, while Florida was the only southern state without a female college. See Farnham, 18; Statistics of Bevier in Young, *A Study of the Curricula of Seven Selected Women's Colleges of the Southern States*, 56; Gov. John Ellis cited in Powell, *Higher Education in North Carolina*, 7.

12. See Schweiger, *A Literate South* and "The Literate South," and Wells, *Women Writers and Journalists in the Nineteenth-Century South*. Historian Anya Jabour likewise underscores the theme of intellectual development among adolescent southern females in chapter 2 of *Scarlett's Sisters* as well as in "'Grown Girls, Highly Cultivated.'"

13. See Junk, "Ladies Arise"; and Bumpass, *Frances Webb Bumpass, Autobiography and Journal*.

14. Historian Jonathan Daniel Wells estimates that there were a "dozen or so women" who edited antebellum southern magazines and newspapers. See chapter 5 of Wells, *Women Writers and Journalists in the Nineteenth-Century South* and chapter 4 of Wells, *The Origins of the Southern Middle Class, 1800–1861*.

15. For discussion of, and praise for, the opening of women's religiously backed

academies and colleges, see Adam Leopold Alexander to Sarah Gilbert Alexander, 13 August 1835, and W. Baud to Adam Leopold Alexander, 13 September 1848, Alexander and Hillhouse Family Papers, 1758–1976.

16. See chapter 3 of Kelley, *Learning to Stand and Speak,* for more detail on purpose, demographics, curriculum, and leadership of antebellum female institutions of higher learning.

17. J. Edwin Spears, speech to the Female College of Bennettsville, South Carolina, 9 June 1859, Louis Manigault Papers.

18. See also Miscellaneous Student Notebooks, 1820–1921, Byrd Family Papers, 1791–1867, and Northen Family Papers, 1832–1944. The Byrd family collection includes letters written by Lucy Carter McGuire, great-granddaughter of William Byrd III, during the 1850s about female education in a seminary setting, while the Northen family collection includes an array of notebooks kept by students, many of which include religious material. Of particular interest are two notebooks kept by Eliza Ann Orr, a student in Caswell County, North Carolina (institutional affiliation unknown). Orr's notebooks include religious poems, exercises, essays, and sermon texts that are reminiscent of the content within Martha Elizabeth Coons's notebook. The latter collection (Northen Family) contains religious essays written by Annie B. Northen during the early 1880s when she was a student at Southern Female College in LaGrange, Georgia.

19. Miscellaneous Student Notebooks, 1859, n.p.

20. See Ellen McAlpin Notebook and Visitors' Book, 1882–1913.

21. Ibid., n.p.

22. Examples of other southern women who used diaries or journals as religious outlets include Laura Beecher Comer of Columbia, Georgia; Mary Jeffreys Bethell of Rockingham County, North Carolina; Jane Evans Elliot of Fayetteville, North Carolina; and Lucila Agnes McCorkle of Talladega, Alabama. See Laura Beecher Comer Papers, 1862–1899; Mary Jeffreys Bethell Diary, 1853–1873; Jane Evans Elliot Diaries, 1837–1882; and William P. McCorkle Papers, 1806–1922. Maria Baker Taylor's private writings and journal offer particular insight and depth into intellectual musings related to evangelical Christianity. Taylor, a devout Baptist and plantation mistress in Beaufort, South Carolina, and Osceola, Florida, was the granddaughter of religious leader Richard Furman. See Schwartz, ed., *Baptist Faith in Action.*

23. An emerging literature exists that considers the practice of journal- and diary-keeping among nineteenth-century women, including southern women. Collectively, it addresses such topics as the politics and conscious construction of, and gendered conceptions found in, women's diaries. See Bunkers, "Diaries"; Fialka, "Textual Healing"; Harrison, "Rhetorical Rehearsals"; and O'Brien, *An Evening When Alone.*

24. See George Galphin Nowlan and Ann Elizabeth Nowlan MacDonnell Diaries.

25. Sarah Wadley's residences between 1859 and 1865 included Amite in Tangipahoa Parish, Monroe, and Oakland in Ouachita Parish, Louisiana, as well as near Macon, Georgia. See Sarah Lois Wadley Papers, 1849–1886; Sarah Wadley Journal, Volume 2, Thursday, December 18, 1862.

26. In addition to her family's library, Sarah referred to her personal "book closet, about a foot wide and seven feet high, but which affords [her] an emmence deal of comfort for its

size." Sarah turned fifteen in November 1859. Wadley Journal, Volume 1, Saturday, December 17, 1859.

27. Wadley Journal, Volume 1, Sunday, March 17, 1861.

28. Wadley Journal, Volume 1, Monday, January 7, 1861. See also journal entries in which Sarah critiqued live sermons: Wadley Journal, Volume 1, Monday, December 10, 1860; Wadley Journal, Volume 1, Monday, December 10, 1860; Wadley Journal, Volume 2, Sunday, July 14, 1861; Wadley Journal, Volume 2, Monday, October 7, 1861; Wadley Journal, Volume 2, Monday, November 11, 1861; Wadley Journal, Volume 3, Sunday, July 26, 1863; and Wadley Journal, Volume 3, Monday, March 12, 1865.

29. Wadley Journal, Volume 2, Sunday, November 30, 1862.

30. Wadley Journal, Volume 3, Thursday, August 13, 1863.

31. Wadley Journal, Volume 1, Tuesday, October 2, 1860.

32. Wadley Journal, Volume 2, Wednesday, September 18, 1862; Wadley Journal, Volume 3, Sunday evening, April 24, 1864.

33. Moore, *Adaptation of Religion to Female Character*, 3.

34. Ibid., 4.

35. Another gendered discourse includes Slaughter, *Man and Woman*.

36. Reverend Moore certainly conveyed such a notion within his discourse. In his words, "the attributes of man's nature stretch out their strong and rugged roots towards the earth … whilst those of woman lift up their graceful stems and unfold their fragrant foliage to the sky." See Moore, *Adaptation of Religion to Female Character*, 4.

37. N.p., religious poetry within Barbour Family Papers, 1810–1890, Section 13.

38. Sallie Didd Beck Johnson Commonplace Book, 1860–1881, n.p. religious poetry.

39. The Methodist Episcopal Church, South, especially when compared to the Episcopal and Presbyterian denominations, enjoyed a "democratic" reputation in which hierarchy played a minimal role. Although the title "Brother" does not signify one as a minister or church leader, Mary Jeffreys Bethell explicitly identifies Bruton and Brother Reid as ministers. One may assume that the Methodist Episcopal Church, South, formally ordained these two men. See Mary Jeffreys Bethell Diary, 12 July 1861.

40. Mary Jeffreys Bethell Diary, 12 July 1861.

41. Mary Jeffreys Bethell Diary, 12 February 1863.

42. For examples of Mrs. Bethell's demonstrated self-doubt, see Mary Jeffreys Bethell Diary, 30 June 1862; 15 May 1863; 29 July 1863.

43. Hebrews 4:16, "Let us therefore come boldly unto the throne of grace, that we may obtain mercy, and find grace to help in time of need" (King James Bible).

44. Mary Jeffreys Bethell Diary, 25 December 1861.

45. Female Mite Societies of South Carolina, p. 1.

46. The first southern female mite society was established on Edisto Island, South Carolina, in 1811. According to Loulie Owens's (admittedly) incomplete list, women organized at least sixteen female mite societies between 1811 and 1844 within South Carolina. Ibid., 1–2. See also Decker, *A Continuing Light, 1813–1963*, 10.

47. Loulie Latimer Owens (1912–1998), the first Special Collections librarian at Furman University and later an assistant manuscript librarian at the South Caroliniana Library at the University of South Carolina, sustained a nearly lifelong interest in the history of the

Baptist faith, particularly South Carolina Baptist women in mission work. Among her projects as an assistant manuscript librarian at the South Caroliniana was her compilation of materials relating to, and historical sketches of, the early Baptist mite societies in South Carolina. See Loulie Latimer Owens Papers, 1940–1989: Biographical Sketch, accessed on April 23, 2024: https://libguides.furman.edu/special-collections/loulie-owens-papers/biography. In Loulie Owens's words, the female mite societies "differed from the woman's missionary society [a postbellum organization] in that it was indigenous and had no affiliation with other societies." See Female Mite Societies, p. 1.

48. Ibid., 3–6.

49. Ibid., 4.

50. See https://warwick.ac.uk/fac/arts/southerncharitiesproject/database/state/ (accessed August 11, 2024).

51. Mathews, *Religion in the Old South*, 19–20.

52. Schweiger, *Gospel Working Up*, 84.

53. Aside from Schweiger's *Gospel Working Up*, two other works that explore this theme of institutional building among evangelicals are Mathews, *Religion in the Old South*, and Quist, *Restless Visionaries*.

54. Historian Emily Wright adds to this discussion of activist women engaged in religious work outside of the home during the antebellum era. Wright examines what she calls public female stewardship, namely women who used their "time, talent, and treasure to build and furnish church structures" in the Gulf South (Alabama, Mississippi, and Louisiana). Such women exercised authority regarding church furnishing and architecture as well as church maintenance and decoration. In Wright's words, "the movement to build and furnish new churches in the region was not the moment of Protestant women's religious domestication, but rather an opportunity for a new type of public stewardship of the church, one that encouraged female collective action." See Wright, "'A Doorkeeper in the House of My God,'" https://jsreligion.org/vo121/wright/ (accessed August 11, 2024).

55. Lebsock, *The Free Women of Petersburg*, 196.

2. EVANGELIZING THE ENSLAVED

1. In spite of the immense scholarship on elite southern women, historians have largely failed to address the role that antebellum plantation mistresses played relative to the religious instruction of their enslaved. In the over fifty years since Anne Firor Scott published *The Southern Lady: From Pedestal to Politics, 1830–1930*, historians have examined antebellum elite white southern women in virtually all of the South's subregions, have studied these women as daughters, sisters, wives, and parents, have portrayed these women as benevolent slave mistresses, abusive mistresses, and everything in between, and have considered the numerous types of relationships that mistresses forged with their enslaved men and women. They have remained virtually silent on the religious instruction provided by such women. Notable scholarship on slaveholding women includes Scott, *The Southern Lady*; Clinton, *The Plantation Mistress*; Weiner, *Mistresses and Slaves*; Fox-Genovese, *Within the Plantation Household*; Molloy, *Single, White, Slaveholding Women in the Nineteenth-Century American South*; and Jones-Rogers, *They Were Her Property*.

2. See Mathews, *Religion in the Old South.*

3. Raboteau, *Slave Religion.*

4. Eighteen-thirty is not an entirely random year. My reasons for starting with this year are two-fold. First, a uniquely southern culture had emerged by 1830. Second, religion and the church became more prominent institutions in the South by the end of the third decade of the nineteenth century. The Second Great Awakening had substantively shaped southerners' politics and social, gender, and racial hierarchies and relations in addition to their religious practices and beliefs by this point. See Heyrman, *Southern Cross,* and Part II: Grace, Southern Religion in Transition (particularly chapters 4, 5, and 7) of Wyatt-Brown, *The Shaping of Southern Culture.*

5. Genovese, *Fatal Self-Deception.*

6. See Scott, *The Southern Lady,* and Weiner, *Mistresses and Slaves.*

7. Irons, *The Origins of Proslavery Christianity.*

8. Rohrer, "Slaveholding Women and the Religious Instruction of Slaves in Post-Emancipation Memory."

9. Lucilla Agnes Gamble McCorkle Diary, 1 January 1858, William Parson McCorkle Papers, 1806–1922.

10. See also Mary Jeffreys Bethell Civil War Diary, 1 January 1862; Laura Beecher Comer Papers, 1862–1899, 1 January 1862; Sarah Lois Wadley Papers, 1849–1886, 31 December 1860.

11. "The Diary of an Episcopalian, the Rev. Francis Hanson," August 1858 quoted in Boles, ed., *Masters & Slaves in the House of the Lord,* 116.

12. McTyeire, *Duties of Christian Masters,* 170. McTyeire later served as a bishop to the Methodist Episcopal Church, South, assisted in the organization of the Colored Methodist Episcopal Church South and cofounded Vanderbilt University. See https://tennessee encyclopedia.net/entries/holland-n-mctyeire/ (accessed August 11, 2024).

13. Lounsbury, ed., *Louisa S. McCord,* 152. McCord's piece appeared shortly after the Seneca Falls Convention (1848), the first meeting of significance which discussed women's rights. McCord's contentions about the white female role were antithetical to most of those advanced by Susan B. Anthony and Elizabeth Cady Stanton.

14. Ella Noland MacKenzie Miscellaneous Papers, "On Obedience," November 24, 1849.

15. Mary Boykin Chesnut was one southern-born plantation mistress who would strongly disagree with the more conservative Louisa S. McCord. While Chesnut identified with the omnipotent planter class, she was not reticent to criticize the institution of slavery and patriarchy. See Woodward and Muhlenfeld, eds., *The Private Mary Chesnut.* Likewise, contemporary scholars readily accept the reality of subordination of women and the enslaved in antebellum society and the role that evangelical Christianity played in reinforcing this dual phenomenon. Examples include: chapter 4 in Blum and Harvey, *The Color of Christ;* chapters 4 and 5 in Carney, *Ministers and Masters;* chapters 2, 5, 10, and 11 in Clinton, *The Plantation Mistress;* and chapters 3, 4, and 5 in Heyrman, *Southern Cross.*

16. Lucilla Agnes Gamble McCorkle Diary, no date (p. 1).

17. These northern texts doubtlessly were referring to free, nonenslaved servants, but elite white southern women nonetheless took such advice and applied it to their enslaved people.

18. Wise, *Bridal Greetings*, 111. See also Wise, *The Young Lady's Counsellor.*

19. It is impossible to estimate the frequency of plantation behavior which prohibited work on Sunday. In reality, some masters would have granted the enslaved complete, or even partial, rest on the Sabbath Day.

20. Maria Southgate Hawes Diary, 8 March 1863.

21. Cornelius, *When I Can Read My Title Clear.*

22. Caroline Elizabeth Burgwin Clitherall Diary, 1 January 1854.

23. Richard Furman was an unabashed defender of slavery. However, he deeply cared about the spiritual welfare of enslaved people. In wake of the Denmark Vesey Conspiracy in 1822, an alleged enslaved rebellion in Charleston, some white South Carolinians wondered whether evangelization of the enslaved encouraged violent resistance. Furman, however, remained ever more committed to his Christian mission to the enslaved. See https://libguides.furman.edu/legacyofslavery/richardfurmanexposition (accessed August 11, 2024).

24. Schwartz, ed., *Baptist Faith in Action.*

25. Everard Green Baker Diaries, 1 June 1849. Note: Although the source cited reflects the sentiments of Everard Baker—and not Laura Alexander Baker—he explicitly noted that both he and his wife were in agreement relative to this issue.

26. Mary Jeffreys Bethell Diary, 30 November 1856.

27. Mississippian Katherine Polk Gale is another slaveholding woman notable for her support of enslaved salvation. See Gale and Polk Family Papers, 1815–1940.

28. Rawick, ed., *The American Slave: Supplement, Series 1, Vol. 12*, 59–60.

29. Mary Jeffreys Bethell Diary, 4 October 1857.

30. Ingraham, ed. *The Sunny South*, 210.

31. Caroline Elizabeth Burgwin Clitherall Diary, 29 January 1854.

32. To a significant degree, these realities applied to slaveholding women who recorded their experiences before the Second Great Awakening and the rise of evangelism in the antebellum South.

33. Moore, ed., *A Plantation Mistress on the Eve of the Civil War*, 86.

34. See Mary Bateman Diary, 10 February 1856; Cyrena Bailey Stone Diary, 1864.

35. Burr, ed., *The Secret Eye*, 236.

36. Moore, ed., *A Plantation Mistress on the Eve of the Civil War*, 85.

37. Antebellum enslaved narratives contended that plantation mistresses who conducted Sabbath Schools did not do so out of a genuine concern for the spiritual welfare nor the ultimate salvation of their enslaved people. They complained about difficult mistress/enslaved relationships and the inability and/or unwillingness of mistresses to contemplate those cultural differences that separated them from the Black population. See Lane, *The Narrative of Lunsford Lane*, 19–20, and Stroyer, *My Life in the South*, 46.

38. Robinson, *From Log Cabin to the Pulpit*, 86.

39. For examples of enslaved people who completely resisted their mistresses' religious instruction, see: Brown, *Narrative of William W. Brown*, 34; Drew, *A North-side View of Slavery*, 62–63; French, *Slavery in South Carolina and the Ex-Slaves*, 162. For a more general discussion of those enslaved who rejected mistress-directed religious education, see Raboteau, *Slave Religion*, 293–95.

40. Susan Cornwall Diary, 7 March 1857. Note: Entire discussion of Susan Cornwall is based upon this one lengthy journal entry.

41. Fox-Genovese, *Within the Plantation Household*. See also White, *Ar'n't I a Woman*.

42. Susan Cornwall Diary, 7 March 1857.

43. Susan Cornwall Diary, 1 May 1857.

44. Andrews, ed., *Memoirs of Mrs. Ann R. Page*, 47–48.

45. Mary Eliza Eve Carmichael Diary, 6 March 1842.

46. Examples include Mary Jeffreys Bethell, Mary Eliza Eve Carmichael, Lucilla Agnes Gamble McCorkle, and Sarah Lois Wadley. Elite white women continued to hold such internalized beliefs about African American religion—particularly perceptions of "excessive emotionalism" and the need for white women to correct such emotional religious expression—long after the Civil War. South Carolinian Sudie Miller Furman Dabbs received an illustrative letter in 1890 in which her aunt wrote: "I was quite entertained by your account of the Colored [Baptist] Association. There is certainly no lack of enthusiasm among them. Many of them, have yet to learn, that religion is not a thing of mere emotion. There is a great deal yet to be done for those people, and in doing it, we must be governed by the law of Christian love." See "Aunt Ann of Greenville, SC" to Susan "Sudie" Miller Furman Dabbs, 9 November 1890, Sudie Miller Furman Dabbs papers, 1858–1926.

47. LeClercq, ed., *Between North and South*, 31.

48. Woodward and Muhlenfeld, eds., *The Private Mary Chesnut*, 167–68.

49. Those mistress diaries which specifically referred to enslaved preachers included passages in which the author certainly acknowledged her awareness of them and their activities. This is not to say that mistresses described religious interaction between themselves and enslaved clergymen, but rather that they expressed a horror that the enslaved clergy-directed expressions and practices were very different from their own.

50. Christine Leigh Heyrman cites many instances in which nonevangelical slaveholding whites—both male and female—found African American religious displays "uncomfortable" and "threatening." Evangelical whites may have explained their religious expressions and even talents as the "divine power" alone enabling "black virtuosos to transcend their 'natural inferiority.'" Nonevangelicals, however, saw in Black religious performances evidence of "innate talents all too disturbing to such masters when African Americans, especially their own enslaved, suddenly shed poses of submission to reveal potent selves compelling people of both races." See Heyrman, *Southern Cross*, 220, and chapter 5.

51. LeClercq, ed., *Between North and South*, 22.

52. Ibid., 44.

53. See Jones, *The Religious Instruction of Negroes*, as one example.

54. Kemble, *Journal of a Residence on a Georgian Plantation in 1838–1839*, 125–26.

55. Smedes, *Memorials of a Southern Planter*, 191.

56. "Slave of Slaves" is the title of chapter 2 of Catherine Clinton's *The Plantation Mistress*. While the entire book highlights the underappreciated challenges that slaveholding women faced, chapter 2 offers a particularly sympathetic interpretation. Included here is a discussion of their difficulties regarding plantation administration (which included, among others, financial and housekeeping responsibilities); management of the enslaved; and caring for and educating their own biological families. Exacerbating this was the

reality that such women could often not rely on their husbands—who were frequently out of town—for any assistance. Unfortunately, this chapter does not incorporate any discussion of religion, let alone any treatment of mistresses' religious instruction of the enslaved.

3. FOREIGN MISSION WORK IN LIBERIA

1. According to a March 1860 *New York Times* article that covered Bishop John Payne's lecture on the Episcopal mission in Africa, there existed "eight female assistants," at least half of whom were missionary wives. The Episcopal mission "and their field cover[ed] 300 miles of coast and 90 miles in the interior." See No author, "Missions in Africa; INTERESTING ADDRESS ON AFRICA BY BISHOP PAYNE, MISSIONARY BISHOP TO AFRICA FROM THE EPISCOPAL CHURCH," *New York Times,* March 13, 1860.

2. Martha Jane Williford to Martha Stackhouse Williford Service, 4 August 1849, Emma Maria Service Papers, 1803–1892.

3. I reconstructed Martha Jane Williford's early life through Georgia Property Tax Digests, 1793–1892; the 1850 U.S. Federal Census—Slave Schedules; and the 1860 United States Federal Census. See www.ancestry.com/.

4. See https://www.georgiahistory.com/ghmi_marker_updated/montpelier-institute/ (accessed August 12, 2024).

5. See Farnham, *The Education of the Southern Belle, 75.*

6. Martha Jane Williford to Martha Stackhouse Williford Service, 4 August 1849.

7. *Missionary Register for MDCCCLI, 16.*

8. Martha Jane Williford to Martha Stackhouse Williford Service, 11 January 1850.

9. *Missionary Register for MDCCCL, 11–12.*

10. See Koppen Climate Classification System, the most accepted system used to classify the climates of places on Earth. See https://w2.weather.gov/media/jetstream/global /Koppen-Geiger.pdf (accessed May 6, 2024).

11. The state of Maryland has particular ties to the section of Liberia where the Episcopal Church established the Cape Palmas Mission. By the 1820s, the institution of slavery was enduring a slow death in the Upper South, and, in response, the Maryland state legislature, in 1831, appropriated $10,000 (over the course of twenty-six years) for the transportation of free Blacks and formerly enslaved people from the United States to Africa. Soon after this, the Maryland State Colonization Society—originally a branch of ACS—established a settlement, a colony, apart from the ACS that could accommodate its emigrants. African American intellectual and political leaders, James W. C. Pennington included, argued that southern whites who supported emigration did so not out of any sympathy toward African Americans but because of their economic, political, and social interests. For example, emigration of newly freed enslaved people and free Blacks would reduce competition for jobs among the poorer class of whites. For information regarding the State of Maryland's role in establishing the colony, see Latrobe, *Maryland in Liberia.* For more general information regarding the African American community's divergent reaction to issues of emigration, see Davis, *The Problem of Slavery in the Age of Emancipation;* Kinshasa, *Emigration vs. Assimilation;* Levine, *Martin Delany, Frederick Douglass, and the*

Politics of Representative Identity; Moses, *Liberian Dreams;* and Power-Greene, *Against Wind and Tide.*

12. This prompts another question: what were the demographics within Liberia and/or Cape Palmas at the time of Martha Williford and Reverend John Payne's tenure? Although official statistics are unavailable, evidence suggests that, by the 1850s, an increasing number of Blacks considered emigration a more attractive option. Many Blacks continued to embrace an anti-emigrationist stance into the early 1850s. Others concluded that conditions for Blacks in the United States had deteriorated to such a degree that emigration was actually an increasingly attractive and, for some, only option. See sources from note no. 11.

13. Similar to the organization of the United States Congress, the governing body of the Episcopal Church (called the General Convention) consists of two houses. They are the House of Bishops and the House of Deputies, the former of which (today) includes approximately one hundred and forty members. These two bodies meet and act separately. All bishops of the Episcopal Church, active or retired, comprise the House of Bishops. Responsibilities of the House of Bishops include: electing the presiding bishop, chairing the executive council of the General Convention, establishing church policies, enacting canon (i.e., laws), and overseeing the ecclesiastical courts. During Payne's tenure, the House of Bishops prioritized church expansion, both domestically and internationally. See Bernardin, *An Introduction to the Episcopal Church.*

14. Payne, *History of the Greboes.*

15. Information obtained from www.ancestry.com/ (both posted information and through conversation with a descendent in the summer of 2014). Unfortunately, I could not substantiate these claims with any relevant documentation.

16. See Batterson, *A Scetch-book of the American Episcopate,* 161–62; www.ancestry.com/

17. Martha Jane Williford to Martha Stackhouse Williford Service, 4 July 1850.

18. According to the *Spirit of Missions,* an Episcopal publication on their foreign missions, Martha Williford's school included, there were twenty-six "scholars in the female department." See Episcopal Church, Domestic and Foreign Missionary Society, Board of Mission, *Spirit of Missions* 16 (1851): 360. As a point of comparison, this publication indicates a roughly identical number of students in the male department.

19. Martha Jane Williford to Martha Stackhouse Williford Service, 4 July 1850.

20. Scott, *Day Dawns in Africa,* 167.

21. Clarke, *By the Rivers of Water,* 163.

22. See Episcopal Church, Domestic and Foreign Missionary Society, Board of Mission, *Spirit of Missions* 16 (1851): 360.

23. Clarke, *By the Rivers of Water.*

24. Martha Jane Williford to Martha Stackhouse Williford Service, 4 July 1850.

25. Mrs. Anna M. Steele Scott, a Virginian, and her husband, Rev. Hugh Roy Scott, also of Virginia, were Episcopal missionaries in Liberia. Mrs. Scott's brother, Dr. T. R. Steele, a medical missionary, died while serving in Liberia.

26. Scott, *Day Dawns in Africa,* 66.

27. Ibid., 45. See also Clarke, *By the Rivers of Water.*

28. Blassingame, *The Slave Community.*

29. Martha Jane Williford to Martha Stackhouse Williford Service, 4 July 1850.

30. Scott, *Day Dawns in Africa*, 50.

31. Ibid.

32. Martha Jane Williford to Martha Stackhouse Williford Service, 4 July 1850.

33. Martha Jane Williford to Martha Stackhouse Williford Service, 18 July 1850.

34. No (known) surviving letter written by Martha Williford discusses the nature of her sickness in Liberia, her voyage back to the United States, or her stay with family in Georgia, including her recovery. Rather, I found this information in Scott, *Day Dawns in Africa*, 38–39.

35. Martha Jane Williford to Emma M. Service, 31 May 1855.

36. Ibid.

37. Irons, *The Origins of Pro-Slavery Christianity*, 125.

38. Scott, *Day Dawns in Africa*, 167.

39. See Episcopal Church, Domestic and Foreign Missionary Society, Board of Mission, *Spirit of Missions* 21 (1856): 605. Included within this volume of the *Spirit of Missions* are some of Bishop Payne's reports on the state of the Cavalla Mission.

40. Martha Williford Payne to Emma M. Service, 6 May 1858.

41. "Missions in Africa; INTERESTING ADDRESS ON AFRICA BY BISHOP PAYNE, MISSIONARY BISHOP TO AFRICA FROM THE EPISCOPAL CHURCH." No extant source confirms that the Paynes journeyed down to Georgia during their 1859–60 visit to the States. Martha wrote a letter to her sister, Margaret, in June 1859 in which she briefly discussed her schedule once they had arrived in the States: "We expect to stay only over the Sabbath in New York, and then on to Alexandria, from which place I hope to write again. Oh! how I wish we could go right on, and see you all, but my Husband must be at Alexandria at the close of the term to deliver an address to the Students. Our plans cannot be decided till we reach that point." She later wrote to Margaret in January 1861, apologizing for her scanty correspondence since "our return home." "Home" might simply mean the United States, but, considering that Martha had not seen her family for ten years, it is likely that the Paynes made the five-hundred-mile trip between the Northern Neck of Virginia and Augusta. See Martha Williford Payne to Margaret E. Williford, 25 June 1859, and Martha Williford Payne to Margaret E. Williford, 4 January 1861.

42. Martha Williford Payne to Margaret E. Williford, 4 January 1861.

43. Martha Williford Payne to Emma M. Service, 13 March 1861.

44. Ibid.

45. Ibid.

46. Ibid.

47. For example, throughout the 1850s, Martha Payne consistently praised Virginia Hale Hoffman—a native of Glastonbury, Connecticut—for her devotion and contributions to the Mission. In her acclaim for Mrs. Hoffman, Payne never cited her fellow missionary's New England origins, let alone complained about her regional and/or political differences.

48. See Bearden, "The Episcopal Church in the Confederate States"; Bond, "Slavery in the Diocese of Mississippi's Convention Journals, 1826–1861"; Graebner, "The Episcopal Church and Race in Nineteenth-Century North Carolina"; Mason, "Separation and Reunion of the Episcopal Church, 1860–1865"; Mohler, "The Episcopal Church and National Reconciliation, 1865"; Shanks, "The Reunion of the Episcopal Church, 1865."

49. Hopkins, "A Scriptural, Ecclesiastical, and Historical View of Slavery"; Hyer, *Bishop Hopkins' Letter on Slavery Ripped Up and His Misuse of the Sacred Scriptures Exposed.*

50. Martha Williford Payne to Emma M. Service, 6 December 1861.

51. Ibid.

52. Ibid.

53. See https://saintpauls.org/who-we-are/history/ (accessed August 14, 2024).

54. Martha Williford Payne to Emma M. Service, 16 September 1861.

55. See Scott, *The Southern Lady;* and Faust, *Mothers of Invention,* 242–43; 252–53. Faust, for example, cites Confederate mother, Mary Scales, who looked forward to the postbellum years in which she hoped the South would reinstate "the moral economy of gender in which women traded 'helplessness' and subservience for care and protection." See Faust, 242.

56. Martha Williford Payne to Margaret E. Williford, 4 June 1866.

57. Martha Williford Payne to Emma M. Service, 4 March 1868.

58. Martha Williford Payne to Margaret E. Williford, 4 June 1866.

59. Martha Williford Payne to Emma M. Service, 16 September 1868.

60. Martha Williford Payne to Emma M. Service, 4 March 1868.

61. Ibid.

62. *Handbooks on the Missions of the Episcopal Church.* Part of the Canterbury Project; accessed April 23, 2024: http://anglicanhistory.org/africa/lb/missions1928/. That said, the so-called back-to-Africa movement did not reach its highest levels until the period between the end of Reconstruction in the late 1870s—after it became well apparent that the promises of Reconstruction would never become realities for African Americans—and the 1890s, a time of revived racism and violence, including a record number of lynchings. See Barnes, *Journey of Hope.*

63. Martha Williford Payne to Emma M. Service, 4 March 1868.

64. William C. Burke to Ralph Randolph Gurley, February 9, 1867, Mary Custis Lee Papers, 1694–1917.

65. Martha Williford Payne to Emma M. Service, 10 September 1868.

66. Martha Williford Payne to Emma M. Service, 16 June 1868.

67. Martha Williford Payne to Emma M. Service, 20 October 1868.

68. In support of the latter comment, Martha informed her sister Emma that "the Bishop remarked yesterday, that my pen was the principal support of our schools." See ibid.

69. Graduates of Williams College founded the American Board of Commissioners for Foreign Missions, whose objective was to spread Christianity worldwide, in 1811. Although Congregationalist in origin, the ABCFM accepted prospective missionaries whose membership fell with the Presbyterian, Dutch Reform, and apparently the Episcopal Church. ABCFM did send missionaries to a diverse collection of places throughout the world but including Cape Palmas. See Peabody, *The American Board of Commissioners for Foreign Missions.* Note: Publication is an exact reproduction of the "pre-1923" copy.

70. Martha Williford Payne to Emma M. Service, 16 June 1868.

71. Martha Williford Payne to Emma M. Service, 10 September 1868.

72. Martha Williford Payne to Emma M. Service, 19 March 1869.

73. *Handbooks on the Missions of the Episcopal Church: Liberia;* accessed April 23, 2024, http://anglicanhistory.org/africa/lb/missions1928/.

4. INTERREGNUM AND TRANSITION

1. At times, I will use the following abbreviations for each of these churches: PCUS for Presbyterian Church of the United States (Southern Presbyterians); MEC, South for Methodist Episcopal Church, South; and SBC for Southern Baptist Convention.

2. Thompson, *Presbyterian Missions in the Southern United States*, 96.

3. The general observations within this paragraph are based upon many primary sources including a document dated 19 August (year not specified) that served as the formation of a mission society in Powhatan County, Virginia, for the relief of Confederate soldiers. See Elizabeth Gilmer Grattan to Virginia Eppes Dance Campbell, 20 October 1865, Virginia Eppes Dance Campbell Papers, 1858–1865. Another relevant primary source includes "Scrapbook, 1866–1911—Mary Washington Cabell Early, 1846–1917."

4. McMillen, *To Raise Up the South*.

5. Elizabeth Gilmer Grattan to Virginia Eppes Dance Campbell, 20 October 1865.

6. A clear and concise overview of southern denominations during, and immediately after, the Civil War is Daniel W. Stowell's essay "Religion in the South: An Overview, Post-bellum Period," included within Hill and Lippy, eds., *Encyclopedia of Religion in the South*, 2nd ed., 19–29.

7. Heck, *In Royal Service*, 85–87.

8. The SBC, for example, sent no foreign missionaries between 1861 and 1870. It dispatched five women to China in 1872–73 and two women in Italy in the early 1870s. See Heck, *In Royal Service*, Appendix A.

9. For more insight into the ways by which notions of gender—specifically masculinity—shaped southern religion after the Civil War, see Allen, *A Century to Celebrate*; Friend and Glover, eds., *Southern Masculinity*; Hardesty, *Women Called to Witness*; Ownby, *Subduing Satan*; Stowell, *Rebuilding Zion*; and Wilson, *Baptized in Blood*. For an excellent, more general, account of the gendered climate in the postbellum South, see Edwards, *Gendered Strife and Confusion*.

10. In addition to sources cited in note no. 9, see Carney, *Ministers and Masters*.

11. Huff, *Greenville*, 204.

12. Allen, *A Century to Celebrate*, 30–31, and Raley, "'On the Same Basis as the Men,'" https://jsr.fsu.edu/Volume7/Raley1.htm (accessed April 23, 2024).

13. Farnham, *The Education of the Southern Belle*. Farnham's epilogue provides insight into the changes occurring in female higher education after 1860.

14. Battle, *Piety*, 11.

15. Lile, "More than Daughters," 3.

16. Heck, *In Royal Service*, 73.

17. See Censer, *The Reconstruction of White Southern Womanhood, 1865–1895*; Scott, *The Southern Lady*; and "Women, Religion and Social Change in the South, 1830–1930," in Hill, ed., *Religion in the Solid South*.

18. See chapter 5, "Door after Door Is Being Flung Open . . . ," of Scott's *The Southern Lady* for broad discussion of women's evolving roles during the first generation after the Civil War.

19. Scott, *The Southern Lady*, 129.

20. Censer, *The Reconstruction of White Southern Womanhood, 1865–1895*, 9.

21. Sims, *The Power of Femininity in the New South*, 1.

22. See chapter 1 of Censer, *The Reconstruction of White Southern Womanhood, 1865–1895*.

23. Although Haygood's quote comes from a speech in which she addressed "the relation of female education to home mission work," her comments apply to both home and foreign mission work (anything ensconced in the public sphere). At the time of writing the essay in which this quote is taken, Haygood was preparing for what would turn out to be a sixteen-year life as a teacher, administrator, and religious mentor at a girls' school in Shanghai. See Brown and Brown, eds., *Life and Letters of Laura Askew Haygood*, 89.

24. Ibid.

25. Vickers, "Models of Womanhood and the Early Woman's Missionary Union."

26. Blum, *Reforging the White Republic*, and Blum and Poole, *Vale of Tears*.

27. Harvey, *Freedom's Coming*.

28. See Olive Elliott Bagby Papers, 1904–1915.

29. Excerpts came from a single newspaper article written by Mary Washington Cabell Early. The article was glued in her scrapbook, which she kept between 1866 and 1911. Unfortunately, the clipping did not include the article's title, date, or newspaper name. Early most likely wrote this article during the later 1870s or early 1880s. Within the piece, she referred to the "epizootic panic of 1872," confirming that the article postdated that economic depression. [Note: Early may be confused about the timing and/or denotation of the financial instability of the early 1870s. "The Great Epizootic of 1872" and the "Panic of 1873" were two events; the former was a debilitating equine flu while the latter was a devastating global depression.] One can only speculate on the newspaper that printed this article. However, it is possible that she published it in Lynchburg's morning newspaper, *The News & Advance* (established in 1866), or its evening newspaper, *The Daily Advance* (established in 1880). The description of Mrs. Early ("a person of deep spiritual and intellectual gifts") came from her obituary clipping (undated, no newspaper name) that was also included in the scrapbook. See Scrapbook, 1866–1911—Mary Washington Cabell Early, 1846–1917.

30. Ibid.

31. Marie Gordon "Gordy" Pryor Rice to Franklina Gray Bartlett, 3 February 1886, Franklina Gray Bartlett Papers, 1870–1930.

32. Pope-Levison, *Building the Old Time Religion*.

33. John Patrick McDowell acknowledges the establishment of the Woman's Bible Mission of Nashville, Tennessee (which included women from multiple Methodist churches within the district), in 1874 as one of the first successfully planted Methodist mission societies in the South. Nonetheless, home missionary women remained a minority within the Protestant denominations' total female membership. According to McDowell, despite significant strides, a majority of southern Methodist women remained indifferent to mission work. He estimates that in the year 1898 approximately 15,000 women were actively involved in home mission work, while there were approximately 700,000 southern women who belonged to the MEC, South. See McDowell, *The Social Gospel in the South*, 9–11, 16.

34. Ibid., 3.

35. By the first decade of the twentieth century, Southern Methodist leader Belle Bennett feared that the term "settlement house" was too secular. In 1906, she recommended to the Home Mission Board that it consider applying the name "Wesley House" to existing settlement houses in the South. Nonetheless, home missionaries based Wesley Houses upon the concepts and goals associated with the settlement movement. See McDowell, *The Social Gospel in the South*, 62.

36. For more information on these home mission projects in Virginia, see Born, "Candlesticks." Another valuable source about women's roles in home mission work in Virginia is Mrs. Henry Walker Decker's sesquicentennial history of the Woman's Missionary Society of the First Baptist Church of Richmond. See Decker, *A Continuing Light*.

37. Additional sources drawn from to make this broad assertion include Brown and Brown, *Life and Letters of Laura Askew Haygood;* MacDonell, *Belle Harris Bennett;* and Williams, *The Morning-Glory*. Laura Haygood established the Trinity Home Mission in Atlanta in 1882. Belle Bennett served as president of both the Home Mission Society and the Missionary Council (MEC, South, organizations) during the first two decades of the twentieth century. Mae McKenzie administered a mission in an Arkansas lumber mill town.

38. For additional statistical information about the Woman's Parsonage and Home Mission Society of the MEC, South (later known simply as the Woman's Home Mission Society of the MEC, South), and similar Christian organizations, see World Missionary Conference, *Statistical Atlas of Christian Missions*, 18. For more information on Lucinda Helm, see Alexander, *The Life and Word of Lucinda B. Helm*.

39. The Woman's Missionary Union instituted the week of self-denial in 1894–95. See Decker, *A Continuing Light*, 33–34. For more insight into the activities and organization of local WMU societies, see Turkey Creek Baptist Church (Abbeville County, S.C.), Women's Missionary Society, Minute Book. That local WMU, under the administration of a president, vice president, treasurer, and secretary, held meetings on the second Saturday of each month or second Sunday of each month. It collected money for state missions, home missions, the WMU training school, the Sunday School Board, the Connie Maxwell Orphanage, and other projects. Occasionally, the Turkey Creek WMU raised money for church maintenance, special events, and purposes (i.e., collecting for a scholarship fund for Anderson College or at North Greenville Academy). Finally, it sent a delegate from the WMU Auxiliary to the South Carolina Convention, which met in such locations as Columbia, Belton, and Orangeburg.

40. Examples include Cannon III, *History of Southern Methodist Missions;* Ragsdale, *Story of Georgia Baptists; Our Home Field*. Somewhat in contrast, Presbyterians' histories and compendiums, some of which women authored, were typically ahead of the Methodists and Baptists in their acknowledgment of women's efforts.

41. Abby Manly Gwathmey worked as a bookkeeper for the *Foreign Mission Journal* prior to her administrative responsibilities with the Woman's Missionary Union. After her service as president of the WMU, Gwathmey served as president of the Central Committee for Woman's Work in Virginia and as vice president of the Southern Woman's Missionary Union.

42. Decker, *A Continuing Light*, 33–34.

43. Ibid., 34. See also Sudie Miller Furman Dabbs Papers, 1858–1926 (especially Box 1, Folder 15). This collection offers many letters in which Dabbs, a prominent Southern Baptist missionary, encourages women's leadership skills, and their efforts in the "planting" of missionary societies across South Carolina.

44. Woman's Missionary Union, *A Century of Service*, 9, 49.

45. See Doyle, *Presbyterian Home Missions,* specifically page 196, for more information on Bible-reader women within the Presbyterian Church. The general observations within this paragraph are based upon many primary sources, many of which have already been cited. Additional consulted collections include Copp Family Papers, 1820–1917, Folder 3; Drury Lacy Papers, 1823–1965, particularly Series 3 Volumes, 1826–1896 and undated, Folders 40, 42; C. H. Wiley Papers, 1774–1962, especially subseries 2.4 Religious Writings; Sudie Miller Furman Dabbs Papers, 1858–1926, Box 1, Folders 15 and 21; and the George Galphin Nowlan and Ann Elizabeth Nowlan MacDonnell Diaries. The Copp Family Papers comprised the papers of Mary Copp Wilbur (1866–1900) about family life, local faith-based charities, and Presbyterian Sunday School matters in Savannah, Georgia. The Drury Lacy Papers included personal correspondence of Bessie Dewey—the daughter of Drury Lacy, a Presbyterian minister, educator, and Confederate army chaplain—and her home mission work in Charlotte, N.C. And the C. H. Wiley papers comprised postbellum correspondence, the majority of which was religious in nature (written in central North Carolina).

46. See Susan Dabney Smedes Papers, 1860–1930, Folders 1 and 2. Folder 1 included a biographical sketch of Smedes written by Kline H. Smith, a student in American literature at George Washington University, in 1930. Smith's sketch incompletely cites many primary sources attributed to Smedes (correspondence, her memoirs). While I have access to Smedes's oft-cited memorial to her father and the irrecoverable antebellum southern civilization, *Memorials of a Southern Planter* (1887), I could not locate some of this relevant correspondence. Folder 2 included Smedes's diary and memoranda (1888–89) from her missionary work in Helena, Montana.

47. While Smedes identified herself as a Christian (Episcopal) missionary, the federal government funded this position.

48. For more information on the federally funded Rosebud Agency (1886–1976), see Anderson, *Crying for a Vision;* Biolosi, *Deadliest Enemies;* Dyck, *Brule, The Sioux People of the Rosebud;* Foley, "Father Francis M. Craft and the Indian Sisters"; Fusco, "The Last Hunt of Gen. George A. Crook"; McBride, "Hoosier Schoolmaster among the Sioux"; and Weinberg, *The Real Rosebud.*

49. Susan Dabney Smedes Papers, 1860–1930, Folders 1 and 2. More specifically, this paragraph incorporated additional biographical information from the biographical sketch of Smedes (Folder 1, pp. 14–18) as well as the 1888–89 diary kept by Smedes while a resident of Helena, Montana. Unfortunately, no known primary sources exist that would shed further light on her fourteen-month period as a missionary in South Dakota.

50. For more information on the community of "Confederate carpetbaggers," see Sutherland, *The Confederate Carpetbaggers* and Blight, *Race and Reunion,* 90–91.

51. See James, ed., *Notable American Women, 1607–1950,* 103–4.

52. According to Mrs. Pryor's memoir, the family moved to Brooklyn in 1868. The

earliest letter referring to the home was dated May 15, 1870. See Marie Gordon "Gordy" Pryor to Franklina Gray, 15 May 1870.

53. Although never explicitly stated, this "home" presumably catered to illiterate or poorly educated, widowed, and even battered women. Furthermore, never does either Sara Pryor or Marie Rice use the term "settlement house" to describe their "Home," which technically predated the settlement house movement. That movement started in Great Britain in 1884 when middle-class London reformers established Toynbee Hall. The first settlement house, it provided education and social services to the impoverished workers who lived and worked in East London. American social reformers subsequently founded settlement houses beginning in the late 1880s, largely as a response to growing industrial poverty. For further insight into the settlement house model/settlement movement, see Carson, *Settlement Folk*; Davis, *Spearheads for Reform*; and Trolander, *Professionalism and Social Change*.

54. Sara Agnes Rice Pryor, *My Day*, 339.

55. Beckert, *The Monied Metropolis*, 253. I could not access the Pryors' net worth via the 1870 or 1880 U.S. Census (it was not denoted), but these two censuses did reveal that the Pryors kept two live-in Irish servants. See www.ancestry.com.

56. Marie Gordon "Gordy" Pryor to Franklina Gray Bartlett, 9 February 1878.

57. Ibid.

58. See chapter 8, "The Culture of Capital," of Beckert, *The Monied Metropolis* for greater insight into the leisure and social life enjoyed by New York's bourgeoisie.

59. Marie Gordon "Gordy" Pryor to Franklina Gray Bartlett, 25 May 1878.

60. Marie Gordon "Gordy" Pryor to Franklina Gray Bartlett, 5 March 1889.

61. Marie Gordon "Gordy" Pryor Rice to Franklina Gray Bartlett, 24 November 1891.

62. Marie Gordon "Gordy" Pryor Rice to Franklina Gray Bartlett, 21 May 1891.

63. Marie Gordon "Gordy" Pryor Rice to Franklina Gray Bartlett, 8 February 1891.

64. Ibid.

65. Marie Gordon "Gordy" Pryor Price to Franklina Gray Bartlett, 8 February 1891; Marie Gordon "Gordy" Pryor Price to Franklina Gray Bartlett, 1 January 1893; Marie Gordon "Gordy" Pryor Price to Franklina Gray Bartlett, 29 December 1894. See also Marie Gordon Rice, "The Negro's Greatest Need," 123-24. *The Home Mission Monthly* was a Presbyterian (Woman's Executive Committee of Home Missions) publication.

66. Marie Gordon "Gordy" Pryor Rice to Franklina Gray Bartlett, 8 February 1891.

5. HOME MISSION WORK MEETS CONSERVATIVE PROGRESSIVISM

1. The literature on southern progressivism, specifically as it relates to the Social Gospel, remains in its infancy. Scholars who have studied the Social Gospel have disproportionately focused upon the East and Midwest. Nonetheless, influential studies on southern progressivism include Ayers, *The Promise of the New South*; Bailey, *Liberalism in the New South*; Grantham, *Southern Progressivism*; Kirby, *Darkness at the Dawning*; and Link, *The Paradox of Southern Progressivism, 1880-1930*.

2. See Link, *The Paradox of Southern Progressivism, 1880–1930*. Link contends that the South did not see such widespread, progressive reforms as did other regions in the United States due to strong cultural conflicts between social reformers—those who promoted social reform through the development of centralized government power—and "traditional" southern communities whose residents accepted social reform only at the local level and who tended to deeply resent outsiders and any threats to their autonomy.

3. Sims, *The Power of Femininity in the New South*, 3.

4. Eliza Y. Hyde to Sudie Miller Furman, 9 November 1891, Sudie Miller Furman Dabbs Papers, 1858–1926.

5. Friedman, *The Enclosed Garden*, xvi.

6. See McDowell, *The Social Gospel in the South*, and chapter 6 of Scott, *The Southern Lady*. During these years, women representing different Protestant sects were also attending their respective denominations' summer conferences, at which home and foreign mission works and women's role within them were discussed.

7. Cott, *The Grounding of Modern Feminism*, 3.

8. Vickers, "Models of Womanhood and the Early Woman's Missionary Union," 52.

9. Decker, *A Continuing Light, 1813–1963*, 28.

10. Observation based upon the following primary sources: the George Galphin Nowlan and Ann Elizabeth Nowlan MacDonnell Diaries; pp. 7–8 in "Ninth Annual Announcement of the Mission Training College, Clinton, S.C., 1902-'03," Mission Training College for Inner and Foreign Missions; Woman's Missionary Union, *A Century of Service;* Franklina Gray Bartlett Papers, 1870–1930; and Mary Washington Cabell Early Scrapbook, 1866–1911. I also referred to Born, "Candlesticks," 21–39; chapter 9 of Cannon, *History of Southern Methodist Missions;* and chapters 3 and 4 of McDowell, *The Social Gospel in the South*.

11. McDowell, *The Social Gospel in the South*, 61.

12. Maxey, *Miss Ora and Miss Etta*, 1. Note: Source is a thirty-seven-page unpublished history (typescript) about Caryetta Louisa Davis and Ora Harrison as well as the development of two mission schools, St. John's-in-the-Mountains at Endicott and St. Peter's-in-the-Mountains at Callaway in southwestern Franklin County, Virginia, during the early twentieth century. The author of the informal history apparently interviewed Miss Davis and Miss Harrison—along with several of their contemporary female missionaries—at some point after the Great Depression.

13. See McCauley, *Appalachian Mountain Religion*, 400–410, and Williams, *Appalachia*, 200–202.

14. Silber, "'What Does America Need So Much as Americans?'" in Inscoe, ed., *Appalachians and Race*.

15. Maxey, *Miss Ora and Miss Etta*, pp. 14–19.

16. See Appalachian School, Penland, North Carolina, January 1923 Cover, Appalachian Industrial Schools Records, Hunter Library Digital Collections, Western Carolina University. See https://southernappalachiandigitalcollections.org/browse/search /appalachian-school-penland-north-carolina-january-1923-cover (accessed May 5, 2024). For more information on Morgan and her work, see her memoir, Morgan, *Gift from the Hills*

and http://www.wcu.edu/library/DigitalCollections/CraftRevival/people/lucymorgan.html (accessed April 24, 2024).

17. Whisnant, *All That Is Native and Fine* and *Modernizing the Mountaineer*. Other sources on Appalachian education, particularly craft, trade, and industrial education, include Campbell, *The Future of Church and Independent Schools in the Southern Highlands*; Ritchie, *The Rabun Industrial School and Mountain School Extension Work among the Mountain Whites by One of Them*; Stephenson, *The Home Industrial School, Asheville, North Carolina*; Stoddart, *Challenge and Change in Appalachia*; and Williams, ed., *Appalachian Travels*.

18. Shapiro, *Appalachia on Our Minds*.

19. Although this is not confirmed, I have not identified any evidence that this school admitted Black girls.

20. "Domestic science" and "industrial education" are similar terms. At industrial schools, girls and young women would focus on one or more trades, for example broom making, sewing, or weaving.

21. See Vashti School Postcard. See also http://www.vashti.org/about-us/history/ (accessed May 5, 2024) for more information on the school's history.

22. Unfortunately, I do not have access to any of Sudie Furman's letters. Rather, I am making this assertion based upon comments made by friends, family, and society members that referred to Furman's correspondence (still found within Sudie Miller Furman Dabbs Papers, 1858–1926).

23. Aunt Ann [last name unknown] to Sudie Miller Furman, 9 November 1890.

24. I obtained significant information on Caryetta Davis's elite ancestral background through a 1986 application for acceptance of Carywood, Caryetta's grandfather's large Italianate mansion in Campbell County, Virginia, to the National Register of Historic Places. Miss Davis's grandfather, Robert Saunders, was a graduate of New London Academy and the University of Virginia, a significant slaveholder, a member of the Virginia House of Delegates, a Confederate officer, and, after the Civil War, was the first superintendent of schools of Campbell County. See https://www.dhr.virginia.gov/historic-registers/015-5147/ (accessed April 28, 2024).

25. According to the 1900 U.S. Census, Ora's father, Joseph Harrison, rented a farm in Rocky Mount, Virginia (Franklin County). See www.ancestry.com/.

26. Maxey, *Miss Ora and Miss Etta*, p. 10. For further analysis of mission work in Appalachia performed by southern women representing other Protestant denominations, see Inscoe, "Memories of a Presbyterian Mission Worker in the Kentucky Mountains, 1918–1921"; Carter, ed., *Virginia Broughton*; and Withoft, *Oak and Laurel*.

27. Maxey, *Miss Ora and Miss Etta*, pp. 13–14.

28. In contrast, women who had labored for many months or even years as missionaries typically had come to know those whom they served as people as opposed to mere voiceless victims. For example, such women had labored as midwives (when no physician was present) or as nurses to sick and dying members of households in their greater community in addition to the prescribed teaching responsibilities. See Maxey, *Miss Ora and Miss Etta*, p. 20.

29. For a multiperspective assessment of the solidification of the Jim Crow South, see Dailey, Gilmore, and Simon, eds., *Jumpin' Jim Crow*.

30. Pamphlet: "W.M.U. Interest in Inter-Racial Relations" by Mrs. W. J. Neel, Georgia within "Turkey Creek Baptist Church (Abbeville County, S.C.) Women's Missionary Society, Minute Book Minute Book, 1911–1925.

31. "The Story of Mrs. W. J. Neel," Baptist Woman's Missionary Union, n.d.

32. Mrs. Neel likely delivered the pamphlet at (or prepared it just after having attended) the twenty-fourth annual meeting of the WMU in Birmingham, Alabama, in November 1917. At this meeting, there "was a registered attendance of 800 delegates and visitors." See *American Baptist Year-Book 1917, 50.*

33. Pamphlet: "W.M.U. Interest in Inter-Racial Relations" by Mrs. W. J. Neel, Georgia.

34. Much of the secondary literature that examines the intersection of southern progressivism and race complements Mrs. Neel's elitist (and often condescending) brand of racial uplift. See Castorph, *Republicans, Negroes, and Progressives in the South, 1912–1916;* Feldman, *The Irony of the Solid South;* Frankel and Dye, eds., *Gender, Class, Race, and Reform in the Progressive Era;* Harris, "Racists and Reformers" (Ph.D. diss., University of Michigan, 1967); Link, *The Paradox of Southern Progressivism, 1880–1930;* and Southern, *The Progressive Era and Race.*

35. For additional biographical information about Isa Beall Williams Neel, see Gruver, *From This High Pinnacle,* and Pryor, "Mrs. W. J. Neel."

36. Pamphlet: "W.M.U. Interest in Inter-Racial Relations."

37. Ibid. Note: Neel's pamphlet never provides an explicit definition for "interracial movement," but one may safely assume that the term refers to the methods by which white Southern Baptists (mostly women) would reach Blacks.

38. Pamphlet: "W.M.U. Interest in Inter-Racial Relations." Joel Williamson and Glenda Elizabeth Gilmore have made similar points. See Gilmore, *Gender and Jim Crow,* and Williamson, *The Crucible of Race.*

39. Rice, "The Negro's Greatest Need."

40. Pamphlet: "W.M.U. Interest in Inter-Racial Relations."

41. Ibid.

42. Baptist Woman's Missionary Union of Georgia Records, 1878–2020.

43. See Franklina Gray Bartlett Papers.

44. See Pryor, *Reminiscences of Peace,* and Gardner, *Blood & Irony,* 128–30. The UDC also recommended pro-Confederate memoirs written by Virginia Clay-Clopton and Louise Wigfall Wright. See Clay-Clopton, *A Belle of the Fifties,* and Wright, *A Southern Girl in '61.*

45. Pryor, *My Day,* 258.

46. Ibid., 325.

47. Peacock, "Nellie Peters Black," and Shellman, "Nellie Peters Black."

48. To get a reasonable sampling of women involved in mission work and heritage organizations, I consulted: 1) *American Baptist Year-Book 1917,* 2) Haskin, *Women and Missions in the Methodist Episcopal Church, South* and 3) The Woman's Home Missionary Society, *Thirty-Ninth Annual Report of the Board of Managers for the Year 1919–1920* for a listing of names of female officers in state chapters of the Woman's Missionary Union and officers and prominent Methodist home missionaries and then proceeded to locate, for such women, on-line obituaries or biographies (from newspaper databases and ancestry .com) that mentioned involvement in heritage organizations.

49. Gardner, *Blood & Irony*.

50. Chapter 4, "The Imperative of Historical Inquiry, 1895–1905," of Gardner's *Blood & Irony* offers particular extrapolation on this theme. See also Rohrer, "Slaveholding Women and the Religious Instruction of Slaves in Post-Emancipation Memory." For a representative work by U. B. Phillips, see Phillips, *American Negro Slavery*.

51. For examples of southern women engaged in home mission work but who also authored southern histories, biographies, and memoirs between the late nineteenth and early twentieth centuries, see Burwell, *A Girl's Life in Virginia before the War*; Clayton, *White and Black under the Old Regime*; DeSaussure, *Old Plantation Days*; Pringle, *Chronicles of Chicora Wood*; Pryor, *My Day*; and Smedes, *Memorials of a Southern Planter*.

52. See undated and unlabeled obituary on first page within "Scrapbook, 1866–1911– Mary Washington Cabell Early, 1846–1917." Mrs. Early died in Lynchburg, Virginia, in July 1917. Considering this, it is likely that Early's obituary appeared in the *Lynchburg News* or in the *Lynchburg Daily Advance*.

53. See undated article entitled "The Fireside. Old Virginia" within "Scrapbook, 1866– 1911–Mary Washington Cabell Early, 1846–1917." This is a "true" scrapbook–a collection of cut-outs. Nonetheless, I believe this article is from the *Southern Planter* (January 1892).

54. Censer, *The Reconstruction of Southern White Womanhood, 1865–1895*; Edwards, *Gendered Strife and Confusion*; Turner, *Women and Gender in the New South*; and Whites, *Gender Matters*. See also Epstein, *The Politics of Domesticity*, and Ginzberg, *Women and the Work of Benevolence*.

55. South Carolina Woman's Missionary Union, *A Century of Service*, 24.

56. Typical women's missionary societies included the following officers and key members: president, vice president(s), recording secretary, historian, treasurer, and several delegates to the annual denominational/organization conventions.

57. See p. 1, "Women's Foreign Missionary Society of the Methodist Episcopal Church South Records, 1881–1898."

58. Minutes of the Annual Session of the Woman's Missionary Union, Auxiliary to the Baptist State Convention of South Carolina, 7.

59. *Twenty-second Annual Report of the Woman's Home Mission Society*, 162–63, as quoted in McDowell, *The Social Gospel in the South*, 46.

60. *Fourth Annual Report of the Woman's Missionary Council*, 161, as quoted in McDowell, *The Social Gospel in the South*, 46.

61. While Stanton did not hold widely accepted views about divorce, she was also not a rarity among northern feminists in the late nineteenth and early twentieth centuries. See Riegel, *American Feminists*.

62. Issues of marriage status and work are discussed in this letter: Marie Gordon "Gordy" Pryor Rice to Franklina Gray Bartlett, 31 December 1877.

63. Marie Gordon "Gordy" Pryor Rice to Franklina Gray Bartlett, 14 January 1893. Mr. Casaubon is a character from George Eliot's *Middlemarch, A Study of Provincial Life*. Significant themes running throughout *Middlemarch* ran through Gordy's writings. These included the status of women, the nature of marriage, idealism, self-interest, religion, hypocrisy, political reform, and education. See Eliot, *Middlemarch*.

64. Marie Gordon "Gordy" Pryor Rice to Franklina Gray Bartlett, 24 November 1891.

65. Woman's Missionary Union, *A Century of Service*, 6.

66. J. William McCain to Marie Gordon "Gordy" Pryor Rice, 9 November 1891.

67. Maxwell, *The Woman I Am*, 9.

68. Examples of southern women's religious societies that cite male clergy speakers at their meetings include the Ladies Benevolent and Missionary Society of the Presbyterian Church, Athens, Georgia; and the Ladies Aid Society of Savannah, Georgia. See Ladies Benevolent and Missionary Society of the Presbyterian Church (Athens, Ga.) Record Book and George Galphin Nowlan and Ann Elizabeth Nowlan MacDonnell Diaries.

6. RECRUITMENT

1. While the time frame for this chapter is 1890–1930, the "selling" and "marketing" of mission work particularly peaked between 1890 and World War I. Consequently, the majority of my examples (and sources) are from that period.

2. See Maxwell, *The Woman I Am*, 9, and McBeth, *Women in Baptist Life*, 113.

3. During this time, men authored virtually all published religious materials. The Library Company of Philadelphia recently assembled a website entitled "Portraits of American Religion That Appeared in Print before 1861." According to the site, "the project initially emerged as part of the 'Picturing Women' exhibition, a multi-institution exhibition that was the culmination of many years work by art historian Dr. Susan Shifrin." Compared to the thousands of American men who published religious materials before the Civil War, approximately forty women appear in the Library Company of Philadelphia project. Most of these women lived outside of the South, including enslaved women Jarena Lee and Sojourner Truth. Although the Library Company of Philadelphia makes no claims that their collection comprises all American women who published religious material before 1861, their research suggests that antebellum southern women read religious books, poetry, lectures, and sermons that were almost entirely authored by men. See http://www .librarycompany.org/women/portraits_religion/intro.htm (accessed May 5, 2024).

4. A more comprehensive list of religious publications read by southern women at this time include: *Alabama Baptist; Baltimore Baptist; Baptist Basket; Baptist Standard; Biblical Recorder; the Christian Observatory: A Religious and Literary Magazine; Heathen Helper; Home Missions; Ladies' Repository; the Methodist Review; The Missionary, a Monthly Periodical, Devoted to Literature, Art, and Religion Light and Life for Women; Our Home Field; Our Mission Fields; Religious Herald; Royal Service; The State; the Sunday School Times; The Survey; Western Recorder; Woman's Work for Woman*. See https://libraryguides.missouri .edu/newspapers/historicalnews (accessed May 13, 2024).

5. Maxwell, *The Woman I Am*, 7.

6. Woman's Missionary Union, *A Century of Service*, 49. Note: This is an informal booklet assembled by the South Carolina WMU with incomplete publication information.

7. Maxwell, *The Woman I Am*, 27. See chapters 1 and 2 of *this book* for a more general analysis of the themes, as they applied to women, present in religious publications of the early twentieth century. Monthly magazine *Royal Service*, for example, included information on "mission programs for each grade of society … news from our home and foreign

women missionaries, from the [WMU] Training School, the Margaret Home Fund [to support children of missionaries], Woman's Missionary Union Headquarters, an exchange of society methods, a department of Personal Service [social ministry], a department of Bible study and brief items of current events in the missionary world." See Maxwell, 18.

8. "Report of the Twenty-Eighth Annual Meeting of the Woman's Baptist Missionary Union, Auxiliary to Georgia Baptist Convention, 1910," Woman Missionary Union of Georgia Records, 1878–2020.

9. Single-sex and coed mission training institutions existed throughout the United States. See Robert, *American Women in Mission*, 199–200.

10. For more information on these respective institutions' histories, see Cannon III, *History of Southern Methodist Missions;* Miller, *Piety and Profession;* Scales, *All That Fits a Woman;* and Van West, "Scarritt College for Christian Workers." See https://tennessee encyclopedia.net/entries/scarritt-college-for-christian-workers/ (accessed August 28, 2024).

11. Southern women entered mission work directly out of one of the many women's denominational colleges, including but not limited to Agnes Scott College (Presbyterian), Blue Mountain College (Baptist), Brenau College (Baptist), Charlotte Female Institute/ Queen's College (Presbyterian), Columbia College (Methodist), Greensboro Female College (Methodist), Judson College (Baptist), LaGrange College (Methodist), Louisburg College (Methodist), Meredith College (Baptist), Randolph-Macon Woman's College (Methodist), Synodical College (Presbyterian), Wesleyan College (Methodist), and Wofford College (Methodist).

12. Oral History Interview with Thelma Stevens, February 13, 1972, Southern Oral History Program Collection.

13. Heck, *In Royal Service*, 205. Fannie Heck, a mission leader, educator, and administrator, was influential in Baptist women's circles during the late nineteenth and early twentieth centuries. She was born in Lithonia Springs, Virginia, in 1862, but her family moved to North Carolina when she was just a few months old. She received her education at Professor F. P. Hobgood's seminary in Raleigh and at Hollins Institute in Virginia. An active member of Raleigh's First Baptist Church, Heck sustained an intense passion for mission work. In addition to her work with the WMU Training School, Heck served as president of both the North Carolina Mission Board and the North Carolina WMU. Fannie Heck never married and died in 1915. For more information, see Farmer, *Hitherto*, and Powell, ed., *Dictionary of North Carolina Biography, vol. 3, H–K*, 92.

14. Solomon, *In the Company of Educated Women*, xix.

15. Miller, *Piety and Profession*, 219.

16. See pp 56–57 of "Minutes of the Woman's Baptist Missionary Union, Auxiliary to the Georgia Baptist Convention, 1912."

17. Scales, *All That Fits a Woman*, 68.

18. Ibid., 69–81.

19. See Woman's Missionary Union, *A Century of Service*, 37.

20. See pp. 7–8 in "Ninth Annual Announcement of the Mission Training College, Clinton, S.C., 1902-'03," Mission Training College for Inner and Foreign Missions. In the words of the institution: "The expenses of the pupil will be regulated somewhat by the

advancement and usefulness of the pupil, and by the part they take in the work." Furthermore, the Clinton, SC, school did not charge its students for "room rent, fuel or lights," and all bed clothes were free.

21. Oral History Interview with Thelma Stevens, February 13, 1972. Interview G-0058. Southern Oral History Program Collection.

22. In addition, "young ladies who are already accepted by the Committee of Foreign Missions, if in need of [further] aid," could apply to the Executive Committee of Education of the Southern Assembly. See "Ninth Annual Announcement of the Mission Training College, Clinton S.C., 1902–'03," 4–6, 8.

23. Scales, *All That Fits a Woman*, 87.

24. "Announcement" refers to the title that the Mission Training College chose to name its annual brochure.

25. See pp. 4–6, 8 in "Ninth Annual Announcement of the Mission Training College, Clinton, S.C., 1902–'03."

26. Membership in the Baptist Church was also a requirement of admission at the Woman's Missionary Union Training School in Louisville, Kentucky.

27. Scales, *All That Fits a Woman*, 96.

28. See pp. 10–11 in "Ninth Annual Announcement of the Mission Training College, Clinton, S.C., 1902–'03." Among the religious readings and textbooks that women read at Mission Training College were James Wharey's *Church History*, Archibald Alexander's *Evidence of Christianity*, Robert Flint's *Theism*, Archibald Alexander Hodge's *Commentary on the Confession of Faith*, and John H. Muirhead's *Elements of Ethics*. Included within this two-year biblical course was instruction in (and textbooks on) psychology.

29. Scarritt alumna Thelma Stevens further refers to her enrollment in several sociology classes. See Oral History Interview with Thelma Stevens, February 13, 1972.

30. Carney, *Ministers and Masters*, 7.

31. According to historian Paul Stephen Hudson, Presbyterian women worked at the Thornwell Orphanage from its opening in 1875. The orphanage's first teacher was Miss Emma Witherspoon, who was the granddaughter of a distinguished Presbyterian minister and a president of Princeton University. See Hudson, "From Old South to New South," 21.

32. Mission Training College also paid for students' "room rent, fuel and lights" as well as their bed-clothes." According to promotional literature, at the turn of the twentieth century, students could expect to pay ten dollars per year on books and five dollars per month for food.

33. Scales, *All That Fits a Woman*, 179–80.

34. See "Ninth Annual Announcement of the Mission Training College, Clinton, S.C., 1902–'03," 7. Further research confirms the successes of some of the Mission Training College alumnae. For example, Miss Emma Lee McKnight served as a missionary—along with four single women and one (presumably) widowed woman, three clerics (and their wives) and one male physician (and his wife)—with the American Presbyterian Mission (South) in 1903. Miss Ruth B., another alumna, worked as a missionary in the East Brazil mission (headquartered in Lavras)—along with two single and two (presumably) widowed women, one married couple, and two clerics (one of whom was a physician) and their

wives—with the Presbyterian Church. See also *Directory of Protestant Missionaries in China, Japan and Corea* and *the Missionary Survey*.

35. "Ninth Annual Announcement of the Mission Training College, Clinton, S.C., 1902-'03," 16.

36. By the 1920s, Scarritt had relocated to Nashville, and it had formal administrative ties to both Vanderbilt and Peabody College.

37. Oral History Interview with Thelma Stevens, February 13, 1972.

38. Miller, *Piety and Profession*, 218. According to Miller, Scarritt remained "as a school for Christian workers until 1988."

39. Note: I was unable to locate a precise closing date for the Mission Training College for Inner and Foreign Missions in Clinton, South Carolina, but approximated a date based on information from a history of Thornwell Orphanage. It operated as Thornwell Mission College at least as late as the mid-1920s. See Lynn, *The Story of Thornwell Orphanage*, 138–39.

40. See Moore, *Adaptation of Religion to Female Character*, and Slaughter, *Man and Woman*.

41. An apt example is Methodist minister J. William McCain, the friend of Marie Gordon "Gordy" Pryor Rice from chapter 5. See J. William McCain to Marie Gordon "Gordy" Pryor Rice, 9 November 1891, Franklina Gray Bartlett Papers, 1870-1930.

42. See speech Douglas delivered to churches throughout North and South Carolina, included within "Mission to Brazil: The Journal of Margaret Moore Douglas, 1906-1915."

43. Heyrman, *Southern Cross*, 19. For further discussion of the highly democratic nature (and marketing) of evangelical Protestant sects at the turn of the nineteenth century and beyond, see Calhoon, *Evangelicals and Conservatives in the Early South*, and Hill, ed., *Religion in the Southern States*.

44. See "Catalogue of the Officers, Students and Patrons of Monroe Female College, Forsyth, Georgia, 1874-1875," n.p.

45. See Emma L. Amos speech before the Women's Baptist Missionary Society in Athens, Georgia, in the James M. Chiles Family Papers, 1880-1919. For biographical information on Amos, see "Memorial Service in Honor of Miss Emma L. Amos," Baptist Woman's Missionary Union of Georgia Records, 1878-2020.

46. Ibid.

47. Ibid.

48. Emma L. Amos speech before the Women's Baptist Missionary Society in Athens, Georgia.

49. Ibid.

50. Emma Amos was certainly not the only southern woman who voiced concern about the leadership and administration of female church and missionary organizations. For discussion of similar problems within southern women's religious groups, see "Historical Sketch of the Woman's Home Missionary Society of the South Carolina Conference: Read by Mrs. W. L. Wait to the Women of the Missionary Societies of South Carolina Conference at Florence, S.C., January, 1915." Within this sketch was an excerpt (quote) from the Annual Report of the Corresponding Secretary (then Mrs. Wait) in 1900 in which she lamented the lack of consistent leadership—including frequent resignations—within the society.

51. Emma L. Amos speech before the Women's Baptist Missionary Society in Athens, Georgia.

52. Amos 6:1: "Woe to them that are at ease in Zion" (King James Bible).

53. Emma L. Amos speech before the Women's Baptist Missionary Society in Athens, Georgia.

54. Ibid.

55. During the 1920s, Pernambuco—located eight degrees south of the equator—was a city of approximately 240,000 residents. See "Mission to Brazil: The Journal of Margaret Moore Douglas, 1906–1915." Note: While this chapter focuses upon the ways by which Margaret Moore Douglas marketed mission work, chapter 7 will include fuller analysis of her experiences in Brazil and how she fit relative to the group of women engaging in foreign mission work in the very late nineteenth and early twentieth centuries.

56. Note: I located this biographical information on Margaret Moore Douglas in the "Introduction" to her transcribed journal (kept between 1906 and 1915 when she served as a missionary and teacher in Pernambuco, Brazil, and transcribed by her niece, Mary Craig Douglas Stauffer, in 1988). See ibid.

57. Ibid. While Douglas lived the life that she promoted, she often refrained from divulging her professional accomplishments to those to whom she lectured.

58. Speech within "Mission to Brazil."

59. Ibid.

60. See Turkey Creek Baptist Church (Abbeville County, S.C.) Woman's Missionary Society, Minute Book. Papers or meeting themes were not uncommonly read, or commented upon, at Woman's Missionary Society meetings and community events. Some titles of papers written or given by members and meeting themes acknowledged include: 1) "Finance in Missions" (open discussion on August 8, 1920); 2) "Our State's Part in the Campaign for Denominational Education" (open discussion on September 12, 1920); 3) "The Development of Christian Education" (paper given by Miss Annie Moore—September 12, 1920); 4) "Christian Education" (paper given by Mrs. R. L. Beasley—September 12, 1920); 5) "The Cure of Bodies and Souls" (paper given by Mrs. R. L. Beasley on November 14, 1920); 6) "Foreign Missions as a Dying Soldier Sees Them" (paper given by Miss Annie Moore on November 14, 1920); 7) "Foreign Missions" (open discussion on December 12, 1920); 8) "The Call to China for Me" (paper given by Miss Annie Moore on December 12, 1920); 9) "Things that are Lovely in Chinese Character" (paper given by Mrs. J. T. Cochran on December 12, 1920); 10) "What God thinks of Missions" (paper given by Mrs. J. W. Kirkpatrick on January 25, 1921); 11) "The Baptist Conception of Christian Citizenship" (paper given by multiple members on March 13, 1921); 12) "How the Union Fell" (poem read by Miss Inez Agnew on February 13, 1921); 13) "Can a Man be a Christian and not believe in Missions?" (paper given by Annie Moore on August 14, 1921). See also Martha Virginia McNair Evans Patterson Papers, 1858–1992, folder 35, for further examples of papers given by women at the First Presbyterian Church of Augusta, Georgia.

61. Ladies Benevolent and Missionary Society of the Presbyterian Church (Athens, Ga.) Record Book, 1882–1885.

62. See "Mt. Zion Academy" among many applicable writings about religious organizations, institutions, and people within the Northen Family Papers, 1832–1944. See also a

history of the Woman's Missionary Union Auxiliary to the Rappahannock Baptist Association written by Olive Elliott Bagby, a single woman from King and Queen County, Virginia, who twice served as a Baptist missionary to China. See Olive Elliott Bagby Papers, 1904–1915.

63. See *Missionary Circles, No. 2* in Martha Virginia McNair Evans Patterson Papers, 1858–1992. While no date is ascribed to *Missionary Circles*, it likely dates to the very late nineteenth or very early twentieth century. The folder in which I found this copy of *Missionary Circles* included a variety of printed sources from the last decade of the nineteenth and the first decade of the twentieth century.

64. Examples of non-Presbyterian and/or non-southern-authored lectures and leaflets in or alongside *Missionary Circles* include "The Responsibility of Not Doing," by Mrs. G. P. Durham of New Haven, Connecticut, read at the sixteenth annual meeting of the Woman's Baptist Foreign Missionary, 1887; and "India: Questions and Answers for Mission Circles and Bands," by Mrs. John Newton, Philadelphia, 1895. There existed similar leaflets on other foreign mission locations, including Africa, China, Chinese in America, Japan, Mexico, Persia, Siam and Laos, South America, and Syria. The leaflet on India was forty-two pages in length and included some vocabulary and information about currency, geography, Indian cultural values, and the history of Protestant missions in India.

65. Mrs. G. P. Durham, "The Responsibility of Not Doing," 8 in Martha Virginia McNair Evans Patterson Papers, 1858–1992.

66. See "Report of Woman's Missionary Society of Fayetteville (NC) Presbytery, 1897," in Martha Virginia McNair Evans Patterson Papers, 1858–1992.

67. Martha Virginia McNair Evans Patterson Papers, 1858–1992, folder 35.

68. "Talks About Christian Giving, No. 3, Thanksgiving Ann," by Mrs. Kate W. Hamilton, pp. 10–11 in Martha Virginia McNair Evans Patterson Papers, 1858–1992, folder 35.

69. Although no date is ascribed to the pamphlet, based on materials in the Turkey Creek, SC, Baptist Church minute book, it is likely that it dates to the 1910s. See "W.M.U. Interest in Inter-Racial Relations" by Mrs. W. J. Neel, Georgia, Turkey Creek Baptist Church (Abbeville County, S.C.). Women's Missionary Society, Minute Book. For a fuller biography of Isa Beall Williams Neel, see chapter 5.

70. Ibid.

71. Ibid.

72. Ibid.

73. See Phillips, *American Negro Slavery*.

74. Gardner, *Blood & Irony*, 4–5; see also chapter 5, "Righting the Wrongs of History, 1905–1915."

7. FOREIGN MISSION WORK AT HOME AND IN THE FIELD

1. At times, I will use the following abbreviations for each of these churches: PCUS for Presbyterian Church of the United States (Southern Presbyterians); MEC, South, for Methodist Episcopal Church, South; and SBC for Southern Baptist Convention.

2. Heck, *In Royal Service*, 85.

3. For an applicable sample of southern female missionaries—including concise biographies—who possessed higher-level educations, see Appendix: Missionary Biographies, pp. 349–67, in Flynt and Berkley, *Taking Christianity to China*.

4. 17 November 1906 entry in "Mission to Brazil: The Journal of Margaret Moore Douglas, 1906–1915."

5. Frances McBryde Worth to Kathryn Worth, Mary Josephine McBryde Worth "Mama" and Dave, 3 May 1926, James Spencer Worth Papers, 1849–1969.

6. See Durway, "'The Field Is Endless,'" 207–19. While this article focuses upon those Presbyterian women who engaged in home mission work, Durway does cite a few foreign missionaries and their more progressive racial politics.

7. In the words of the first SBC president, William Bullein Johnson, the church created the Foreign Mission Board in 1845 "for the purpose of organizing an efficient and practical plan, on which the energies of the whole Baptist denomination, throughout America, may be elicited, combined and directed in one sacred effort for sending the word of life to idolatrous lands." See "Southern Baptist Convention—International Mission Board," http://www.sbc.net/aboutus/entities/imb.asp (accessed September 4, 2024).

8. See Heck, *In Royal Service*, 371.

9. See Colby and Peck, eds., *The International Year Book*, 601. Although highly eclectic, this source provides compact, yet detailed, information on each of the denomination-wide foreign mission societies throughout the United States. Specific details for each society (or board) include: 1) date of organization, 2) income from home sources, 3) income from foreign sources, 4) total number of missionaries, 5) total number of denomination-organized churches, 6) number of communicants, and 7) native contributions (in U.S. dollars). See also: 1) *Statistical Atlas of Christian Missions* for similar information for the year 1910, and 2) "Early Methodist Protestant Foreign Missions," in *Virginia United Methodist Heritage*, 17–26. The latter source is a brochure-length source.

10. See T. B. Ray (Foreign Secretary of the SBC Foreign Mission Board) to L. R. Bagby, 21 June 1915, in Olive Elliot Bagby Papers, 1904–1915.

11. Trueheart, *Brief History of the Woman's Foreign Missionary Society*, 1.

12. Daggett, ed., *Historical Sketches of Woman's Missionary Societies in America and England*, 143.

13. For information on the early years of the WMU, see Heck, *In Royal Service*, 109–19. According to Heck, "the first vague hint of a general woman's organization came from an early Committee on Woman's Work, appointed by the Southern Baptist Convention in 1879." This proposal was too bold at the time. However, a couple years later, in 1881, the Committee on Woman's Work recommended that the Foreign Mission Board designate a woman as "superintendent of Woman's Work." This development ultimately led to greater things, including their greater influence in the male-led Foreign Mission Board of the SBC as well as the founding of the WMU. One should consult Boyd, *Presbyterian Women in America*, 39–42, for additional information on the establishment of the Women of the Church (PCUS).

14. Donovan, "Women as Foreign Missionaries in the Episcopal Church, 1820-1920," 20.

15. Ladies Benevolent and Missionary Society of the Presbyterian Church (Athens, Ga.) Record Book, 1882–1885.

16. See p. 1 of "History of Woman's Missionary Union, Auxiliary to Rappahannock Baptist Association," in Olive Elliot Bagby Papers.

17. Ibid., 2.

18. A few secondary sources that focus upon gender discrimination faced by female missionaries whose ties were not with the American South include Hill, *The World Their Household;* Huber and Lutkehaus, eds., *Gendered Missions;* chapter 5 of Robert, *American Women in Mission;* and Robert, ed., *Gospel Bearers, Gender.* This latter source, however, focuses on the period after 1930 and may not be as applicable as the first three identified sources.

19. Emma L. Amos speech before the Women's Baptist Missionary Society in Athens, Georgia, in the James M. Chiles Family Papers, 1880–1919. Unfortunately, I have no date for this speech. For more information on Amos, see chapter 6, note 45.

20. See "Relation of Female Education to Home Mission Work" (August 1884), included in Brown and Brown, eds., *Life and Letters of Laura Askew Haygood,* 89.

21. Methodist bishop Holland McTyeire was an important figure in the history of the MEC, South. A native of South Carolina, McTyeire attended Randolph-Macon College in the 1840s and then, upon receiving his license to preach, served as a minister, first in Virginia and later in Alabama. During the 1850s, McTyeire edited the *New Orleans Christian Advocate* and the *Nashville Christian Advocate,* the central mouthpiece of the MEC, South. After the Civil War, McTyeire reentered the pastorate in the Alabama Conference and was soon elected a bishop of the Church. In later life he, played a pivotal role in the founding of Vanderbilt University. See Fitzgerald, *Holland N. McTyeire.*

22. Bishop McTyeire to Mrs. D. H. McGavock, General Secretary of the Woman's Foreign Missionary Society [date unknown], as quoted in Trueheart, *Brief History of the Woman's Foreign Missionary Society,* 5–6. Although Trueheart did not identify a date for the letter exchanged between McTyeire and McGavock, I am surmising that the bishop wrote it in either 1888 or very early 1889. My reason is two-fold: First, the bishop refers to the ten-year anniversary of the Woman's Foreign Missionary Society, MEC, South (which would have been in May 1888) and 2) Bishop McTyeire died in February 1889.

23. Woman's Foreign Missionary Society of the Methodist Episcopal Church, South Records, 1881–1889. According to *Minutes of the Annual Conferences of the Methodist Episcopal Church, South,* Reverend Dillard enjoyed strong relationships with women and appreciated their intellectual capabilities as well as their strong characters and religious convictions. As such, his praises for the Cherokee Corner Women's Foreign Missionary Society (MEC, South) were likely genuine. See *Minutes of the Annual Conferences of the Methodist Episcopal Church, South for the Year 1898,* 135–37. I identified further evidence of male clerics' support for the Woman's Foreign Missionary Society and its public "missionary expressions" in one officer's "Report of Delegate to the Missionary Conference held at Decatur." She referred to Atlanta pastor Reverend T. R. Kendall of Grace Methodist Church and his missionary sermon, which was full of "encouragement and approbation" of the women of the church in their efforts to spread the Gospel. See p. 16, "Report of Delegate to

the Missionary Conference held at Decatur" in Woman's Foreign Missionary Society of the Methodist Episcopal Church, South Records, 1881–1889.

24. Stuart McGuire, MD to MEC, South Foreign Mission Board, 27 February 1907, Emily Earl Chenault Runyan Papers, 1857–1956.

25. Trueheart, *Brief History of the Woman's Foreign Missionary Society*, 7–8.

26. See Appendix E (Woman's Missionary Union—Cash and Box Contributions for 25 Years) in Heck, *In Royal Service*, 376–77.

27. Heck included financial information re: foreign missions for other denominations. Ibid., 135.

28. Hill, *The World Their Household*, 3.

29. Woman's Missionary Society of the Lexington Methodist Church (Lexington, Ga.) minutes (1929–1939).

30. After examining several sources, I concluded that most such positions were held by married women. These included the Ladies Benevolent and Missionary Society of the Presbyterian Church (Athens, Ga.) Record Book, 1882–1885; Woman's Foreign Missionary Society of the Methodist Episcopal Church South Records, 1881–1889; Woman's Missionary Society of the Lexington Methodist Church (Lexington, Ga.) minutes (1929–1939); Olive Elliot Bagby Papers, 1904–1915.

31. Women's Foreign Missionary Society of the Methodist Episcopal Church South Records, 1881–1889. This source is a single notebook consisting of approximately seventy pages of notes kept by one of the secretaries for this organization. It gives a detailed accounting of each monthly meeting, identifying the organization's activities, speeches given by its members and by guests, summaries of annual denomination-wide missionary meetings, and regular updates on fundraising progress/financial health. The *Woman's Missionary Advocate* was published by the Woman's Missionary Society of the MEC, South (headquartered in Nashville). The Woman's Missionary Society published its first edition of the *Advocate*, "a neat sixteen-page paper," in 1880. By the end of its second year, the *Advocate* counted 8,500 subscribers. In one person's estimation the society had produced "three hundred and forty-nine thousand eight hundred and seventy-two pages of missionary reading, in the form of leaflets, tracts, and cards have been issued and distributed." See Daggett, ed., *Historical Sketches of Woman's Missionary Societies in America and England*, 145.

32. Ibid.

33. See Decker, *A Continuing Light, 1813–1963*, 30. Likewise, female attendees of annual conventions—for example, the Annual Convention of the Woman's Home and Foreign Missionary Society of the Evangelical Lutheran Synod of Southwestern Virginia—wrote reports that were published in *The Lutheran Visitor, Our Church Paper, the Southern Lutheran*, and *Wytheville Paper*. These female-authored articles were largely based upon the many reports and speeches given by those Lutheran women who administered the Committees on President's Report, Treasurer's Report, Last Year's Minutes, Auxiliaries' Reports, Letters and Papers, and others.

34. See Olive Elliot Bagby Papers, 1904–1915.

35. Trueheart, *Brief History of the Woman's Foreign Missionary Society*, 7–8; Heck, *In Royal Service*, 366–67.

36. Technically, one of the denoted nations, "Africa," was a continent. Of course, this did

not signify that each denomination sent 40+ women missionaries abroad *each year.* Rather, it meant that in any given year there were 40+ women representing each denomination via active foreign service.

37. See Heuser, "Presbyterian Women and the Missionary Call, 1870–1923."

38. Consulted sources for basic information on locations and dates of southern foreign missions include *The Missionary Survey: The Presbyterian Church in the U.S. at Home and Abroad, February 1920;* Brown, "Overseas Mission Program and Policies of the Presbyterian Church in the U.S., 1861–1983"; Heck, *In Royal Service;* and Trueheart, *Brief History of the Woman's Foreign Missionary Society.*

39. See Emily Earl Chenault Runyan Papers, 1857–1956. See also Woman's Medical College of Chicago, *The Institution and Its Founders: Class Histories, 1870–1896,* and Crane, "A Century of PCUS Medical Mission, 1881–1983."

40. See "The Entry of Women into Medicine in America," https://www.hws.edu/about /history/elizabeth-blackwell/entry-of-women-into-medicine.aspx (accessed September 6, 2024).

41. Numerous extant letters from 1909, written by Runyon's friends, colleagues, and professionals within the Richmond community, pled the MEC, South, Foreign Mission Board to reconsider its decision to release her. Some went as far as to state that the church had unfairly accused Runyon. These include those written by Alma M. Cecil, Russell M. Cecil (pastor, Second Presbyterian Church, Richmond), Anne Clay-Crenshaw, S.W. Crenshaw, William S. Gordon (medical doctor in Richmond, in his words the "leading nerve specialist in Virginia") and D. Saussure (Richmond lawyer). See Emily Earl Chenault Runyan Papers, 1857–1956.

42. Huntley, "Presbyterian Women's Work and Rights in the Korean Mission."

43. Crane, "A Century of PCUS Medical Mission, 1881–1983."

44. For more information on these early MEC, South/Woman's Missionary Society pursuits, see Daggett, ed., *Historical Sketches of Woman's Missionary Societies in America and England,* 147–48.

45. For example, each appeared to enjoy a respectful, yet subordinate, relationship with male leadership within their respective denominations.

46. Rev. Egbert W. Smith, D.D., "Margaret Douglas: An Appreciation," the *Presbyterian Survey* (September 1940): 405–7, included within "Mission to Brazil: The Journal of Margaret Moore Douglas, 1906–1915."

47. On October 16, 1848, the First Baptist Church of Charleston appointed its first missionaries—B. W. Whilden and his family—to serve in China. Sadly, Mr. Whilden suffered the loss of his wife and, later, a second wife, to illness there. See "First Church Charleston Notes Historic Commissioning—South Carolina Baptist Convention": http://www.scbaptist .org/first-church-charleston-notes-historic-commissioning/ (accessed August 4, 2015).

48. Sources of biographical information for Lula Whilden include Heck, *In Royal Service,* 253–62; Huff, *Greenville,* 252; and Lula F. Whilden, *Life Sketches from a Heathen Land.*

49. Mildred Rutherford, unknown date in Brown and Brown, eds., *Life and Letters of Laura Askew Haygood,* 27.

50. The major source of biographical information for Laura Askew Haygood is chapters 1–3 in Brown and Brown, eds., *Life and Letters of Laura Askew Haygood.*

51. For biographical information on Margaret Moore Douglas, see: 1) "Introduction" to Douglas's transcribed journal (kept between 1906 and 1915 when she served as a missionary and teacher in Pernambuco, and transcribed by her niece, Mary Craig Douglas Stauffer, in 1988), and 2) Rev. Egbert W. Smith, D.D., "Margaret Douglas: An Appreciation." Both sources are part of "Mission to Brazil: The Journal of Margaret Moore Douglas, 1906–1915," edited by Mary Douglas Stauffer.

52. Miss Worth entered foreign mission work before she was thirty. Little evidence exists that might shed light on her life experiences between the end of her formal education and her acceptance as a Presbyterian foreign missionary in 1924. I gleaned this biographical information on Frances McBryde Worth from: 1) miscellaneous letters written by Miss Worth from the *James Spencer Worth Papers,* and 2) miscellaneous sources attached to her on *Ancestry.com.* The latter included her obituary in the *Greensboro News & Record* from February 21, 1989, Salem Academy yearbooks from the 1910s, and her U.S. passport application from 1924. See James Spencer Worth Papers, 1849–1969.

53. Laura Haygood to Miss Mollie Stevens, 17 March 1885, in Brown and Brown, eds., *Life and Letters of Laura Askew Haygood,* 126.

54. Similarly, Haygood recorded in October 1884, on the eve of her voyage to China: "Within the last ten days I have come to feel that if the work of God in China needs women, there is no woman in all the world under more obligation to go than I am. As far as the decision rests with me, I am ready." See Brown and Brown, eds., *Life and Letters of Laura Askew Haygood,* 99.

55. See "Intro," p. vii in "Mission to Brazil: The Journal of Margaret Moore Douglas, 1906–1915."

56. Heck, *In Royal Service,* 258.

57. Laura Askew Haygood to MEC, South, Woman's Board, 22 March 1886, in Brown and Brown, eds., *Life and Letters of Laura Askew Haygood,* 150.

58. Technically, the Shanghai District also included missions in Nanziang and Soochow. In 1900, Shanghai was a large city with a population approximating 1 million.

59. Ya-chen, ed., *New Modern Chinese Women and Gender Politics.*

60. Laura Askew Haygood to Mrs. F. A. Butler, 30 October 1885, in Brown and Brown, eds., *Life and Letters of Laura Askew Haygood,* 156–57.

61. See 1891 and 1893 reports on the Shanghai District prepared by Laura Askew Haygood for the MEC, South, in Brown and Brown, eds., *Life and Letters of Laura Askew Haygood,* 147–49.

62. Laura Askew Haygood to MEC, South, Woman's Board, 22 March 1886, in Brown and Brown, eds., *Life and Letters of Laura Askew Haygood,* 150.

63. Ibid.

64. Laura Askew Haygood to Mrs. D. H. McGavock, 10 March 1885, in Brown and Brown, eds., *Life and Letters of Laura Askew Haygood,* 154. As an aside, Mrs. McGavock made the first donation ($4,000) for what became the Clopton School in the early 1880s. See Trueheart, *Brief History of the Woman's Foreign Missionary Society,* 2.

65. Laura Askew Haygood to MEC, South, Woman's Board, 22 March 1886, in Brown and Brown, eds., *Life and Letters of Laura Askew Haygood,* 152.

66. 1891 Report (prepared by Laura Haygood) to the Foreign Mission Board, MEC, South, in Brown and Brown, eds., *Life and Letters of Laura Askew Haygood*, 148.

67. 1893 Report (prepared by Laura Haygood) to the Foreign Mission Board, MEC, South, in Brown and Brown, eds., *Life and Letters of Laura Askew Haygood*, 148–49.

68. Oswald Eugene Brown and Anna Muse Brown, the author-editors of *Life and Letters of Laura Askew Haygood,* made this observation in 1904. See p. 164.

69. See Heck, *In Royal Service,* Appendix A ("Women Missionaries of Southern Baptist Convention, Table II—On the Field in 1913"), 366–69. For an example of a Baptist woman in education/education management, see Griggs, "Margie Shumate: A Virginia Missionary's Experiences in Asia, 1915–1958."

70. Most of the biographical content in this paragraph came from Heck, *In Royal Service,* 257–59.

71. Heck, *In Royal Service,* 262.

72. Whilden, *Life Sketches from a Heathen Land,* 11.

73. Assertion made by Lula Whilden and corroborated by Fannie Heck. See Whilden, *Life Sketches from a Heathen Land,* chapters 2 and 6, and Heck, *In Royal Service,* 260.

74. Lula Whilden as quoted in Heck, *In Royal Service,* 260.

75. Lula Whilden, *Life Sketches from a Heathen Land,* 26, 29. Other negative descriptors and phrases concerning heathen Chinese mothers included "selfish" and "gross darkness covers [them]."

76. Again, it is impossible to determine the extent to which Lula Whilden sanitized her remembrances for public consumption. Fellow Baptist missionary in China Miss Margie Shumate made mention of women who did not display a "professional" character. Shumate particularly disliked a Miss Alvada Gunn of Crawfordville, Georgia, who referred to Chinese students at her school as the "little brown girls."

77. For more insight into late Qing Dynasty China and particularly relevant issues of gender, see Huang, *Negotiating Masculinities in Late Imperial China;* Pruitt, *A Daughter of Han;* Qian, Fong, and Smith, eds., *Different Worlds of Discourse;* and Ya-chen, ed., *New Modern Chinese Women and Gender Politics.*

78. See p. 41 (9 January 1907), "Mission to Brazil: The Journal of Margaret Moore Douglas, 1906–1915," edited by Mary Douglas Stauffer, hereafter "Mission to Brazil."

79. The American College of Pernambuco was later renamed the Agnes Erskine School, sometimes also denoted as Agnes Erskine College or the Agnes Erskine Presbyterian College.

80. For decades, Margaret Douglas exhibited a strong dislike for Catholicism. On no occasion did she concede that Christianity encompassed those who did not identify with Protestant churches.

81. pp. 56–57 (18 May 1907), "Mission to Brazil."

82. p. 149 (15 January 1911), "Mission to Brazil."

83. p. 33 (23 December 1906), "Mission to Brazil."

84. pp. 48–50 (23 March 1907), "Mission to Brazil."

85. While I know that Douglas distributed these parables to her students, I do not know whether she published them or simply printed them.

86. p. 100, "Corinna's Dolls," in "Mission to Brazil."

87. p. 143 (2 October 1910), "Mission to Brazil."

88. p. 90 (24 May 1908), "Mission to Brazil."

89. Pp. H1-H26, "History of the Agnes Erskine School" by Margaret Douglas, in "Mission to Brazil." Note: Douglas prepared this institutional history in 1933.

90. Details about the growth of the Agnes Erskine Presbyterian College came from a speech given by Douglas to various Presbyterian churches in North and South Carolina in 1925 when she was on furlough. See p. S4, "Mission to Brazil."

91. In an unknown year, the American College of Pernambuco was renamed the Agnes Erskine Presbyterian College. Curiously, Douglas omits any discussion of the name change for the school in the institutional history she produced in 1933.

92. C. Darby Fulton to Janie W. McGaughey, 12 September 1935, "Mission to Brazil."

93. Examples, some of whom denominations have celebrated for generations, include Mary Raleigh Anderson (Southern Baptist missionary in China between 1917 and 1937); Virginia Atkinson (Southern Methodist missionary in China between 1884 and 1941); Virginia Leftwich Bell (Southern Presbyterian in China between 1917 and 1941); Addie Cox (Southern Baptist missionary in China between 1918 and 1951); Sophie Stephens Lanneau (Southern Baptist in China between 1907 and 1950); Charlotte "Lottie" Digges Moon (Southern Baptist missionary in China between 1873 and 1912); and Anna Cunningham Safford (Southern Presbyterian missionary in China between 1873 and her death in 1890). See Hazen, *In Memoriam: Anna C. Safford; Sullivan and Moon: A Southern Baptist Missionary in China in History and Legend;* "Biographical Dictionary of Chinese Christianity," http://www.bdcc online.net/en/ (accessed May 14, 2024).

94. Frances McBryde Worth to Mary Josephine McBryde Worth "Ma" and Kathryn Worth, 22 March 1925, James Spencer Worth Papers, 1849–1969.

95. Frances McBryde Worth to Kathryn Worth, 3 May 1925.

96. Frances McBryde Worth to Mary Josephine McBryde Worth "Ma" and Kathryn Worth, 15 March 1925.

97. Frances McBryde Worth to Mary Josephine McBryde Worth "Ma" and Kathryn Worth, 22 March 1925.

98. Frances McBryde Worth to Kathryn Worth, Mary Josephine McBryde Worth "Mama" and Dave, 3 May 1926.

99. At this time, I do not know of the circumstances surrounding her departure from the Belgian Congo. Additional research is necessary.

100. Frances McBryde Worth Obituary, *Greensboro News & Record,* February 21, 1989, located on www.ancestry.com/.

EPILOGUE: FROM PEDESTAL TO PULPIT

1. A few consulted sources to make this point include Decker, *A Continuing Light, 1813–1963;* Doyle, D.D., Ph.D., *Presbyterian Home Missions;* Fairchild, *Memoir of Mrs. Louisa A. Lowrie, of the Northern India Mission;* Thompson, *Presbyterian Missions in the Southern United States;* Whilden, *Life Sketches from a Heathen Land;* and a pamphlet, "W.M.U. Interest

in Inter-Racial Relations" by Mrs. W.J. Neel, Georgia, within "Turkey Creek Baptist Church (Abbeville County, S.C.) Women's Missionary Society, Minute Book Minute Book, 1911–1925.

2. Many but fewer sources exist that shed light on the more private lives and thoughts among southern women engaged in faith-based activities and careers. In order to fully unveil the white southern female mission worker—that is, her identity beyond her constructed image—scholars will need to locate and carefully study her personal materials, such as diaries, scrapbooks, and correspondence with family and friends not directly tied to missionary work. A good example of the latter would be the extensive personal correspondence of Frances McBryde Worth, a Presbyterian missionary who served in the Belgian Congo in the 1920s. One focus of chapter 7, Worth was a whiny, self-centered, impatient, and arrogant woman who exuded little interest in, and perhaps contempt for, those whom she served. While Worth may not have been typical among her colleagues, her sources challenge the lofty position which female mission workers assumed and marketed.

3. "Memorial Service in Honor of Miss Emma L. Amos," Baptist Woman's Missionary Union of Georgia Records, 1878–2020.

4. Rev. Egbert W. Smith, D.D., "Margaret Douglas: An Appreciation," the *Presbyterian Survey* (September 1940): 405–7, included within "Mission to Brazil: The Journal of Margaret Moore Douglas, 1906–1915."

5. Incidentally, this merger also incorporated most congregations from the much smaller Methodist Protestant Church (MPC). The MPC formed in 1828. It identifies with Wesleyan doctrine but ascribes to congregational governance. As of 2024, a few dozen Methodist Protestant Church congregations, mostly in the Deep South, remain. See https://www.themethodistprotestantchurch.org/about-us/ (accessed September 18, 2024).

6. See Chaffin, "A Southern Advocate of Methodist Unification in 1865"; and Moore, "Church Efficiency."

7. See Davis, *The Methodist Unification;* and Knotts, "The Debates over Race and Women's Ordination in the 1939 Methodist Merger."

8. Hess and McCarthy, "A Life Lived in Response."

9. In 1967, the Watts Street Baptist Church left the SBC and aligned with the American Baptist Churches USA.

10. Durso, "Journey to Ordination."

11. Griffith, *God's Daughters.*

12. Johnson, *This Is Our Message.*

BIBLIOGRAPHY

PRIMARY SOURCES

MANUSCRIPTS AND RARE BOOKS

Duke University, Perkins Library, Durham, NC

Louis Manigault Papers, 1776–1883

Georgia Historical Society, Savannah, GA

Sallie Didd Beck Johnson Commonplace Book, 1860–1881
George Galphin Nowlan and Ann Elizabeth Nowlan MacDonnell Diaries, 1851–1905
Ellen McAlpin Notebook and Visitors' Book, 1882–1913
Miscellaneous Student Notebooks, 1820–1921
Northen Family Papers, 1832–1944

Mercer University, Tarver Library, Archives, Special Collections, & Digital Initiatives, Macon, GA

Baptist Woman's Missionary Union of Georgia Records, 1878–2020
Ruth Jinks Papers, 1911–1936

University of Georgia, Special Collections Libraries, Athens, GA—Hargrett Rare Book & Manuscript Library

Nellie Peters Black Papers, 1875–1920
James M. Chiles Family Papers, 1880–1919
Cyrena Bailey Stone Diary, 1864
Ladies Benevolent and Missionary Society of the Presbyterian Church (Athens, Ga.) Record Book, 1882–1885
Vashti School Postcard, 1928

Woman's Foreign Missionary Society of the Methodist Episcopal Church
South Records, 1881–1898
Woman's Missionary Society of the Lexington Methodist Church
(Lexington, Ga.) Minutes, 1929–1939

University of North Carolina at Chapel Hill, Wilson Library,
Chapel Hill, NC—Southern Historical Collection

Alexander and Hillhouse Family Papers, 1758–1976
Elizabeth Willis Gloster Anderson Memoranda, 1822–1862
Everard Green Baker Papers, 1848–1876
Mary E. Bateman Diary, 1856
Mary Jeffreys Bethell Diary, 1853–1873
Bumpass Family Papers, 1838–1972
Carmichael Family Diaries and Commonplace Books, 1803–1850
Caroline Elizabeth Burgwin Clitherall Diaries, 1751–1860
Laura Beecher Comer Papers, 1862–1899
Copp Family Papers, 1820–1917
Susan Cornwall Diary, 1857–1866
Jane Evans Elliot Diaries, 1837–1882
Gale and Polk Family Papers, 1815–1940
Maria Southgate Hawes Reminiscences, 1914
Drury Lacy Papers, 1823–1965
Ella Noland MacKenzie Miscellaneous Papers, 1851–1905
William Parson McCorkle Papers, 1806–1922
Martha Virginia McNair Evans Patterson Papers, 1858–1992
Emma Maria Service Papers, 1803–1892
Susan Dabney Smedes Papers, 1860–1930
Sarah Lois Wadley Papers, 1849–1886
C. H. Wiley Papers, 1774–1962
Oral History Interview with Thelma Stevens, February 13, 1972

University of South Carolina, South Caroliniana Library, Columbia, SC

"Catalogue and Announcement of the Mission Training College for Inner and
Foreign Missions"
"The Development of the South Carolina Woman's Missionary Union as I have
known it, 1902–1912," Mrs. J. D. Chapman
Margaret Moore Douglas, "Mission to Brazil: The Journal of Margaret Moore
Douglas, 1906–1915"
Female Mite Societies of South Carolina
"Historical Sketch of the Woman's Home Missionary Society of the South
Carolina Conference," Read by Mrs. W. L. Wait to the Women of the

Missionary Societies of South Carolina Conference at Florence, S.C., January 1915
Minutes of the ... Annual Session of the Woman's Missionary Union, Auxiliary to the Baptist State Convention of South Carolina
Minnie Webb Spearman Papers, 1903–1960
Maria Baker Taylor Papers, 1829–1990
Turkey Creek Baptist Church (Abbeville County, S.C.). Women's Missionary Society, Minute Book
Woman's Missionary Union, "A Century of Service" (pamphlet)

Virginia Museum of History & Culture, Richmond, VA
Sallie Ann Acree Scrapbook, 1863–1865
Olive Elliott Bagby Papers, 1904–1915
Barbour Family Papers, 1810–1890
Franklina Gray Bartlett Papers, 1870–1930
Byrd Family Papers, 1791–1867
Virginia Eppes Dance Campbell Papers, 1858–1865
Emily Dupuy Papers, 1810–1866
Mary Washington Cabell Early Scrapbook, 1866–1911
Mary Custis Lee Papers, 1694–1917
Esther Fox Maxey, "Miss Ora and Miss Etta: A Folk History of the Women at the Episcopal Mission Schools" (unpublished manuscript)
Proceedings of the Annual Convention of the Woman's Home and Foreign Missionary Society of the Evangelical Lutheran Synod of Southwestern Virginia

Western Carolina University, Hunter Library Digital Collections
Appalachian Industrial Schools Records

PERIODICALS

Home Mission Monthly   *Southern Christian Advocate*
New York Times   *Southern Literary Magazine*
Our Home Field   *Spirit of Missions*

PUBLISHED PRIMARY SOURCES

American Baptist Year-Book 1917. Philadelphia: American Baptist Publication Society, 1917.
Andrews, C. W., ed. *Memoirs of Mrs. Ann R. Page.* New York: Garland Publishing, Inc, 1987.

Battle, A. J. *Piety, the True Ornament and Dignity of Woman*. Marion, AL: Dennis Dyk-ous, 1857.

Brown, Oswald Eugene, and Anna Muse Brown. *Life and Letters of Laura Askew Hay-good*. Nashville: Smith & Lamar, 1904.

Brown, William Wells Brown. *Narrative of William W. Brown, A Fugitive Slave*. Boston: Anti-slavery Office, 1847.

Bumpass, Frances M., Eugenia H. Bumpass, and F. A. Bumpass. *Autobiography and Journal*. Nashville: M.E. Church, South, 1899.

Burr, Virginia Ingraham, ed. *The Secret Eye: The Journal of Ella Gertrude Clanton Thomas, 1848–1889*. Chapel Hill: University of North Carolina Press, 1990.

Burwell, Letitia M. *A Girl's Life in Virginia Before the War*. New York: Frederick A. Stokes Company, 1895.

Carter, Tomeiko Ashford, ed., *Virginia Broughton: The Life and Writings of a National Baptist Missionary*. Knoxville: University of Tennessee Press, 2010.

Clay-Clopton, Virginia. *A Belle of the Fifties; Memoirs of Mrs. Clay of Alabama, Covering Social and Political Life in Washington and the South, 1853–66*. New York: Double-day, Page & Company, 1904.

Clayton, Victoria V. *White and Black under the Old Regime*. Milwaukee: Young Churchman Co., 1899.

Colby, Frank Moore, and Harry Thurston Peck, eds. *The International Year Book: A Compendium of the World's Progress during the Year 1901*. New York: Dodd, Mead & Company, 1901.

DeSaussure, Nancy Bostwick. *Old Plantation Days: Being Recollections of Southern Life efore the Civil War*. New York: Duffield & Company, 1909.

Directory of Protestant Missionaries in China, Japan and Corea. Hong Kong: Hong Kong Daily Press Office, 1903.

Drew, Benjamin. *A North-side View of Slavery. The Refugee; or, The Narratives of Fu-gitive Slaves in Canada Related by Themselves. With an Account of the History and Condition of the Colored Population of Upper Canada*. Boston: J. P. Jewett & Co.; New York: Sheldon, Lamport & Blakeman, 1856.

Eliot, George. *Middlemarch: A Study of Provincial Life*. New York: Harper, 1876.

French, A. M. *Slavery in South Carolina and the Ex-Slaves; or, The Port Royal Mission*. New York: W. M. French, 1862.

Handbooks on the Missions of the Episcopal Church: Liberia. New York: National Coun-cil of the Protestant Episcopal Church, 1928.

Haskin, Sara Estelle. *Women and Missions in the Methodist Episcopal Church, South*. Nashville: Publishing House of the Methodist Episcopal Church, South, 1925.

Heck, Fannie E. S. *In Royal Service*. Richmond, VA: Foreign Mission Board of the Southern Baptist Convention, 1913.

Hopkins, John Henry. "A Scriptural, Ecclesiastical, and Historical View of Slavery: From the Days of the Patriarch Abraham, to the Nineteenth Century: Addressed to the Right Rev. Alonzo Potter." New York: W. I. Pooley, 1861, 1864.

Hyer, G. W. *Bishop Hopkins' Letter on Slavery Ripped Up and His Misuse of the Sacred Scriptures Exposed.* New York: John F. Trow, 1863.

Jones, Charles C. *The Religious Instruction of the Negroes. In the United States.* Savannah, GA: Thomas Purse, printer, 1844.

Kemble, Frances Anne. *Journal of a Residence on a Georgian Plantation in 1838–1839,* edited by John A. Scott. Athens: University of Georgia Press, 1984.

Lane, Lunsford. *The Narrative of Lunsford Lane, Formerly of Raleigh, N.C.: Embracing an account of his early life, the redemption of purchase of himself and family from slavery, And his banishment from the place of his birth for the crime of wearing a colored skin.* Boston: Published by the Author, 1842.

LeClercq, Anne Sinkler Whaley, ed. *Between North and South: The Letters of Emily Wharton Sinkler, 1842–1865.* Columbia: University of South Carolina Press, 2001.

Lounsbury, Richard C., ed. *Louisa S. McCord: Poems, Drama, Biography, Letters.* Charlottesville: University Press of Virginia, 1996.

Marcus, Jacob R. *Memoirs of American Jews, 1773–1865.* Philadelphia: Jewish Publication Society of America, 1955–56.

McTyeire, Holland Nimmons, D.D. *Duties of Christian Masters.* Nashville: Southern Methodist Publishing House, 1855.

Minutes of the Annual Conferences of the Methodist Episcopal Church, South for the Year 1898. Nashville: Publishing House of the Methodist Episcopal Church, South, 1898.

Missionary Register for MDCCCLI, Containing the Principal Transactions of the Various Institutions for Propagating the Gospel: With the Proceedings at Large, of the Church Missionary Society. London: Seeleys, 1851.

Missionary Survey. Richmond, VA: Presbyterian Committee of Publication, 1915.

Missionary Survey: The Presbyterian Church in the U.S. at Home and Abroad, February 1920. Richmond, VA: Presbyterian Committee of Publications, 1920.

Moore, Thomas Verner, *Adaptation of Religion to Female Character: A Discourse to Young Ladies, Delivered in the First Presbyterian Church, Richmond, Virginia, February 29th, 1852.* Richmond, VA: H. K. Ellyson, Printer, 1852.

Morgan, Lucy. *Gift from the Hills: Miss Lucy's Story of Her Unique Penland School.* New York: Bobbs-Merrill, 1958.

O'Brien, Michael. *An Evening When Alone: Four Journals of Single Women in the South, 1827–67.* Charlottesville: University of Virginia Press, 1997.

Olmsted, Frederick Law, *A Journey in the Seaboard Slave States; With Remarks on Their Economy.* New York; London: Dix & Edwards; Sampson Low, Son & Co., 1856.

Powell, William S. *Higher Education in North Carolina.* Raleigh, NC: State Department of Archives and History, 1964.

Pringle, Elizabeth W. Allston. *Chronicles of Chicora Wood.* New York: Charles Scribner's Sons, 1922.

Pruitt, Ida. *A Daughter of Han: The Autobiography of a Chinese Working Woman.* Stanford, CA: Stanford University Press, 1967.

Pryor, Sara Agnes Rice. *My Day: Reminiscences of Peace and War.* New York: MacMillan Company, 1905.

Rawick, George P., ed., *The American Slave: A Composite Autobiography: Supplement, Series 1, Vol. 12.* Westport, CT: Greenwood Press, 1979.

Robinson, Rev. William H. *From Log Cabin to the Pulpit, or, Fifteen Years in Slavery, 3rd ed.* Eau Claire, WI: Published by Author, 1913.

Schwartz, Kathryn Carlisle, ed. *Baptist Faith in Action: The Private Writings of Maria Baker Taylor.* Columbia: University of South Carolina Press, 2003.

Slaughter, Reverend Philip. *Man and Woman; Or, The law of honor applied to the solution of the problem, why are so many more women than men Christians? By the Rev. Philip Slaughter. With an introduction by A. T. Bledsoe.* Philadelphia: J. B. Lippincott & Co., 1860.

Smedes, Susan Dabney. *Memorials of a Southern Planter.* Baltimore: Cushings & Bailey, 1887.

Statistical Atlas of Christian Missions. Edinburgh: World Missionary Conference, 1910.

Stroyer, Jacob. *My Life in the South.* Salem, MA: Newcomb & Gauss, 1898.

Whilden, Lula F. *Life Sketches from a Heathen Land.* Greenville, SC: Woman's Missionary Union, Auxiliary to the Baptist State Convention of South Carolina, 1917.

Williams, Elizabeth McCutchen, ed. *Appalachian Travels: The Diary of Olive Dame Campbell.* Lexington: University Press of Kentucky, 2012.

Woman's Home Missionary Society. *Thirty-Ninth Annual Report of the Board of Managers for the Year 1919–1920.* Cincinnati, OH: Methodist Book Concern Press, 1920.

Woodward, C. Vann, and Elisabeth Muhlenfeld, eds. *The Private Mary Chesnut: The Unpublished Civil War Diaries.* New York: Oxford University Press, 1984.

World Missionary Conference. *Statistical Atlas of Christian Missions; Containing a Directory of Missionary Societies, a Classified Summary of Statistics, an Index of Mission Stations, and a Series of Specially Prepared Maps of Mission Fields.* Edinburgh: World Missionary Conference, 1910.

Wright, Louise Wigfall. *A Southern Girl in '61: The War-time Memories of a Confederate Senator's Daughter.* New York: Doubleday, Page & Company, 1905.

SECONDARY SOURCES

BOOKS

Alexander, Arabel Wilbur. *The Life and Word of Lucinda B. Helm, Founder of the Woman's Parsonage and Home Mission Society of the M.E. Church, South.* Nashville: Publishing House of the Methodist Episcopal Church, South, 1898.

Allen, Catherine. *A Century to Celebrate: History of Woman's Missionary Union.* Birmingham, AL: Woman's Missionary Union, 1987.

Anderson, J. A. *Crying for a Vision: A Rosebud Sioux Trilogy 1886–1976.* Dobbs Ferry, NY: Morgan & Morgan, 1976.

Ayers, Edward L. *The Promise of the New South: Life after Reconstruction.* New York: Oxford University Press, 1992.

Bailey, Hugh C. *Liberalism in the New South: Southern Social Reformers and the Progressive Movement.* Coral Gables, FL: University of Miami Press, 1969.

Barnes, Kenneth C. *Journey of Hope: The Back-to-Africa Movement in Arkansas in the Late 1800s.* Chapel Hill: University of North Carolina Press, 2004.

Batterson, Hermon Griswold. *A Scetch-book of the American Episcopate.* Philadelphia: J. P. Lippencott & Co., 1878.

Beckert, Sven. *The Monied Metropolis: New York City and the Consolidation of the American Bourgeoisie, 1850–1896.* Cambridge: Cambridge University Press, 2001.

Bernardin, Joseph B. *An Introduction to the Episcopal Church: Revised Edition.* New York: Morehouse Publishing, 1990.

Biolosi, Thomas. *Deadliest Enemies: Law and Race Relations on and off Rosebud Reservation.* Minneapolis: University of Minnesota Press, 2007.

Blassingame, John W. *The Slave Community: Plantation Life in the Antebellum South.* Oxford: Oxford University Press, 1972.

Blight, David. *Race and Reunion: The Civil War in American Memory.* Cambridge, MA: Belknap Press of Harvard University Press, 2001.

Blum, Edward J. *Reforging the White Republic: Race, Religion, and American Nationalism, 1865–1898.* Baton Rouge: Louisiana State University Press, 2005.

Blum, Edward J., and Paul Harvey. *The Color of Christ: The Son of God and the Saga of Race in America.* Chapel Hill: University of North Carolina Press, 2012.

Blum, Edward J., and W. Scott Poole. *Vale of Tears: New Essays on Religion and Reconstruction.* Macon, GA: Mercer University Press, 2005.

Boles, John B. *The Great Revival: Beginnings of the Bible Belt.* Lexington: University Press of Kentucky, 1996.

Boles, John B., ed. *Masters & Slaves in the House of the Lord: Race and Religion in the American South, 1740–1870.* Lexington: University Press of Kentucky, 1988.

Boyd, Lois A. *Presbyterian Women in America: Two Centuries of a Quest for Status.* Greenwood, CT: Greenwood Press, 1996.

Broadus, John Albert. *Should Women Speak in Mixed Public Assemblies?* Louisville: Baptist Book Concern, 1880.

Calhoon, Robert M. *Evangelicals and Conservatives in the Early South, 1740–1861.* Columbia: University of South Carolina Press, 1988.

Campbell, John C. *The Future of Church and Independent Schools in the Southern Highlands.* New York: Russell Sage Foundation, 1917.

Cannon, James, III. *History of Southern Methodist Missions.* Nashville: Cokesbury Press, 1926.

Carney, Charity R. *Ministers and Masters: Methodism, Manhood and Honor in the Old South.* Baton Rouge: Louisiana State University Press, 2011.

Carson, Mina Julia. *Settlement Folk: Social Thought and the American Settlement Movement, 1885–1930.* Chicago: University of Chicago Press, 1990.

Carter, Tomeiko Ashford, ed. *Virginia Broughton: The Life and Writings of a National Baptist Missionary.* Knoxville: University of Tennessee Press, 2010.

Cash, W. J. *The Mind of the South.* New York: Knopf, 1941.

Castorph, Paul D. *Republicans, Negroes, and Progressives in the South, 1912–1916.* Tuscaloosa: University of Alabama Press, 1981.

Censer, Jane Turner. *The Reconstruction of Southern White Womanhood, 1865–1895.* Baton Rouge: Louisiana State University Press, 2003.

Chapell, Colin B. *Ye That Are Men Now Serve Him: Radical Holiness Theology and Gender in the South.* Tuscaloosa: University of Alabama Press, 2016.

Clarke, Erskine. *By the Rivers of Water: A Nineteenth-Century Atlantic Odyssey.* New York: Basic Books, 2013.

——. *Wrestlin' Jacob: A Portrait of Religion in the Old South.* Louisville: Westminster John Knox Press, 1979.

Clinton, Catherine. *The Plantation Mistress: Woman's World in the Old South.* New York: Pantheon Books, 1982.

Cornelius, Janet Duitsman. *When I Can Read My Title Clear: Literacy, Slavery and Religion in the Antebellum South.* Columbia: University of South Carolina Press, 1992.

Cott, Nancy F. *The Grounding of Modern Feminism.* New Haven, CT: Yale University Press, 1987.

Cox, Karen L. *Dixie's Daughters: The United Daughters of the Confederacy and the Preservation of Confederate Culture.* Gainesville: University Press of Florida, 2003.

Dailey, Jane, Glenda Elizabeth Gilmore, and Bryant Simon, eds. *Jumpin' Jim Crow: Southern Politics from Civil War to Civil Rights.* Princeton, NJ: Princeton University Press, 2001.

Daggett, Mrs. L. H., ed. *Historical Sketches of Woman's Missionary Societies in America and England.* Boston: Woman's Union Missionary Society, 1883.

Davis, Allen Freeman. *Spearheads for Reform: The Social Settlements and the Progressive Movement, 1890–1914.* New York: Oxford University Press, 1967.

Davis, David Brion. *The Problem of Slavery in the Age of Emancipation.* New York: Knopf Doubleday Publishing Group, 2014.

Davis, Morris L. *The Methodist Unification: Christianity and the Politics of Race in the Jim Crow Era.* New York: New York University Press, 2008.

Decker, Mrs. Henry Walker, *A Continuing Light, 1813–1963.* Richmond, VA: Woman's Missionary Society, First Baptist Church, 1963.

Doyle, Sherman H. *Presbyterian Home Missions: An Account of the Home Missions of the Presbyterian Church in the U.S.A.* Philadelphia: Presbyterian Board of Publication and Sabbath-school Work, 1902.

Drury, George H. *The Historical Guide to North American Railroads.* Milwaukee, WI: Kalmbach Publishing Company, 1985.

Dyck, Paul. *Brule, The Sioux People of the Rosebud.* Flagstaff, AZ: Northland Press, 1971.

Edwards, Laura F. *Gendered Strife and Confusion: The Political Culture of Reconstruction.* Urbana-Champaign: University of Illinois Press, 1997.

Elder, Angela Esco. *Love and Duty: Confederate Widows and the Emotional Politics of Loss.* Chapel Hill: University of North Carolina Press, 2022.

Epstein, Barbara. *The Politics of Domesticity.* Middletown, CT: Wesleyan University Press, 1981.

Farmer, Foy J. *Hitherto: History of North Carolina Woman's Missionary Union.* Raleigh, NC: Woman's Missionary Union of North Carolina, 1952.

Farnham, Christie Anne. *The Education of the Southern Belle: Higher Education and Student Socialization in the Antebellum South.* New York: New York University Press, 1994.

Faust, Drew Gilpin. *Mothers of Invention: Women of the Slaveholding South in the American Civil War.* Chapel Hill: University of North Carolina Press, 1996.

Feldman, Glenn. *The Irony of the Solid South: Democrats, Republican, and Race, 1865–1944.* Tuscaloosa: University of Alabama Press, 2013.

Fitzgerald, O. P. *Holland N. McTyeire.* Nashville: Southern Methodist Pub. House, 1896.

Flynt, Wayne, and Gerald W. Berkley, *Taking Christianity to China: Alabama Missionaries in the Middle Kingdom, 1850–1950.* Tuscaloosa: University of Alabama Press, 1997.

Fox-Genovese, Elizabeth. *Within the Plantation Household: Black and White Women of the Old South.* Chapel Hill: University of North Carolina Press, 1985.

Fox-Genovese, Elizabeth, and Eugene D. Genovese. *The Mind of the Master Class: History and Faith in the Southern Slaveholders' Worldview.* Cambridge: Cambridge University Press, 2005.

Frankel, Noralee, and Nancy S. Dye, eds. *Gender, Class, Race, and Reform in the Progressive Era.* Lexington: University Press of Kentucky, 1991.

Fredette, Allison. *Marriage on the Border: Love, Mutuality, and Divorce during the Civil War Era.* Lexington: University Press of Kentucky, 2020.

Friedman, Jean E. *The Enclosed Garden: Women and Community in the Evangelical South, 1830–1900.* Chapel Hill: University of North Carolina Press, 1985.

Friend, Craig Thompson, and Lorri Glover, eds. *Southern Masculinity: Perspectives on Manhood in the South since Reconstruction.* Athens: University of Georgia Press, 2008.

Gardner, Sarah E. *Blood & Irony: Southern White Women's Narratives of the Civil War, 1861–1937.* Chapel Hill: University of North Carolina Press, 2004.

Genovese, Eugene. *Fatal Self-Deception: Slaveholding Paternalism in the Old South.* Cambridge: Cambridge University Press, 2011.

Gilmore, Glenda Elizabeth. *Gender and Jim Crow: Women and the Politics of White Supremacy in North Carolina, 1896-1920.* Chapel Hill: University of North Carolina Press, 1996.

Ginzberg, Lori. *Women and the Work of Benevolence: Morality, Politics, and Class in the Nineteenth-Century United States.* New Haven, CT: Yale University Press, 1990.

Grantham, Dewey W. *Southern Progressivism: The Reconciliation of Progress and Tradition.* Knoxville: University of Tennessee Press, 1983.

Griffith, R. Marie. *God's Daughters: Evangelical Women and the Power of Submission.* Berkeley: University of California Press, 2000.

Gruver, Kate Ellen. *From This High Pinnacle: One Hundred Years with Georgia Baptist Woman's Missionary Union.* Decatur, GA: Woman's Missionary Union, Auxiliary to Georgia Baptist Convention.

Hardesty, Nancy A. *Women Called to Witness: Evangelical Feminism in the 19th Century.* Nashville: Abingdon Press, 1984.

Harlow, Luke E. *Religion, Race, and the Making of Confederate Kentucky, 1830–1880.* Cambridge: Cambridge University Press, 2014.

Harvey, Paul. *Freedom's Coming: Religious Culture and the Shaping of the South from the Civil War through the Civil Rights Era.* Chapel Hill: University of North Carolina Press, 2005.

Heyrman, Christine Leigh. *American Apostles: When American Evangelicals Entered the World of Islam.* New York: Hill & Wang, 2015.

———. *Southern Cross: The Beginnings of the Bible Belt.* Chapel Hill: University of North Carolina Press, 1997.

Higginbotham, Evelyn Brooks. *Righteous Discontent: The Women's Movement in the Black Baptist Church, 1880–1920.* Cambridge, MA: Harvard University Press, 1993.

Hill, Patricia R. *The World Their Household: The American Woman's Foreign Mission Movement and Cultural Transformation, 1870–1920.* Ann Arbor: University of Michigan Press, 1985.

Hill, Samuel S. *Religion in the Southern States: A Historical Survey.* Macon, GA: Mercer University Press, 1983.

Hill, Samuel S., and Charles H. Lippy, eds. *Encyclopedia of Religion in the South.* 2nd ed. Macon, GA: Mercer University Press, 2005.

Huang, Martin W. *Negotiating Masculinities in Late Imperial China.* Honolulu: University of Hawaii Press, 2006.

Huber, Mary Taylor, and Nancy C. Lutkehaus, eds. *Gendered Missions: Women and Men in Missionary Discourse and Practice.* Ann Arbor: University of Michigan Press, 1999.

Huff, Archie Vernon, Jr. *Greenville: The History of the City and the County in the South Carolina Piedmont.* Columbia: University of South Carolina Press, 1995.

Ingraham, Joseph Holt, ed. *The Sunny South; or, The Southerner at Home.* Philadelphia: G. G. Evans, 1860.

Inscoe, John C., ed. *Appalachians and Race: The Mountain South from Slavery to Segregation.* Lexington: University Press of Kentucky, 2001.

Irons, Charles F. *The Origins of Proslavery Christianity: White and Black Evangelicals in Colonial and Antebellum Virginia.* Chapel Hill: University of North Carolina Press, 2008.

Jabour, Anya. *Scarlett's Sisters: Young Women in the Old South.* Chapel Hill: University of North Carolina Press, 2007.

Janney, Caroline E. *Burying the Dead but Not the Past: Ladies' Memorial Associations and the Lost Cause.* Chapel Hill: University of North Carolina Press, 2008.

Johnson, Emily S. *This Is Our Message: The Politics of Women's Leadership in the New Christian Right.* Oxford: Oxford University Press, 2019.

Jones-Rogers, Stephanie E. *They Were Her Property: White Women as Slave Owners in the American South.* New Haven, CT: Yale University Press, 2019.

Kelley, Mary. *Learning to Stand and Speak: Women, Education, and Public Life in America's Republic.* Chapel Hill: University of North Carolina Press, 2008.

Kierner, Cynthia A. *Beyond the Household: Women's Place in the Early South, 1700–1835.* Ithaca, NY: Cornell University Press, 1998.

Kinshasa, Kwando Mbiassi. *Emigration vs. Assimilation: The Debate in the African American Press, 1827–1861.* Jefferson, NC: McFarland, 1988.

Kirby, Jack Temple. *Darkness at the Dawning: Race and Reform in the Progressive South.* Philadelphia: Lippincott, 1972.

Latrobe, John H. B. *Maryland in Liberia: A History of the Colony Planted by the Maryland State Colonization Society under the Auspices of the State of Maryland, U.S. at Cape Palmas on the South-West Coast of Africa, 1833–1853: A Paper Read Before the Maryland Historical Society.* Baltimore: Maryland Historical Society, 1885.

Lebsock, Suzanne. *The Free Women of Petersburg: Status and Culture in a Southern Town, 1784–1860.* New York: W. W. Norton & Company, 1984.

Levine, Robert S. *Martin Delany, Frederick Douglass, and the Politics of Representative Identity.* Chapel Hill: University of North Carolina Press, 1997.

Link, William A. *The Paradox of Southern Progressivism, 1880–1930.* Chapel Hill: University of North Carolina Press, 1992.

Lyerly, Cynthia. *Methodism and the Southern Mind.* Oxford: Oxford University Press, 1998.

Lynn, Lucius Ross. *The Story of Thornwell Orphanage, Clinton, SC, 1875–1925.* Richmond, VA: Presbyterian Committee of Publication, 1924.

MacDonell, Mrs. R. W. *Belle Harris Bennett: Her Life Work.* Nashville: Woman's Section of the Board of Missions, 1928.

Mathews, Donald G. *Religion in the Old South.* Chicago: University of Chicago Press, 1977.

Maxwell, Melody. *The Woman I Am: Southern Baptist Women's Writings, 1906–2006.* Tuscaloosa: University of Alabama Press, 2014.

McBeth, Leon. *Women in Baptist Life.* Nashville: Broadman Press, 1979.

McCauley, Deborah Vansau. *Appalachian Mountain Religion: A History.* Urbana: University of Illinois Press, 1995.

McDowell, John Patrick. *The Social Gospel in the South: The Woman's Home Mission-*

ary Movement in the Methodist Episcopal Church South, 1886–1939. Baton Rouge: Louisiana State University Press, 1982.

McMillen, Sally G. *To Raise Up the South: Sunday Schools in Black and White Churches, 1865–1915.* Baton Rouge: Louisiana State University Press, 2001.

Miller, Glenn T. *Piety and Profession: American Protestant Theological Education, 1870–1970.* Cambridge: Wm. B. Eerdmans Publishing Co., 2007.

Molloy, Marie S. *Single, White, Slaveholding Women in the Nineteenth-Century American South.* Columbia: University of South Carolina Press, 2018.

Moses, Wilson Jeremiah. *Liberian Dreams: Back-to-Africa Narratives from the 1850s.* University Park, PA: Penn State University Press, 2010.

Noll, Mark A. *The Civil War as a Theological Crisis.* Chapel Hill: University of North Carolina, 2006.

Ownby, Ted. *Subduing Satan: Religion, Recreation, and Manhood in the Rural South, 1865–1920.* Chapel Hill: University of North Carolina Press, 1993.

Payne, John. *History of the Greboes.* New York: Printed by E. O. Jenkins, 1860.

Peabody, Andrew P. *The American Board of Commissioners for Foreign Missions.* Charleston, SC: Nabu, 2009.

Phillips, Ulrich Bonnell. *American Negro Slavery: A Survey of the Supply, Employment and Control of Negro Labor as Determined by the Plantation Regime.* New York: D. Appleton & Company, 1918.

———. *The Central Theme of Southern History.* Lancaster, PA: Lancaster Press, 1928.

Pope-Levison. *Building the Old Time Religion: Women Evangelists in the Progressive Era.* New York: New York University Press, 2014.

Powell, William S., ed. *Dictionary of North Carolina Biography, vol. 3, H–K.* Chapel Hill: University of North Carolina Press, 1988.

Power-Greene, Ousmane. *Against Wind and Tide: The African American Struggle against the Colonization Movement.* New York: New York University Press, 2014.

Qian, Nanxiu Grace S. Fong, and Richard J. Smith, eds. *Different Worlds of Discourse: Transformations of Gender and Genre in Late Qing and Early Republican China.* Leiden: Brill, 2008.

Quist, John W. *Restless Visionaries: The Social Roots of Antebellum Reform in Alabama and Michigan.* Baton Rouge: Louisiana State University Press, 1998.

Raboteau, Albert J. *Slave Religion: The "Invisible Institution" in the Antebellum South.* Oxford: Oxford University Press, 1972.

Ragsdale, B. D. *Story of Georgia Baptists.* Atlanta: Georgia Baptist Convention, 1932.

Rankin, Richard. *Ambivalent Churchmen and Evangelical Churchwomen: The Religion of the Episcopal Elite in North Carolina, 1800–1861.* Columbia: University of South Carolina Press, 1993.

Reznikoff, Charles, and Uriah Engelman. *The Jews of Charleston: A History of an American Jewish Community.* Philadelphia: Jewish Publication Society of America, 1950.

Rice, Connie Park, and Marie Tedesco, eds. *Women of the Mountain South: Identity, Work, and Activism.* Athens: Ohio University Press, 2015.

Riegel, Robert E. *American Feminists.* Lawrence: University Press of Kansas, 1963.

Ritchie, Andrew Jackson. *The Rabun Industrial School and Mountain School Extension Work among the Mountain Whites by One of Them.* Atlanta: Byrd, 1906.

Robert, Dana Lee. *American Women in Mission: A Social History of Their Thought and Practice.* Macon, GA: Mercer University Press, 1996.

———, ed. *Gospel Bearers, Gender Barriers: Missionary Women in the Twentieth Century.* Maryknoll, NY: Orbis Books, 2002.

Scales, T. Laine. *All That Fits a Woman: Training Southern Baptist Women for Charity and Mission, 1907–1926.* Macon, GA: Mercer University Press, 2000.

Scales, T. Laine, and Melody Maxwell. *Doing the Word: Southern Baptists' Carver School of Church Social Work and Its Predecessors, 1907–1997.* Knoxville: University of Tennessee Press, 2019.

Schweiger, Beth Barton. *The Gospel Working Up: Progress and the Pulpit in Nineteenth-Century Virginia.* New York: Oxford University Press, 2000.

———. *A Literate South: Reading before Emancipation.* New Haven, CT: Yale University Press, 2019.

Scott, Anna M., Mrs. *Day Dawns in Africa; or, Progress of the Protestant Episcopal Mission at Cape Palmas, West Africa.* New York: Protestant Episcopal Society for the Promotion of Evangelical Knowledge, 1858.

Scott, Anne Firor. *The Southern Lady: From Pedestal to Politics, 1830–1930.* Chicago: University of Chicago Press, 1970.

Shapiro, Henry D. *Appalachia on Our Mind: The Southern Mountains and Mountaineers in the American Consciousness, 1870–1920.* Chapel Hill: University of North Carolina Press, 1978.

Sims, Anastatia. *The Power of Femininity in the New South: Women's Organizations and Politics in North Carolina.* Columbia: University of South Carolina Press, 1997.

Solomon, Barbara Miller. *In the Company of Educated Women: A History of Women and Higher Education in America.* New Haven, CT: Yale University Press, 1985.

Southern, David W. *The Progressive Era and Race: Reaction and Reform, 1900–1917.* Wheeling, IL: Harland Davidson, 2005.

Stephan, Scott. *Redeeming the Southern Family: Evangelical Women and Domestic Devotion in the Antebellum South.* Athens: University of Georgia Press, 2011.

Stephenson, Florence. *The Home Industrial School, Asheville, North Carolina.* Asheville, NC: Woman's Executive Committee of Home Missions of the Presbyterian Church, 1896.

Stoddart, Jess. *Challenge and Change in Appalachia: The Story of Hindman Settlement School.* Lexington: University Press of Kentucky, 2002.

Stowell, Daniel W. *Rebuilding Zion: The Religious Reconstruction of the South, 1863–1877.* Oxford: Oxford University Press, 2008.

Sutherland, Daniel E. *The Confederate Carpetbaggers*. Baton Rouge: Louisiana State University Press, 1988.

Thelin, John R. *A History of Higher Education*. Baltimore: Johns Hopkins University Press, 2004.

Thompson, Ernest Trice. *Presbyterians in the South*, vols. 1–3. Richmond, VA: John Knox Press, 1963–73.

——. *Presbyterian Missions in the Southern United States*. Richmond, VA, and Texarkana, AR: Presbyterian Committee of Publication, 1934.

Trolander, Judith Ann. *Professionalism and Social Change: From the Settlement House Movement to Neighborhood Centers, 1886 to the Present*. New York: Columbia University Press, 1987.

Trueheart, Mrs. S. C. *Brief History of the Woman's Foreign Missionary Society, Methodist Episcopal Church, South, from May, 1878, to May, 1910*. Nashville: Board of Missions M. E. Church, South, Foreign Department of Woman's Work, 1911.

Turner, Elizabeth Hayes. *Women and Gender in the New South: 1865–1945*. New York: Wiley-Blackwell, 2008.

Weinberg, Marjorie. *The Real Rosebud: The Triumph of a Lokota Woman*. Lincoln: University of Nebraska Press, 2004.

Weiner, Marli F. *Mistresses and Slaves: Plantation Women in South Carolina, 1830–80*. Urbana: University of Illinois Press, 1998.

Wells, Jonathan Daniel. *The Origins of the Southern Middle Class, 1800–1861*. Chapel Hill: University of North Carolina Press, 2004.

——. *Women Writers and Journalists in the Nineteenth-Century South*. Cambridge: Cambridge University Press, 2011.

Wesley, Timothy L. *The Politics of Faith during the Civil War*. Baton Rouge: Louisiana State University Press, 2013.

Whisnant, David. *All That Is Native and Fine: The Politics of Culture in an American Region*. Chapel Hill: University of North Carolina Press, 1983.

White, Deborah Gray. *Ar'n't I a Woman? Female Slaves in the Plantation South*. New York: W. W. Norton, 1985.

Whites, LeeAnn. *The Civil War as a Crisis in Gender: Augusta, Georgia, 1860–1890*. Athens: University of Georgia Press, 1995.

——. *Gender Matters: Civil War, Reconstruction, and the Making of the New South*. New York: Palgrave Macmillan, 2005.

Williams, Cora G. *The Morning-Glory: Life and Work of Miss Mae McKenzie, Deaconess*. Nashville: Publishing House of the MEC, 1910.

Williams, John Alexander. *Appalachia: A History*. Chapel Hill: University of North Carolina Press, 2002.

Williamson, Joel. *The Crucible of Race: Black/White Relations in the American South since Emancipation*. New York: Oxford University Press, 1984.

Wilson, Charles Reagan. *Baptized in Blood: The Religion of the Lost Cause, 1865–1920.* Athens: University of Georgia Press, 2009.

Wise, Daniel. *Bridal Greetings: A Marriage Gift in Which the Mutual Duties of Husband and Wife are Familiarly Illustrated and Enforced.* New York: Carlton & Phillips, 1854.

———. *The Young Lady's Counsellor: or, Outlines and Illustrations of the Sphere, the Duties, and the Dangers of Young Women.* New York: Carlton & Porter, 1855.

Withoft, Mabel Swartz. *Oak and Laurel: A Study of the Mountain Mission Schools of Southern Baptists.* Nashville: Sunday School Board of the Southern Baptist Convention, 1923.

Wood, Kirsten E. *Masterful Women: Slaveholding Widows from the American Revolution through the Civil War.* Chapel Hill: University of North Carolina Press, 2004.

Wyatt-Brown, Bertram. *The Shaping of Southern Culture: Honor, Grace, and War 1760s–1880s.* Chapel Hill: University of North Carolina Press, 2001.

Ya-chen, Chen, ed. *New Modern Chinese Women and Gender Politics: The Centennial of the End of the Qing Dynasty.* New York: Routledge, 2014.

Young, Elizabeth Barber. *A Study of the Curricula of Seven Selected Women's Colleges of the Southern States.* New York: Teachers College, Columbia University Press, 1932.

ARTICLES AND BOOK CHAPTERS

Barber, Mrs. R. W. "Home Missions." *Southern Christian Advocate* 71 (April 4, 1907): 6.

Bearden, Robert E. L., Jr. "The Episcopal Church in the Confederate States." *Arkansas Historical Quarterly* 4 (Winter 1945): 269–75.

Bederman, Gail. "'The Women Have Had Charge of the Church Work Long Enough': The Men and Religion Forward Movement and the Masculinization of Middle-Class Protestantism." *American Quarterly* 41 (September 1989): 432–65.

Bode, Frederick A. "A Common Sphere: White Evangelicals and Gender in Antebellum Georgia." *Georgia Historical Quarterly* 79 (Winter 1995): 775–805.

Bond, Edward L. "Slavery in the Diocese of Mississippi's Convention Journals, 1826–1861." *Anglican and Episcopal History* 78 (March 2009): 94–104.

Born, Ethel Wolfe. "Candlesticks: Methodist Women Putting Faith to Work in Virginia." *Virginia United Methodist Heritage: Bulletin of the Virginia Conference Historical Society* 31 (Spring 2005): 21–39.

Brown, G. Thompson. "Overseas Mission Program and Policies of the Presbyterian Church in the U.S., 1861–1983." *American Presbyterians* 65 (Summer 1987): 157–70.

Bunkers, Suzanne L. "Diaries: Public and Private Records of Women's Lives." *Legacy* 7 (1990): 17–26.

Chaffin, Nora C. "A Southern Advocate of Methodist Unification in 1865." *North Carolina Historical Review* 18 (January 1941): 38–47.

Clinton, Catherine. "Equally Their Due: The Education of the Planter Daughter in the Early Republic." *Journal of the Early Republic* 11 (1982): 39–60.

Corley, Florence Fleming. "The Presbyterian Quest: Higher Education for Georgia Women." *American Presbyterians: Journal of Presbyterian History* 69 (1991): 83–96.

Court, Mrs. William. "Social Service Lines of Home Mission Work." *Methodist Quarterly Review* 62 (October 1913): 764–67.

Crane, Sophie Montgomery. "A Century of PCUS Medical Mission, 1881–1983." *American Presbyterians* 65 (Summer 1987): 135–46.

Donovan, Mary Sudman. "Women as Foreign Missionaries in the Episcopal Church, 1830–1920." *Anglican and Episcopal History* 61 (March 1992): 16–39.

Down, Francis A. "The Greatest Woman in Southern Methodism." *Methodist Quarterly Review* 64 (April 1915): 255–66.

Durso, Pamela R. "Journey to Ordination: Addie Davis and Watts Street Baptist Church." *Baptist History & Heritage* 46 (Spring 2016): 27–36.

Durway, Julie. "'The Field Is Endless': Hallie Paxson Winsborough and Interracial Work in the PCUS Woman's Auxiliary, 1912–1940." *Journal of Presbyterian History* 78 (Fall 2000): 207–19.

"Early Methodist Protestant Foreign Missions." *Virginia United Methodist Heritage: Bulletin of the Virginia Conference Historical Society, Arlington, VA* 9 (Spring 1981): 17–26.

Foley, Thomas. "Father Francis M. Craft and the Indian Sisters." *US Catholic Historian* 16 (Spring 1998): 41–55.

Forderhase, Nancy K. "Eve Returns to the Garden: Women Reformers in Appalachian Kentucky in the Early Twentieth Century." *Register of the Kentucky Historical Society* 85 (Summer 1987): 237–61.

Fox-Genovese, Elizabeth. "Religion in the Lives of Slaveholding Women of the Antebellum South." In Lynda L. Coon, Katherine J. Haldane, and Elisabeth W. Sommer, eds., *That Gentle Strength: Historical Perspectives on Women in Christianity.* Charlottesville: University of Virginia Press, 1990.

Fusco, Eugene. "The Last Hunt of Gen. George A. Crook." *Montana: The Magazine of Western History* 12 (Autumn 1962): 36–46.

Genovese, Eugene D., and Elizabeth Fox-Genovese. "The Religious Ideals of Southern Slave Society." *Georgia Historical Quarterly* 70 (Spring 1986): 1–16.

Goodman, Mrs. W. F. "Our Broadened Opportunities." *North Carolina Christian Advocate* 56 (December 8, 1910): 11.

Graebner, N. Brooks. "The Episcopal Church and Race in Nineteenth-Century North Carolina." *Anglican and Episcopal History* 78 (March 2009): 85–93.

Griggs, Cara. "Margie Shumate: A Virginia Missionary's Experiences in Asia, 1915–1958." *Douglas Southall Freeman Historical Review* (Spring 2000): 86–190.

Harrison, Kimberly. "Rhetorical Rehearsals: The Construction of Ethos in Confederate Women's Civil War Diaries." *Rhetoric Review* 22 (2003): 243–63.

Hess, Carol Lakey, and Estelle Rountree McCarthy. "A Life Lived in Response: Rachel Henderlite, Christian Educator, Advocate for Justice, Ecumenist, and

First Woman Ordained in the PCUS." *American Presbyterians* 69 (Summer 1991): 133–43.

Heuser, Frederick J., Jr. "Presbyterian Women and the Missionary Call, 1870–1923." *American Presbyterians* 73 (Spring 1995): 23–34.

Huntley, Martha. "Presbyterian Women's Work and Rights in the Korean Mission." *American Presbyterians* 65 (Spring 1987): 37–48.

Inscoe, John C. "Memories of a Presbyterian Mission Worker in the Kentucky Mountains, 1918–1921: An Interview with Rubie R. Cunningham." *Appalachian Journal* 15 (Winter 1988): 144–60.

Jabour, Anya. "'Grown Girls, Highly Cultivated': Female Education in an Antebellum Southern Family." *Journal of Southern History* 64 (February 1998): 23–64.

Kierner, Cynthia A. "Woman's Piety within Patriarchy: The Religious Life of Martha Hancock Wheat of Bedford County." *Virginia Magazine of History and Biography* 100 (January 1992): 79–98.

Kirkley, Evelyn A. "'This Work Is God's Cause': Religion in the Southern Woman Suffrage Movement, 1880–1920." *Church History* 59 (December 1990): 507–22.

Knotts, Alice. "The Debates over Race and Women's Ordination in the 1939 Methodist Merger." *Methodist History* 29 (October 1990): 37–43.

Lawless, Elaine J. "Transforming the Master Narrative: How Women Shift the Religious Subject." *Frontiers: A Journal of Women Studies* 24 (2003): 61–75.

Lile, Joanna. "More Than Daughters: Women's Experiences at Southern Baptist Colleges during the Progressive Era." *Religions* 15, no. 8: 966.

MacDonell, Mrs. R. W., and Mrs. J. B. Cobb. "The Board of Missions and the Woman's Work of the Church." *North Carolina Christian Advocate* 55 (April 4, 1910): 6.

Mason, Lockert B. "Separation and Reunion of the Episcopal Church, 1860–1865: The Role of Bishop Thomas Atkinson." *Anglican and Episcopal History* 59 (September 1990): 345–65.

McBride, Dorothy McFatridge. "Hoosier Schoolmaster among the Sioux," *Montana: The Magazine of Western History* 20 (Autumn 1970): 78–86.

McGowan, Lucy. "Women in Kentucky Home Missions." In I. Cochran Hunt, ed., *Presbyterian Home Missions in Kentucky: A Case Book for Mission Study.* Lexington, KY: Transylvanian Printing Co., 1914.

McKinney, Gordon B. "Women's Role in Civil War Western North Carolina." *North Carolina Historical Review* 69 (January 1992): 37–56.

McRae, Elizabeth Gillespie. "Caretakers of Southern Civilization: Georgia Women and the Anti-Suffrage Campaign, 1914–1920." *Georgia Historical Quarterly* 82 (Winter 1998): 801–28.

Mohler, Mark. "The Episcopal Church and National Reconciliation, 1865." *Political Science Quarterly* 41 (December 1926): 567–95.

Moore, John M. "Church Efficiency." *Biblical World* 48 (November 1916): 304–5.

Morgan, Catherine D. "Grow We Must: The Journey Toward Full Clergy Rights for

Women in Virginia." *Virginia United Methodist Heritage, Bulletin of the Virginia Conference Historical Society of the United Methodist Church* 32 (Spring 2006): 1–5.

Peacock, Jane Bonner. "Nellie Peters Black: Turn of the Century 'Mover and Shaker.'" *Atlanta Historical Journal* 23 (Winter 1979/80): 7–16.

Perry, Elisabeth Israels. "Men Are from the Gilded Age, Women Are from the Progressive Era." *Journal of the Gilded Age and the Progressive Era* 1 (January 2002): 25–48.

Pryor, Dorothy. "Mrs. W. J. Neel: Georgia WMU Leader." *Viewpoints: Georgia Baptist History* 14 (1994): 5–15.

Raley, J. Michael. "'On the Same Basis as the Men': The Campaign to Reinstate Women as Messengers to the Southern Baptist Convention, 1885–1918." *Journal of Southern Religion* 7 (2005): https://jsr.fsu.edu/Volume7/Raley1.htm.

Ready, Milton. "Forgotten Sisters: Mountain Women in the South." *Journal of the Appalachian Studies Association* 3 (1991): 61–67.

Rice, Marie Gordon. "The Negro's Greatest Need." *Home Mission Monthly* 14 (1900): 123–24.

Robert, Dana L. "The Influence of American Missionary Women on the World Back Home." *Religion and American Culture: A Journal of Interpretation* 12 (Winter 2002): 59–89.

Robins, Glenn. "Lost Cause Motherhood: Southern Women Writers." *Louisiana History: The Journal of the Louisiana Historical Association* 44 (Summer 2003): 275–300.

Rohrer, Katherine E. "Slaveholding Women and the Religious Instruction of Slaves in Post-Emancipation Memory." *Journal of Southern Religion* 15 (2013): http://jsr.fsu.edu/issues/vol15/rohrer.html.

Schweiger, Beth Barton. "The Literate South: Reading before Emancipation." *Journal of the Civil War Era* 3 (September 2013): 331–59.

Scott, Anne Firor. "After Suffrage: Southern Women in the Twenties." *Journal of Southern History* 30 (August 1964): 298–318.

Shanks, Henry T. "The Reunion of the Episcopal Church, 1865." *Church History* 9 (June 1940): 120–40.

Shaw, Susan M. "Gracious Submission: Southern Baptist Fundamentalists and Women." *NWSA Journal* 20 (Spring 2008): 51–77.

Shellman, Carey Olmstead. "Nellie Peters Black: Georgia's Pioneer Club Woman." In *Georgia Women: Their Lives and Times,* vol. 1. Edited by Ann Short Chirhart and Betty Wood. Athens: University of Georgia Press, 2009.

Stephan, Scott. "Reconsidering the Boundaries of Maternal Authority in the Evangelical Household: The Davis Family of Antebellum Murfreesboro." *North Carolina Historical Review* 83 (April 2006): 165–92.

Vickers, Gregory. "Models of Womanhood and the Early Woman's Missionary Union." *Baptist History and Heritage* 24 (January 1989): 41–53.

Wright, Emily. "'A Doorkeeper in the House of My God': Female Stewardship of Protestant Sacred Places in the Gulf South, 1830–1861." *Journal of Southern Religion* 21 (2019): https://jsreligion.org/vo121/wright/.

ELECTRONIC SOURCES

"Biographical Dictionary of Chinese Christianity," http://www.bdcconline.net/en/ (14 May 2024).

"The Entry of Women into Medicine in America: Education and Obstacles, 1847–1910," n.d., https://www.hws.edu/about/history/elizabeth-blackwell/entry-of-women-into-medicine.aspx/ (6 September 2024).

"First Church Charleston Notes Historic Commissioning—The South Carolina Baptist Convention," n.d., http://www.scbaptist.org/first-church-charleston-notes-historic-commissioning/ (4 August 2015).

"Genealogy, Family Trees and Family History Records online," n.d., http://home.ancestry.com/ (23 April 2024). From this source, I accessed a number of primary and secondary sources including U.S. Federal Census records, church records, newspaper clippings, family trees, state censuses, local histories and photographs.

"History—Saint Paul's Church Augusta, GA," n.d., https://saintpauls.org/who-we-are/history/ (16 September 2024).

"Holland N. McTyeire" in the *Tennessee Encyclopedia,* March 1, 2018, https://tennesseeencyclopedia.net/entries/holland-n-mctyeire/ (11 August 2024).

"Journals and Magazines by Decade, 1800–1849," n.d., https://libraryguides.missouri.edu/newspapers/historicalnews (13 May 2024).

"Loulie Latimer Owens Papers, 1940–1989: Biographical Sketch," n.d., https://libguides.furman.edu/special-collections/loulie-owens-papers/biography (23 April 2024).

"The Methodist Protestant Church," n.d., https://www.themethodistprotestantchurch.org/about-us/ (18 September 2024).

"Phoebe Needles Center," n.d., http://phoebeneedles.org/ (23 April 2024).

"Portraits of American Women in Religion That Appeared in Print before 1861," n.d., http://www.librarycompany.org/women/portraits_religion/intro.htm (23 April 2024).

"Project Canterbury—Handbooks on the Missions of the Episcopal Church, Liberia (1928)," n.d., http://anglicanhistory.org/africa/lb/missions1928/ (23 April 2024).

"Scarritt College for Christian Workers" in the *Tennessee Encyclopedia,* March 1, 2018, https://tennesseeencyclopedia.net/entries/scarritt-college-for-christian-workers/ (28 August 2024).

"Southern Baptist Convention—International Mission Board," n.d., http://www.sbc.net/aboutus/entities/imb.asp/ (1 August 2015).

"Vashti Center—History," n.d., http://www.vashti.org/about-us/history/ (23 April 2024).

"Virginia Department of Historic Resources—Caryswood," 17 March 2010, https://www.dhr.virginia.gov/historic-registers/015-5147/ (28 April 2024).

"World Map of the Koppen-Geiger Climate Classification System Update," 2006, https://w2.weather.gov/media/jetstream/global/Koppen-Geiger.pdf (6 May 2024).

DISSERTATIONS AND THESES

Fialka, Katherine Brackett. "Textual Healing: Female Readers, Self-Writing, and Sensibility in the American South, 1840–1900." Ph.D. diss., University of Georgia, 2018.

Harris, David Alan. "Racists and Reformers: A Study of Progressivism in Alabama 1896–1911." Ph.D. diss., University of Michigan, 1967.

Hodge, Chelsea. "'Deserting the Broad and Easy Way': Southern Methodist Women, the Social Gospel, and the New Deal State, 1909–1939." Ph.D. diss., University of Arkansas, 2020.

Hudson, Paul Stephen. "From Old South to New South: The Public Career of Thornwell Jacobs, His Life and Times." Ph.D. diss., Georgia State University, 2000.

Junk, Cheryl F. "'Ladies Arise! The World Had Need of You': Frances Bumpass, Religion, and the Power of the Press." Ph.D. diss., University of North Carolina, 2005.

INDEX

Blacks/African Americans (*continued*)
110, 138–39, 174, 175; Black forms of worship,
102; Black Protestant women serving as
missionaries in Africa, 5; Black Sunday
Schools, 91; rise of professional Blacks, 103;
"service" provided to Blacks by home
missionaries, 106
Boles, John B., 4
Boyce, James Petigru, 82
Boyer, Cornelia, 74
Brevard, Keziah Goodwyn Hopkins, 46–47
Bridal Greetings: A Marriage Gift, 41–42
Broadus, Eliza, 122
Broadus, John, 114
Bryant, Anita, 177
Bumpass, Frances Moore Webb, 20
Bumpass, Sidney D., 20
Burke, William C., 74
Burwell, Letitia M., 109

Cape Palmas missionary station, 60, 61, 62,
187–88n11, 188n12
Carmichael, Mary Eliza Eve, 50, 186n46
Carney, Charity R., 4, 124
Cash, W. J., 11–12
Cavalla mission station, 60, 62, 67, 78
Censer, Jane Turner, 84–85
Cherokee Corner Church, 147, 148
Chesnut, Mary Boykin, 51, 184n15
"Christian enlightenment," 53–54
Christianity, 21, 50, 52, 67, 103, 163; American
"brand" of, 27. *See also* evangelical
Protestant Christianity
Christians, 22–23
Church of England, 58
Civil War, 9, 29, 32, 70–71, 72, 76, 80–81, 84, 170
Civil War (antebellum), 32, 36, 42, 110, 117, 173,
180n14; antebellum narratives of the
enslaved, 37–38, 185n37
Civil War (postbellum), 3, 15, 22, 142, 174
Clayton, Victoria V., 109
Clinton, Catherine, 186–87n56
Clitherall, Caroline Elizabeth Burgwin, 43, 44;
relationship of with a house servant, 45–46
Clopton School, 158, 160
Colegio Americano de Pernambuco, 134
colleges, female, 19, 180n7

Colored Methodist Episcopal Church, 174
Congregationalists, 23
Connie Maxwell Orphanage, 90
Coons, Martha Elizabeth, 21–22, 23, 26
"Corinna's Dolls" (Douglas), 165
Cornwell, Susan, 48–49; opinion of Jews and
Africans, 49
Cox, Addie, 212n93
Cox, Karen L., 10
Crenshaw, Henry, 112
"Cult of True Womanhood," 41, 42

Dabbs, Sudie Miller Furman, 186n46
Davis, Addie, 176–77
Davis, Caryetta, 100, 101, 102–3, 197n24
Day Dawns in Africa (A. M. Scott), 63
Dehon (Reverend Dehon), 52–53
Deists, 22
Democrats: Southern Democrats, 99
democracy, 14–15
DeSaussure, Nancy Bostwick, 109
diaries/journals/letters/memoirs (of females),
181nn22–23; memoirs of concerning
evangelization of their enslaved persons,
37–38, 40, 41, 42, 44
Dillard, Miles Hill, 147, 207–8n23
Douglas, John, 133
Douglas, Margaret Moore, 12, 128, 133, 135, 139,
143, 153–54, 155–56, 157, 167–68, 204n56;
"Christlike serenity" of, 172–73; journal of,
165–66; missionary career in Brazil,
163–67
Duties of Christian Masters to their Servants
(McTyeire), 38–39

Eager, Anna, 122
Early, Mary Washington Cabell, 87, 109–10,
192n29
education/educators, 19–20, 181n18; female
colleges and academies, 83–84; student
enrollment and curriculum of female
academies, 20–21. *See also* white southern
women: educated southern women
Ellis, John, 180n11
Episcopal Appalachian School, 101
Episcopal Church of the United States of
America (ECUSA), 57–58, 60, 87, 173,